Phenomenology Explained

Xplained

IDEAS EXPLAINED™

IN PREPARATION

Phenomenology Explained

From Experience to Insight

DAVID DETMER

OPEN COURT
Chicago

Volume 9 in the Ideas Explained™ Series

To order books from Open Court, call toll-free 1-800-815-2280, or visit our website at www.opencourtbooks.com.

Open Court Publishing Company is a division of Carus Publishing Company, dba ePals Media.

Printed and bound in the United States of America.

ISBN: 978-0-8126-9797-1

Library of Congress Control Number: 2013944051

Contents

Acknowledgments

I have had the good fortune to study Husserl and phenomenology with several excellent teachers, most notably Erazim Kohák (the world's foremost authority on Jan Patočka, and author of the best commentary on *Ideas I* known to me, *Idea & Experience*), John Findlay (translator of the *Logical Investigations*), James Edie (author of *Edmund Husserl's Phenomenology: A Critical Commentary*), and David Michael Levin (now Kleinberg-Levin, author of *Reason and Evidence in Husserl's Phenomenology*). While I have learned an enormous amount from each of these four fine scholars, they cannot be blamed for my mistakes.

Also deserving of thanks are my friends in the North American Sartre Society and at *Sartre Studies International*, especially Bruce Baugh and Connie Mui. One does not even have to perform the eidetic reduction to realize that they are the best of colleagues.

My colleagues in philosophy at Purdue University Calumet have helped me to develop my ideas over many years of stimulating philosophical discussions, both informally and through our regular colloquia. In this connection, I would like to thank John Wachala, Connie Sowa-Wachala, Neil Florek, Phyllis Bergiel, John Rowan, Eugene Schlossberger, Renee Conroy, Sam Zinaich, David Turpin, Robin Turpin, Howard Cohen, Charmaine Boswell, Kevin Kliver, Michael Stevens, Jason Melton, and Stephen Meinster. I apologize to anyone I have forgotten.

Finally, as always, my biggest thanks go to Kerri and Arlo, for their love, support, encouragement, ideas, and life-sustaining sense of fun.

Abbreviations

The following abbreviations have been used for frequently cited works. The date in square brackets at the conclusion of each entry is the date of the original publication in the original language. In most cases, where possible, I have included section numbers, in addition to page numbers, for quoted passages, thus enabling readers to find the passages in any edition (and in any language) of the works cited.

By Michael Dummett

P   "Preface" to *Edmund Husserl, Logical Investigations*, trans. J.N. Findlay (New York: Routledge, 2001), 2 volumes (Dummett's "Preface" is in vol. 1).

By Edmund Husserl

AP   "Author's Preface to the English Edition of *Ideas*," in *Husserl: Shorter Works*, trans. W.R. Boyce Gibson, ed. Peter McCormick and Frederick A. Elliston (Notre Dame: University of Notre Dame Press, 1981) [1931].

Crisis   *The Crisis of European Sciences and Transcendental Phenomenology*, trans. David Carr (Evanston: Northwestern University Press, 1970) [1954; portions published 1936].

Ideas I   *Ideas Pertaining to a Pure Phenomenology and to a Phenomenological Philosophy, First Book*, trans. F. Kersten (Boston: Martinus Nijhoff, 1982) [1913].

LI 1   *Logical Investigations*, trans. J. N. Findlay (New York: Routledge, 2001), vol. 1 [1900-1901].

LI 2   *Logical Investigations*, trans. J. N. Findlay (New York: Routledge, 2001), vol. 2 [1901].

OPCIT   *On the Phenomenology of the Consciousness of Internal Time (1893–1917)*, trans. John Barnett Brough (New York: Springer, 2008) [1893–1917].

PN   "Personal Notes," in *Early Writings in the Philosophy of Logic and Mathematics*, trans. Dallas Willard (Boston: Kluwer, 2010) [1906].

PP   *Phenomenological Psychology*, trans. John Scanlon (The Hague: Martinus Nijhoff, 1977) [1925].

PRS   "Philosophy as Rigorous Science," in *Phenomenology and the Crisis of Philosophy*, trans. Quentin Lauer (New York: Harper Torchbooks, 1965) [1911].

TS   *Thing and Space: Lectures of 1907*, trans. R. Rojcewicz (Dordrecht: Kluwer, 1997) [1907].

By Gary B. Madison

PE   "Phenomenology and Existentialism: Husserl and the End of Idealism," in Frederick Elliston and Peter McCormick, eds., *Husserl: Expositions and Appraisals* (Notre Dame: University of Notre Dame Press, 1977), 247–68.

By Maurice Merleau-Ponty

PP   *Phenomenology of Perception*, trans. Colin Smith (London: Routledge & Kegan Paul, 1962) [1945].

By Jean-Paul Sartre

BN   *Being and Nothingness*, trans. Hazel E. Barnes (New York: Washington Square Press, 1992) [1943].

NFE   *Notebooks for an Ethics*, trans. David Pellauer (Chicago: University of Chicago Press, 1992) [1983; written in the 1940s].

Introduction

Phenomenology is one of the most important and influential philosophical movements to have emerged since the dawn of the twentieth century. However, while it remains a major force in contemporary European thought (excluding Great Britain), it is neither well known nor well understood in the English-speaking world. In response to this situation, my goal in this book is to provide a concise, accurate account of phenomenology, one that will be clear enough to be accessible to undergraduates and interested general readers, and yet also sufficiently rigorous and original as to appeal to advanced scholars.

Phenomenology is the study of the essential structures of experience. It seeks to describe the objects of experience and the acts of consciousness (for example, thinking, perceiving, imagining, doubting, questioning, loving, hating, etc.) by and through which these objects are disclosed. Its aim is to focus on the world as given in experience, and to describe it with unprecedented care, rigor, subtlety, and completeness. This applies not only to the objects of sense experience, but to all phenomena: moral, aesthetic, political, mathematical, and so forth.

Phenomenology thus opens up an entirely new field of investigation, never previously explored. Rather than assuming what exists outside the realm of experience, and trying to determine what causal relations pertain to these extra-experiential entities, we can study objects strictly as they are given, that is, as they appear to us in experience. This is a realm to which we have unproblematic access. Any kind of experienced object is thus available for phenomenological study—not just physical objects, but also numbers, values, feelings, time, truth, and so forth. We find upon careful inspection that these phenomenological objects contain essential features, in the sense that certain features cannot be removed from them without their losing the character of being that kind of thing.

There is thus a kind of logical structure to the objects-as-meanings that we encounter experientially. Phenomenology is concerned to uncover and to articulate this logical structure.

Phenomenology began in 1900-1901, with the publication of a massive two-volume work, *Logical Investigations*, by a mathematician-turned-philosopher, Edmund Husserl. It proceeded immediately to exert a strong influence on both philosophy and the social sciences. For example, phenomenology provided the central inspiration for the existentialist movement, as represented by such figures as Martin Heidegger in Germany and Jean-Paul Sartre in France. Subsequent intellectual currents in Europe, when they have not claimed phenomenology as part of their ancestry, have defined themselves in opposition to phenomenology. For example, Theodor Adorno and Max Horkheimer, two of the leading philosophers of the famous "Frankfurt School" of critical theory, both wrote their doctoral dissertations on Husserl; and the first two major publications of Jacques Derrida, the father of deconstruction, were devoted to criticisms of Husserl's phenomenological works.

In the English-speaking world, where "analytic philosophy" dominates, phenomenology has recently begun to attract significant attention after decades of neglect. This has resulted from a dramatic upswing in interest in consciousness, the condition that makes all experience possible. Since the special significance of phenomenology is that it investigates consciousness, analytic philosophers have begun to turn to it as an underutilized resource. For the same reason, cognitive scientists now study Husserl's work.

The current revival of interest in phenomenology also stems from the recognition that not every kind of question can be approached either by means of experimental techniques or through the logical analysis of language. Not all meaningful questions are scientific (in that sense) or linguistic. Thus, if there is to be knowledge in logic, mathematics, ethics, political philosophy, aesthetics, epistemology (theory of knowledge), psychology (from the inside), and the study of consciousness, among others, another method is clearly needed. Hence the importance of phenomenology.

In this book I will attempt to explain what phenomenology is and why it is important. I will focus primarily on the works and ideas of Husserl, but will also briefly discuss important later thinkers, so as to give something of a sense of the range of phenomenological thought, and of the possibilities for further development that are opened up by Husserl's project. While Husserl's greatest contributions were to the philosophical foundations of logic, mathematics, knowledge, and science, I will also address the relatively neglected contribution of phenomenology to ethics, and to value theory more generally.

Husserl's Radicalism

In his last work, *The Crisis of European Sciences and Transcendental Phenomenology*, Husserl writes, "I would like to think that I, the supposed reactionary, am far more radical and far more revolutionary than those who in their words proclaim themselves so radical today" (Crisis, Appendix I: "Philosophy and the Crisis of European Humanity," 290). If by "radical" we mean something like "arising from or going to a root or source; fundamental; basic," Husserl's claim is well founded. And it is equally so if we understand the term to mean "thoroughgoing or extreme, especially as regards change from accepted or traditional forms." Indeed, I would suggest that the power of Husserl's phenomenology, what makes it interesting and important, is precisely its radicalism, which is manifested in at least six ways.

First, Husserl investigates the most basic and fundamental of questions. Whereas a typical researcher might inquire into the meaning of a certain claim in a given subject domain, and then examine the evidence pertaining to that claim, with the ultimate purpose of trying to determine whether or not it is true, Husserl concerns himself with the very nature of meaning, evidence, and truth, and with the relations among them. Referring to himself as a "perpetual beginner," he returns to these and other similarly elementary issues over and over again. In this respect Husserl's work exemplifies the radicalism of philosophy itself. For one of the unique characteristics of philosophy is that it is more general, that is, less specialized, than any other intellectual discipline or subject area. It deals with everything, or at least with the basic principles or foundations of everything. It addresses every significant aspect of human experience in the world. Husserl's phenomenology well captures this radical, general, sweeping quality.

Secondly, whereas most scientists and scholars in conducting their investigations rely on a great number of unexamined assumptions (for example, they might make uncritical use of the theoretical framework that currently prevails in their discipline, reserving their critical efforts for the application of that theory to an unsolved problem or unexplored issue), Husserl's famous motto is "back to the things themselves," by which he means that his intended procedure is to base his conclusions on careful inspection of the "things," whatever they might be, about which we inquire, rather than on debates about the often elaborate and artificial conceptual and theoretical constructions that have been built up around them: "With the radicalism belonging to the essence of genuine philosophical science we accept nothing given in advance, allow nothing traditional to pass as a beginning, nor ourselves to be dazzled by any names however great, but rather seek to attain the beginnings in a free dedication to the problems themselves and to the demands stemming from them" (PRS, 145–46).

Thus, Husserl is a radical both with regard to the issues he addresses and in connection with his approach to evidence in dealing with them. I should point out, however, that while such "going to the roots" of things is universally regarded as radicalism in politics (indeed, those who fail to go this route are routinely derided as mere reformers or liberals by those who do), it is often rejected as "foundationalist" and therefore (allegedly) reactionary in epistemology (that is, theory of knowledge), Husserl's usual domain.

In any case, another way, and an equally controversial one, in which Husserl's thought qualifies as radical, concerns his understanding of reason. One popular stance is to defend the "Enlightenment" conception of reason, which is, roughly, the view that the kind of thinking that is used in the natural sciences should be extended to every human practice and area of inquiry, in part because doing so would have emancipatory effects (for example, by leading to the overthrowing of authoritarian politics and religion, and to the replacement of them with more liberal alternatives). But some, largely those on the social, religious, and/or political right, prefer authority, custom, faith, and tradition to such a robust reliance on reason. Others, mostly coming from a left-of-center standpoint, also reject the Enlightenment view, either because they see the appeal to "reason" as a tool used cynically by the rich and powerful to justify their unearned privileges, or because they think there is no such thing as "reason" in itself, understood as something universal, and neutral with respect to the contingencies of culture, history, race, class, gender, and the like, or, simply because they doubt that reason can exert a potent emancipatory force. As against all of these positions, Husserl, while affirming the Enlightenment view of the liberatory potential of reason, argues that we desperately need a richer, deeper conception of reason, one that would comprehend the "life-world," that is, the world of lived experience, in all its diversity and complexity, as opposed to one that rejects as "subjective" everything that does not lend itself to study by the methods of the natural sciences.

This radicalization of reason harmonizes with an equal radicalization of experience and of experiential philosophy (or empiricism). Thus, while Husserl shares with empiricists of the past the program of trying to base knowledge on experience, he rejects as overly narrow their restriction of what counts as experience to sense experience alone. Rather, as mentioned above, he proposes to make use of all of the evidence of experience, including, for example, logical, ethical, and aesthetic data.

Fifthly, Husserl offers a revolutionary approach to the issue of subjectivity. On the one hand, many philosophers of the past have embraced a naïve objectivism, overlooking the fact that we become conscious of objects "through subjective manners of appearance, or manners of givenness" (Crisis, §38, 144). On the other hand, many other thinkers have seized upon this point in order to defend a facile subjectivism that amounts to a relativism or skepticism, according to which each person simply sees things differently from each other person, and the possibility of objective truth is closed off. As against both of these approaches, Husserl calls for directing a "coherent theoretical interest…toward the universe of the subjective" (Crisis, §38, 146), so that the previously unexplored correlation between world and its subjective manner of givenness might be examined and described rigorously, and an entirely new domain of truth opened up.

Finally, the radicalism of Husserlian phenomenology is not restricted to its subject matter, or to its methodological or programmatic aspects, but extends also to many of its findings. For example, Husserl's analyses of perception, spatiality, and the body from his posthumously published manuscript *Ideas II* have exerted an enormous influence on several of his followers, most notably inspiring the ground-breaking innovations of the French phenomenologist Maurice Merleau-Ponty in his much-celebrated book, *Phenomenology of Perception*.

The Subject Matter of Phenomenology

A good deal of the interest in phenomenology is due to the fact that it investigates neglected subjects of undeniable importance. One of these is consciousness, which has until recently been widely denied or ignored, largely because it seemingly cannot be studied by the methods of science. Behavior, or at least movements of the body, can be observed and measured; the same is now true of activity of the brain. Perhaps as a result, many scientists and philosophers have attempted to reduce consciousness either to behavior or to neurological functioning (or both), and have suggested that research on these renders an investigation of consciousness (that is, of the realm of being aware of things, of perceiving, feeling, and having subjective experiences, and of there being a "what it's like" to undergo experiences of varying kinds) dispensable.

Just as scientists have until recently ignored the subjective pole of experience, so have they regarded many of the objects of experience, specifically those that are not in any straightforward way accessible to the senses, as falling outside of their purview. So, for example, the entire domain of values, including ethical, political, and aesthetic values, has been widely regarded, not only as unscientific, but also as thoroughly subjective, as devoid of facts or objectivity, a sphere in which mere opinion reigns supreme, and in which the only "truth" available to us is a relative one, based on consensus, tradition, and culture. While philosophers have neither ignored the realm of values, nor tended to analyze it in a subjectivist, relativist, or skeptical way, their approach to this topic has rarely been descriptive or in any sense empirical. Rather, philosophers have tended to construct theories about values, and then to judge the theories according to such criteria as simplicity, elegance, comprehensiveness, and their ability to conform to, and to render consistent and coherent, certain widely-shared basic judgments about values.

But phenomenology investigates *all objects* of experience, and not merely those that are accessed by the senses. Moreover, it concerns itself with these objects precisely as we are conscious of them, that is, as experienced, as phenomena. So phenomenology is unique in that it returns us to two fundamental but widely neglected areas of study: (1) consciousness and the entire dimension of subjectivity (that is, experience from a "first-person" standpoint, that of the experiencer, rather than from a third-person standpoint, such as that of an observer of the behavior of others) and (2) all those aspects of objectivity that have either been ignored, assumed to have no factual, knowledge-yielding character, or studied only in a highly theoretical way, without grounding in a careful descriptive inventory of the (nonsensory) experiential evidence concerning them.

Consider, in this regard, the phenomenon of meaning. On a daily basis we find many things meaningful—spoken or written words, facial expressions, clouds that "mean" that rain is imminent, a temperature reading on a thermometer that means that a person has a fever, and so forth. Notice that, while we have to take in information through the senses in order to access these meanings, the meanings themselves are not in any direct or straightforward way given through the senses, and are not to be understood as objects of sense experience. For example, while one has to hear spoken words in order to ascertain their meaning, it appears that every sensory aspect of those words, or of the experience of hearing them, is irrelevant to that meaning. The pitch level, timbre of the voice, and accent of the speaker are irrelevant, and we pay little or no attention to them when we are interested in the speaker's meaning. Even the sounds that make one word distinct from another, such as the difference between the sound of the word "glad" and that of the word "sad," are intrinsically irrelevant, and merely serve the function of directing the listener's attention to the difference in meaning, which could be marked by any convention. The obviousness of this point is rendered clear by considering that the same meaning content could be expressed in the words of a different language, in which case the sensory content that conveyed that identical meaning content would be entirely different. Moreover, the same meaning content could be conveyed in writing, bypassing the sense of hearing entirely, thus proving that none of the sensory content of the spoken utterance, the actual sounds heard, are necessary for the conveying of the meaning in question. In short, we must always *look past* the sensory content of an utterance if we are to grasp its meaning, which is itself not sensory.

The fact that it is possible to study meaning profitably suggests that it can be worthwhile to investigate phenomena, that is, objects of experience, even when they are not objects of sense experience. This point undercuts the assumption that values, for example, must be understood to be subjective, since they cannot be seen, heard, touched, tasted, smelled, or measured.

It is noteworthy in this connection that at the beginning of the twentieth century the two major traditions of contemporary Western philosophy, the analytic tradition that dominates the English-speaking world and the phenomenological tradition of continental Europe, both began to take an intense interest in the study of meaning. But whereas phenomenology studies meaning as a phenomenon, the investigation of which is inseparable from an investigation of consciousness, the analytic tradition bypasses consciousness entirely, and studies meaning almost exclusively in the context of a philosophical analysis of language. The restriction of the study of meaning to the context of language may be motivated by the fact that language is public (and therefore seen as objective) in a way that conscious experience is not. But the phenomenological focus is broader and deeper, since meaning is not exclusively or originally, nor even primarily, linguistic in character. The meanings that we find in language are attempts to express the much more fundamental meanings of lived experience. To attempt to reduce these primitive meanings, with which the investigator is intimately acquainted, to that portion of their expression that is overtly public, is similar to the strategy of attempting to reduce consciousness to behavior. For it is only through conscious experience, the subjective awareness of the different "looks" and qualitative "feels" of the objects of experience, that we can make observations of behavior (or, for that matter, of neural activity).

Philosophy as Rigorous Science

Some may argue that there is no great need for a scientific or philosophical investigation of consciousness, of experience from a first-person perspective, or of values and other similarly "subjective" phenomena, since these matters are extensively pursued by artists of all kinds, including novelists, poets, playwrights, filmmakers, composers, songwriters, painters, and sculptors. While there is no denying that many works of art succeed spectacularly at articulating, clarifying, and/or expressing "from the inside" various aspects of human experience, it must also be said that the aims of art are usually (and appropriately) quite different from those of science. For artists, no matter how concerned they might be with expressing truth, rather than falsehood, in their art, rarely pursue that objective with the methodological rigor that characterizes science. Artists do not typically see it as part of their job to accumulate, assess, and test evidence in support of whatever claims they make in their art. (Thus, a scientist is far more likely than an artist to be worried about something like the possibility of confusing mere correlation with causation.) Moreover, many of the problems that engage artists in the creation of their works, such as those having to do with the formal elements of their art (for example, the painter's concern with color harmony and perspective, the novelist's with creating an engaging plot, the composer's with melody, rhythm, and dynamics, and so forth), appear to be far removed from issues related to the adequacy of the artist's report on some area of human experience. To be sure, good artists will typically be interested in telling the truth as they see it, but they may not be terribly troubled by the question of whether or not the way they see it is the most accurate (or complete, or nuanced, or fair to other possible perspectives) way possible. Rather, they may feel that it is their job simply to express what they see, think, and feel, and, by making skillful use of the formal elements of their art, to do so in a way that results in works of art with which it is interesting and satisfying to engage. And indeed, while we often do seek (and find and appreciate) wisdom and insight in works of art, our appreciation of a particular piece might not be significantly diminished by our judgment that what it reports or implicitly claims is exaggerated, one-sided, standing in need of qualification, or speculative, or expressive of a particular temperament or personality (and thus not expressive of objective, or intersubjectively valid, truths). Granted, we likely will not be able to appreciate a work of art that communicates a message that we find to be stupid, crude, utterly wrongheaded, morally offensive, or one that simply fails to resonate with our own experience in any meaningful way. But a work of art that captures only part of the truth, that articulates only one (plausible) world view among others, that indulges in some speculating that goes well beyond what a scrupulous appraisal of the relevant evidence would warrant, can, when married to an engrossing, well-constructed story, to a haunting melody, or to a dazzling visual image, challenge, stimulate, and delight us, and thus provide us with a fully satisfying aesthetic experience.

The status of philosophy in connection with this distinction between science and art is unclear and contested. Since philosophers usually appeal to evidence and offer rational arguments in an attempt to determine, and to defend, what they take to be the truth, many see philosophy as much more closely resembling science than art. (It is noteworthy, in this connection, that the ancient Greeks used the same word, "philosophy," to refer both to philosophy and to what we now call "science.") But on the other hand, great works of philosophy can also be appreciated as works of art. On this view, such works are to be judged not on the basis of their degree of success at stating the objective truth fairly and completely, but rather on the basis of their ability to communicate one particular (interesting and plausible) world view in a compelling (or provocative, or challenging, or beautiful) way. One might admire the architectural splendor of Plato's *Republic* or Kant's *Critique of Pure Reason*—the way in which each work brings together a huge assortment of interlocking arguments and claims, and arranges them in such a way as to construct one dazzlingly complex edifice—without thinking that either philosopher's vision simply captures the truth, any more than does the vision of Picasso or Rembrandt, or Mozart or Louis Armstrong, or Dostoevsky or Virginia Woolf, or Martin Scorsese or Woody Allen. And some philosophical works, including those of Plato and Nietzsche, can be appreciated from the standpoint of the beauty and power of the writing alone, with consideration of the truth of the philosophical claims made in these works receding to the background.

Husserl's position on this issue is clear and uncompromising. What is lacking, and what is needed, is for philosophy to become a "rigorous science." He offers several reasons in support of this conclusion, but the most important one in the present context is that progress in our understanding of consciousness and subjectivity, of values, of experience and of the objects of experience, depends on philosophical activity conceived along such lines. Scientists take these subjects to be outside of their purview, and consequently ignore them. Artists address them, but do so in an unsystematic and idiosyncratic way, wherein considerations of truth and accuracy are usually subordinated both to concerns of personal expression and to those of formal aesthetic principles. Philosophers either (1) emulate scientists by neglecting these topics, (2) treat them, but emulate scientists by adopting a third-person standpoint that is inappropriate to them, rendering their basic data utterly inaccessible, or (3) treat them, but emulate artists by doing so in an impressionistic way, based more on the unique personality and world view of the philosopher than on a careful, scrupulous, and comprehensive examination of the relevant evidence. (Indeed, Husserl expresses the worry that most, if not all, of the great philosophical systems of the past contain large doses of speculation, artificial constructions of concepts that are not well grounded in experience, and expressions of their creators' idiosyncratic and subjective worldview.) What is needed, then, is an approach that would combine the subject matter and first-person standpoint of the artists with the evidence-based truth-orientation of the scientists. Husserl offers his phenomenology precisely as an attempt to meet this need.

In his later work he offers some historical reflections in an attempt to explain the urgency of this need. He suggests that, beginning with the Galilean revolution in science, and intensifying in the wake of the many spectacular successes of the natural sciences, the view has become widespread that genuine knowledge is factual in character, and limited to matters that can be investigated experimentally. The result has been reductionism and alienation. We have lost sight of the richness of human experience—values, meanings, emotions, strivings—in short, human subjectivity in all of its depth and variety. One of the main goals of phenomenology is to restore all of this, without abandoning (indeed, while greatly strengthening) the ideal of philosophy as rigorous science.

Indeed, a major feature of phenomenology is its insistence on a scientific attitude—the idea that claims should be backed by a rigorous appeal to the relevant evidence. When someone makes a claim, we should ask, "What does that mean? Is it true? How can we find out? What, in experience, would indicate the truth or falsity of the claim?" In Husserl's later works he engages in cultural criticism, decrying our utter failure even to approach this scientific-evidentialist ideal in our social, political, and cultural life. Consider, for example, the following statement by Mitch Daniels, who was at the time governor of my state, Indiana (and subsequently became president of my university!), in his official response to President Barack Obama's 2012 State of the Union address: "We do not accept that ours will ever be a nation of haves and have nots; we must always be a nation of haves and soon to haves."[1] What could this possibly mean? Does it mean that there is no poverty in the United States? That there is no distinction to be drawn between the billionaires, on the one hand, and the penniless homeless, on the other, who live among us? That there is no significant wealth or income disparity in the United States, and less there than in other nations? That there is plentiful economic mobility, or movement from poverty to wealth, in the United States, and more there than elsewhere? That the poor, as a matter of historical fact, have "always" in fact tended to escape poverty "soon" after suffering it? Or does the reference to what we will not "accept" simply mean that we do not (and should not) believe what the evidence clearly shows to be the case, so that the statement amounts to a recommendation that we live in a state of denial, a fantasy land, in which the problems of poverty and economic inequality are to be simply ignored, rather than honestly confronted, thought about, debated, and ultimately solved? In any case, from a Husserlian point of view, the problem is that statements as vacuous as these—statements that are both unclear in meaning and, on any plausible construal, demonstrably false—are the rule, rather than the exception, in many arenas of public discourse today (politics and advertising being perhaps the two most notable). From Husserl's perspective, this phenomenon constitutes a grave spiritual disease, with decidedly ugly and dangerous real-world consequences. One of phenomenology's main tasks is to combat it.

Objectivity, Subjectivity, and Correlativity

Phenomenology also offers unique resources for dealing with issues of objectivity and subjectivity. One way to approach these issues is to think of them in terms of a natural progression. Our initial, default, stance in our dealings with the world is to assume uncriti-

---

[1] http://www.usatoday.com/news/washington/story/2012-01-24/ daniels-republican-response-transcript/52783388/1 (accessed February 11, 2012).

cally that the objects we encounter exist independently of us and contain in themselves precisely those qualities that we find in them, just *as* we find them. But then we may lose confidence in this "naïve" objectivism, perhaps as a result of discovering that other people often see objects differently, and draw different conclusions about them, than we do. We then direct our attention to what we bring to bear—our assumptions, prejudices, hopes, fears, biases, conceptual schemes, and the like—on our experiences of objects, and come to the conclusion that these factors play the dominant role in determining the outcome of such encounters. From the objectivism of "pit bulls are scary," we slide fairly easily into the subjectivism of "I'm afraid of pit bulls." But such subjectivism can, in its way, be as one-sided, and nearly as naïve, as the uncritical objectivism with which we began. While my fear of pit bulls undeniably has something to do with me (after all, some people are not afraid of them), clearly it also has something to do with pit bulls (they have sharp teeth and claws, and are sometimes aggressive, all features that are absent from many other objects of which I am not afraid, such as dandelions, books, and pieces of lint).

This same sliding from one naïve, one-sided extreme to another can be observed in connection with attitudes toward cultural practices. When we are taught from an early age to do certain things in specific ways, when we then grow up doing them in those ways (so that the practices become habitual and effortless), and when we notice, furthermore, that everyone else we know does them in those ways as well, it is easy and natural for us to assume that such ways are the right ones, the ones that best fit with, and are most responsive to, the true nature of the objects with which the practices in question deal. When we learn of other people, perhaps from other times or places, who do things differently, our immediate reaction might well be that these people are simply wrong, out of touch with reality, both in their practices and in their beliefs underlying those practices. But as we begin to learn more about the variety of world cultures, perhaps through sociological, anthropological, or historical study, or simply by getting to know people from different parts of the world, it may dawn on us that many practices that seem strange to us do so only because we are unfamiliar with them, rather than because they are in any obvious way less rational or otherwise inferior to our own way of doing things. Once our thoughts turn in this direction, it is not difficult to go further, and to notice that many common beliefs and ways of doing things seem arbitrary. They appear to be the products of historical accident, reinforced not by a reasoned assessment of evidence, but rather by indoctrination, enculturation, habit, and tradition. From this observation it appears to be but a short step (psychologically, if not logically) to the conclusion that cultural factors, rather than the true natures of the objects about which we think, are primarily responsible for our beliefs about the world. On this view, "truth" is "socially constructed," or "culturally relative," and we can have no hope of achieving objective truth—beliefs that we know, on the basis of a rational assessment of evidence, to express the way things really are.

Phenomenology helps to counter these tendencies toward one-sided objectivism or subjectivism in at least two ways. First, phenomenological investigations are in principle balanced with regard to subjectivity/objectivity issues, both methodologically and in terms of subject matter. For in studying phenomena, phenomenologists must inquire into (1) the objects of experience, (2) consciousness, and, in particular, the conscious acts which present or reveal those objects, and (3) the correlativity of consciousness and object, that is, the reciprocal relations among the two. (Practice in focusing on all three of these may help one to develop skills necessary for the tricky task of distinguishing the merely familiar from the truly evident.) While one might suppose that such an even-handed approach would lead to a uniform, middle-of-the-road position, precluding the reaching of a subjectivist or objectivist conclusion on any given issue, and thus discouraging the drawing of distinctions between different claims or issues in terms of where they fall on a subjective/objective spectrum, this turns out not to be the case. Consider the value judgments, "happiness is intrinsically better than misery" and "the taste of strawberry is better than the taste of grape." A phenomenological investigation might reveal that there is something in the nature of the objects "happiness" and "misery," abstract and ideal as these objects are, that renders the judgment that happiness is intrinsically better than misery obvious and undeniable, necessarily true, true for all subjects, and the contrary judgment, that misery is better than happiness, wrongheaded, perverse, clearly mistaken. A similar investigation of "grape" and "strawberry" might show, by contrast, that there is nothing in these objects that would render any preferences concerning them mandatory on others. No matter how much I might prefer strawberry over grape, I cannot see that those with the contrary preference are making any kind of mistake, as I clearly can with regard to those (if there are any such people) who think that misery is better than happiness. (For example, someone who would cite, as evidence that misery is better than happiness, the fact that we often learn valuable lessons from painful experiences, would be confusing the intrinsic value of misery and happiness with the value of their effects.) The phenomenological approach thus does not stand as an obstacle to the drawing of subjectivist or objectivist conclusions that are based on a careful investigation of both the subjective and objective poles (and the correlativity of the two) of the relevant experiences. But it does stand as an obstacle to the kind of facile, sweeping objectivism or subjectivism (both disturbingly common) that simply ignores one or the other of these poles of experience entirely. For example, phenomenological inquiry strongly suggests that religious fundamentalists and social constructionists, for all their differences, make essentially the same mistake. They tend to ignore the things themselves (the data of experience, in all their complexity), preferring the dogmas of old books (in the case of the fundamentalists), or speculations about the reducibility of thought to history and socialization (in the case of the social constructionists), over a thoughtful confrontation with evidence.

The second way in which phenomenology counters the tendency toward versions of subjectivism or objectivism that are lacking in nuance or evidential grounding is by means of its method of bracketing questions about the nonexperiential existence of experienced objects. The reason for bracketing such questions is to facilitate the study of experienced objects as phenomena, that is, precisely *as* objects of experience. The reason this undermines objectionably simplistic objectivist and subjectivist theories is that many such theories are based, not on the evidence of experience, but rather on ideas about what does and does not exist independently of human subjectivity. For example, many people, because of their conviction that an inventory of all things that exist independently of consciousness would not include aesthetic values, conclude that aesthetic values are entirely subjective, that is, as the cliché has it, that "beauty is in the eye of the beholder." As a result, although in their own experience they find some works of art engrossing, exciting, thrilling, thought-provoking, challenging, soothing, beautiful, intelligent, expressive, well-constructed, daring, dazzling, brilliant, and others dull, lifeless, stupid, insipid, clumsy, thoughtless, vapid, boring, flat, inept, incoherent, ugly, they nonetheless, in attempting to explain or to analyze such experienced distinctions, ignore all the data to be found in investigating the objective pole of their aesthetic experience. But because phenomenology, by contrast, studies the objects of experience (including not only works of art, but also aesthetic values) as *phenomena*, it is able to focus on what is disclosed about them in experience, without the investigation being prejudiced by ontological beliefs (that is, beliefs about what exists) that are *imposed on* the experiences in question, rather than *founded in* them.

An Example of Phenomenological Description

To illustrate this point, consider Jean-Paul Sartre's famous description of the phenomenon of absence. In his massive phenomenological work, *Being and Nothingness*, Sartre recounts, from the inside, what is disclosed in the experience of looking for someone at a certain time and place, only to discover that he is not there. In Sartre's example, I have made an appointment to meet my friend Pierre at a café, but I arrive fifteen minutes late. Knowing that Pierre is a busy person, and always punctual, I worry that he will not have waited for me. And indeed, after looking for him hopefully, I am forced to conclude that he is not present at the café.

What happens during my search for Pierre? What do I observe, and what is my experience like? Sartre's first point is that what I see depends crucially on my focusing activities. While there is much to observe in the café (patrons, tables, booths, mirrors, light, a smoky atmosphere [Sartre was writing in Paris in the 1940s], sounds of voices, rattling saucers and footsteps, smells of food, and so forth), I hardly notice these at all, and definitely do not perceive them in detail. The reason is (and note that this is a phenomenological description; it is an attempt to articulate what is given in experience, and pays no attention to the issue of what does or does not exist outside of experience) that

> in perception there is always the construction of a figure on a ground. No one object, no group of objects is especially designed to be organ-

ized as specifically either ground or figure; all depends on the direction of my attention. When I enter this café to search for Pierre, there
is formed a synthetic organization of all the objects in the café, on the
ground of which Pierre is given as about to appear. . . . Each element
of the setting, a person, a table, a chair, attempts to isolate itself upon
the ground constituted by the totality of the other objects, only to fall
back once more on the undifferentiation of this ground; it melts into
the ground. For the ground is that which is seen only in addition, that
which is the object of a purely marginal attention. Thus the original
nihilation [a technical term coined by Sartre, which means, roughly,
"nothing making"] of all the figures which appear and are swallowed
up in the total neutrality of a ground is the necessary condition for the
appearance of the principal figure, which is here the presence of
Pierre. This nihilation is given to my intuition [meaning that it is
directly perceived]; I am witness to the successive disappearance of all
the objects which I look at—in particular of the faces, which detain
me for an instant (Could this be Pierre?) and which as quickly decom-
pose precisely because they "are not" the face of Pierre. (BN, 41)

Sartre's description to this point places emphasis on the subjective pole of experience. I am able to encounter Pierre's absence
from the café only because I am looking for him and hoping to
find him there. Billions of other people are also absent, but I do
not experience these absences.

But on the other hand, the objective pole of experience is also
crucial here. Had Pierre actually been in the café, I would not have
discovered his absence there. Rather, I would have been "suddenly
arrested by his face," and the entire café would have organized
itself around him (BN, 42).

Moreover, it is important to notice that Pierre's absence is an
object of my experience. It is something I genuinely encounter and
perceive. It is the figure in contrast to which the entire remainder
of the café serves as an undifferentiated ground. Here the bracketing of questions of independent existence comes into play. One
might well take the position that "Pierre's absence from the café"
is not something that exists. After all, an infinite number of entities are absent from an infinite number of locations, but an inventory of all of the contents of the universe, however one might go
about drawing it up, presumably would not include this inter-
minable list of absences. Some then draw the conclusion that since
absences are not "real," that is, they don't exist, then we cannot

encounter or perceive them, but rather only know about them by logical inference, involving the application of the category of negation. But such a conclusion conflicts violently with our experience, and it is our experience that phenomenology attempts to describe, and to do so without prejudice.

The Aims of Phenomenology

In one sense phenomenology is highly ambitious. Husserl proposes it as *the* foundational discipline, *the* master science undergirding all of the others. But in another sense it is quite modest. It makes no claims about anything beyond, or outside of, or underlying, the world of our everyday experience. Its aim is to help us to see more clearly what we have already seen, not by adding to what we have seen some grand theory that would explain it all, but rather by persuading us to remove the confused, or speculative, or prejudicial assumptions or thought constructions that can serve to block our access to what is given in experience. It can aid us in our effort to discard from our thinking (or at least, to set aside temporarily) all that is merely traditional, habitual, familiar, taken on faith, taken on authority, or in some other way believed without having been seen (in the widest sense of "seeing"). Phenomenology strives to return us to what stares us plainly in the face, and then to help us to see that from an up-close, unobstructed vantage point.

One of the principal goals of phenomenology, then, is simply descriptive fidelity. The aim is to describe accurately what is given in experience precisely as it is given, and within the limits of how it is given.

As a result, phenomenological writing is unusually interactive. While any writing worth reading will engage the critical faculties of good readers, provoking them to inquire into the meaning, relevance, and truth status of whatever is being communicated, phenomenological writing is unique in that it deals almost exclusively with matters with which its readers are already intimately familiar. Thus, rather than informing readers of events that happened at distant times or places, or of the results of scientific experiments conducted in laboratories with prohibitively expensive equipment, phenomenology discusses the fundamental data of human experience. Readers are therefore well equipped to think along with phenomenological authors, and to evaluate phenomenological texts by comparing the descriptions they contain to their own experience. Accordingly, phenomenological writings usually contain fewer arguments than do other philosophical works. Rather, they contain maps, guideposts, and the like, to assist readers to find in their own experience what the phenomenological authors find in theirs.

Phenomenology is in that sense less a philosophical theory or position (like utilitarianism, logical positivism, or pragmatism), than a field of inquiry (like epistemology, ethics, logic, or philosophy of science). And the extraordinarily basic nature of its subject matter underscores both the modesty and the audacity of the phenomenological project. Consider, in this regard, James M. Edie's description of the subject matter of phenomenology:

> Phenomenology is neither a science of objects nor a science of the subject; it is a science of *experience*. It does not concentrate exclusively on either the objects of experience or on the subject of experience, but on the point of contact where being and consciousness meet. It is, therefore, a study of consciousness *as intentional*, as directed towards objects, as living in an intentionally constituted world. The subject . . . and the object . . . are studied in their strict correlativity on each level of experience (perception, imagination, categorical thought, etc.). Such a study . . . aims at disclosing the structures of consciousness as consciousness, of experience as experience; it means to unveil the . . . structures which constitute the mysterious subject-object relationship which we call *consciousness of*. . . . In short, phenomenology is a study of *phenomena*. As such it is a more fundamental study than logic or psychology; it goes to the fundamental structures of conscious experience which constitute the very conditions of the possibility of any conscious experience whatsoever.[2]

Phenomenology is humble, then, in that its subject matter is non-technical and accessible to everyone, but audacious in that this same subject matter, lived experience, encompasses, is foundational to, and makes possible, our knowledge of anything else whatsoever.

But in dealing with that subject matter, another goal of phenomenology is to reveal the essential structures of each phenome-

---

[2] "Introduction" to Pierre Thévenaz, *What Is Phenomenology? and Other Essays*, trans. James M. Edie et al. (Chicago: Quadrangle Books, 1962), 19–20.

non, as opposed to detailing contingent particulars pertaining to it. On Husserl's view, this goal follows directly from that of descriptive fidelity. Before one can entertain theories about anything—perception, imagination, temporality, embodiment, value, and so forth—one must, according to Husserl, be able to describe it, to understand just what it is that one is trying to explain. What is the *nature* of the phenomenon in question? Similarly, in its investigations of the natures of various phenomena, and of their interrelations, phenomenology is less concerned with specific facts, with what has happened and is actually the case, than it is with what in general is possible or impossible, necessary or contingent, compatible or incompatible.

Similarly, since it is a fundamental finding of phenomenology that we experience the world as meaningful and structured, a third aim of phenomenology is to uncover the logic of these meanings and structures. Recall in this connection that phenomenology differs from the many schools of analytic philosophy that also focus on meaning in that it does not see meaning as always, or even primarily, something linguistic. For, as Husserl points out, there is meaning and signification in "all acts, be they now combined with expressive acts or not" (Ideas I, §124, 294). To see is, at least typically, to "see-as." To see an apple is to see it as red, as round, as a big or little thing, as a fruit, as an apple, as a kind of apple (for example, Fuji), as something tasty, something nutritious, something to eat, a member of the plant kingdom, a thing on the table, a rotten thing that should be thrown away, or some combination of these, or something else equally significant. The point is that perception is meaningful, whether or not I attempt to communicate that meaning to others, or even think about it explicitly in words. To be engaged in practical pursuits is to be engaged in a world in which things, right from the start, are saturated with meaning—this is an aid, this is an obstacle, this is what I am trying to get. The unleashed snarling dog frightens me because I find meaning—a threat of pain and injury—in the snarls. My practical and emotional life, no less than my rational and theoretical one, is meaningful and reveals a meaningful world.

This point brings us to a fourth goal of phenomenology, that of showing that the world is not only meaningful but also intelligible and accessible to reason. In this aim phenomenology puts itself in opposition to some strains of romanticism, to all varieties of mysticism and irrationalism, and, in general, to all theories, no matter how "profound" they may be, that are vague, speculative, and not well grounded in evidence. It is in reference to such theories that Husserl speaks of "the chaos that genuine science [phenomenology] wants to transform into a cosmos, into a simple, completely clear, lucid order" (PRS, 144).

A fifth aim of phenomenology is to study consciousness, not from an external, third-person perspective, and one in which consciousness is understood to be a thing in nature, or an effect of such a thing, but rather from an internal, first-person perspective, one in which consciousness is understood to be the unique and universal medium of access to whatever exists. This issue puts on full display Husserl's major agreement and disagreement with his predecessor, the great seventeenth-century French philosopher and mathematician, René Descartes. On the one hand, Descartes is rightly credited with opening up consciousness to philosophical scrutiny, and with pointing out that it is only by means of consciousness that we can be aware of anything at all. But on the other hand, he conceived of consciousness as a substance, that is, as a kind of thing. This resulted in a research program within modern Western philosophy of investigating consciousness as if it were a thing, where the major issues concerned how this kind of thing could be related to the other major kind of things—physical bodies. So little attention was paid to conscious experience, or to its structures, or to objects considered strictly as objects of experience. Eventually, by the nineteenth century, subjectivity was largely banished as a respectable philosophical topic. This tradition carried over into the twentieth century, with behaviorism (roughly, the view that everything that organisms do should be understood solely in terms of overt bodily movements, with no reference to internal mental states), eliminative materialism (the idea that such concepts as "belief" and "desire" are dispensable fictions, to be replaced with talk of brain states and other biological concepts), and the like. When consciousness was investigated, it was as an empirical phenomenon appropriately approached by means of the quantitative methods of modern natural science. Phenomenology rejects this approach on the grounds that consciousness is not an "object" of that kind, and that many of the objects of consciousness—many phenomena—cannot be adequately dealt with by such methods.

And indeed, a sixth goal of phenomenology is to study and to describe every conceivable kind of object: natural (rocks, trees, animals), cultural (tools, books, works of art), ideal (mathematical and logical entities), historical, social, political, economic, legal, and so forth. No object of experience is to be excluded on methodological grounds. Whatever can be experienced is to be described in terms of, and within the limits of, what it reveals about itself in experience. Indeed, Husserl defines phenomenology as "the theory of experiences in general, inclusive of all matters . . . given in experiences, and evidently discoverable in them" (LI 2, Investigation VI, Appendix, §5, 343). Part of the rationale for such an approach lies in the recognition that the world contains structures that the methods of empirical science cannot disclose.

Consider, in this regard, the special problems raised by the social sciences. Can freedom be studied by the empirical methods of the natural sciences, which assume universal causation? A human life, as lived, is characterized by conscious awareness, a meaningful and purposive relation to objects, attractions and aversions to values, decisions based on reasons, and so forth, all of which elude the methods of the natural sciences, but all of which are accessible to phenomenology. For, as the great historian of phenomenology, Herbert Spiegelberg, puts it, "phenomenology readmits us to a world in which everything has a claim to recognition, as long as it presents itself in concrete experience."[3]

Phenomenology thus differs from traditional empiricism in investigating the many different ways in which something might be experienced, including memory and imagination, in addition to sense perception. But there are also many objects of experience that are not objects of *sense* experience at all. Numbers, logical concepts, and values are examples. All of these things are capable of being presented "in person," in such a way as to provide warrant for making true statements about them (and for ruling out other statements as false). According to Husserl, to clarify something, even in logic and mathematics, disciplines which deal with abstract entities, is to ground it in direct, lived experience.

Accordingly, a final goal of phenomenology, and by far its boldest one, is to serve as the foundation of all specific sciences.

----

[3] "On Some Human Uses of Phenomenology," in *Phenomenology in Perspective*, ed. F. J. Smith (The Hague: Martinus Nijhoff, 1970), 20.

Phenomenology's intention is to clarify the meanings of the basic concepts and categories of all specialized disciplines and areas of inquiry by grounding them in the essential structures, carefully observed and described, of lived experience. The aim is to trace the development of all such phenomena from their roots in basic, perhaps unarticulated, conscious experience to their expression in the most elegant and sophisticated of scientific theories. This is part of phenomenology's comprehensive project of uncovering the entire range of conscious experience, rendering clear and describing its essential structure, and doing so, not from the outside, from a detached, third-person, perspective, but rather from the inside, from an engaged, first-person perspective, that is, from the standpoint of subjectivity itself.

The Critical Reception of Phenomenology

Husserl wanted to establish phenomenology as a method for investigating a distinct, otherwise unexplored region, so that many researchers could make contributions in a cooperative way, gradually building up a large store of knowledge, in the manner of the natural sciences. In a way, he succeeded spectacularly. Few philosophers have equaled him in exerting such a strong influence on such an impressive (both quantitatively and qualitatively) group of followers. The list of notable figures who have made substantial use of Husserl's ideas, and cited him as a major influence, includes Max Scheler (1874–1928), Nicolai Hartmann (1882–1950), Adolf Reinach (1883–1917), Gabriel Marcel (1889–1973), Martin Heidegger (1889–1976), Edith Stein (1891–1942), Roman Ingarden (1893–1970), Alfred Schütz (1899–1959), Hans-Georg Gadamer (1900–2002), Aron Gurwitsch (1901–1973), Ludwig Landgrebe (1902–1991), Eugen Fink (1905–1975), Jean-Paul Sartre (1905–1980), Emmanuel Lévinas (1906–1995), Jan Patočka (1907–1977), Maurice Merleau-Ponty (1908–1961), Simone de Beauvoir (1908–1986), Paul Ricoeur (1913–2005), Jacques Derrida (1930–2004), Francisco Varela (1946–2001), Jean-Luc Marion (1946–), and countless other perhaps lesser but still impressive and significant, individuals. (As this list suggests, Husserl's influence was especially strong in France, as five of the most celebrated figures in twentieth century French philosophy— Sartre, Levinas, Merleau-Ponty, Ricoeur, and Derrida—all devoted their first significant writings to the study of his work.) Moreover, the reach of phenomenology has extended far beyond philosophy, as it has been widely practiced also in psychology, sociology, literary theory, and art criticism, among other fields. The French philosopher Michel Henry, writing in 1990, asserts that "phenomenology increasingly seems to be the principal movement of the thought of our times." Predicting a "return to Husserl," he goes on to suggest that "phenomenology will be to the twentieth century what German idealism was to the nineteenth, what empiricism was to the eighteenth, what Descartes was to the seventeenth, what Thomas Aquinas and Duns Scotus were to scholasticism, what Plato and Aristotle were to antiquity."[4] Indeed, a good case could be made that Husserl has exerted more influence on subsequent intellectual trends on the European continent than has any other figure in twentieth-century philosophy. He belongs on any short list of candidates for the title of most influential philosopher of that century.

But on the other hand, one could also argue that he failed miserably. Husserl clearly hoped that many successors would accept his framework and use it in fields or subject matters that he had not himself explored. Instead, all of his major followers, and most of his lesser ones, while acknowledging his great influence and inspiration, have nonetheless rejected some of his major claims and methods, and have instead made rather bold innovations of their own. (Perhaps this is not a failing, after all. It is rare to succeed at inspiring such a broad range of truly original thinkers!) The testimony of those who knew Husserl presents a complicated picture of his own reaction to the reception of his work. Some say that he tended to feel hurt and betrayed upon discovering that a former disciple had gone off in an independent direction (this was definitely the case with regard to Heidegger). But others insist that Husserl was not dogmatic, and was quite open to the idea that many of his findings were properly destined to be modified and, in some cases, rejected by later investigators. His aim, on this view, was to initiate a new approach to, and subject matter for, philosophy, rather than to present a finished and perfected system—he wanted to found a research program, not a cult or sect.

---

[4] *Material Phenomenology*, trans. Scott Davidson (New York: Fordham University Press, 2008), 1.

The current reputation and status of phenomenology as a wider movement (going beyond Husserl, and including the somewhat dissident figures mentioned above) is controversial and difficult to determine. On the positive side, given the central role phenomenology played in twentieth-century European philosophy, the number of figures of enduring interest associated with it, the number of important intellectual movements influenced by it (for example, existentialism, hermeneutics, ethnomethodology, and deconstruction), the number of still widely-read masterpieces produced by its practitioners (for example, Heidegger's *Being and Time*, Sartre's *Being and Nothingness*, and Merleau-Ponty's *Phenomenology of Perception*), and the number of famous phenomenological descriptions and analyses of specific phenomena that are still in wide circulation (for example, Heidegger on death, Sartre on freedom, Merleau-Ponty on embodiment, and Beauvoir on feminism), it seems likely that phenomenology will continue to be studied as long as there is interest in the history of philosophy.

But on the negative side, there is some question as to whether phenomenology will remain a vital contemporary force (or even regain momentum in that regard), and be regarded as one of the resources to which we should turn in dealing with present problems, or whether it will instead be studied primarily for its historical interest, along with other great (though essentially dead) philosophical movements of the past. For while phenomenology is practiced all over the world, and original phenomenological descriptions and analyses are produced every year, it must be admitted that by far the most significant activity has been confined to Germany and France, with the greatest contributions having been completed by the mid-point of the twentieth century.

A great complicating factor in assessing the current and future status of phenomenology is that throughout the period of phenomenology's existence Western philosophy has been divided into two often hostile and mutually uncomprehending camps: "analytic philosophy," practiced predominantly in English-speaking countries, and "continental philosophy," affiliated with the European continent. Many philosophers in England and the United States receive little or no education in continental philosopher, and are often taught to mistrust it. Those who are brave and open-minded enough to look into it, frequently find that they cannot appreciate it, because its history, problems, terminology, and references tend to differ substantially from what they are used to. On the continental side, the problem is that there are fads, and a hunger for something new, in philosophy no less than in other areas of culture. Every philosophical school or movement that once is hot and new (as phenomenology undoubtedly was, and to an extraordinary degree) is destined to be eclipsed, at least in the short term, by the next big thing to come along. Some of these eclipsed ideas remain in that condition, and are henceforth either forgotten entirely or else studied merely as part of the history of philosophy. But others (for example, the ethical theories of Aristotle, Kant, and Mill) return as contenders for contemporary assent (in modified form) despite the fact that they are long past being new. Given how relatively young phenomenology is, it is still too early to tell which way it will go in this regard.

There are three factors, however, aside from the high quality of the best phenomenological work, that suggest the possibility of a phenomenological renaissance. One is that the severity of the analytic/continental cultural split seems to be diminishing with each passing year. As analytic philosophers begin to become acquainted with continental philosophy, they seem generally to find phenomenology, and especially the work of Husserl, much more to their liking than the ideas of more recent continental giants, such as Foucault, Derrida, and Lacan. Part of the reason is that Husserl's work, more so than that of the figures just mentioned, is largely devoted to issues in epistemology (theory of knowledge), logic, and the philosophy of science—issues with which most analytic philosophers are quite familiar. Also, as discussed above, Husserl's approach to philosophy is scientific in character, with high aspirations of rigor, and this, too, is more congenial to analytic philosophers than the somewhat looser, more literary and playful, approach of more recent continental thinkers.

Secondly, we are in the midst of a "consciousness boom." While analytic philosophers had largely ignored consciousness for decades, they have now taken an intense interest in it, and are casting about for resources to help them to understand it. This is bringing phenomenology to their attention.

Thirdly, "new" works by Husserl, in the form of previously unpublished posthumous writings, are being regularly produced as part of an ongoing publication project, and these cast his thought in a new light. Many of the standard criticisms of Husserl (for example, that he is too much an idealist, too Cartesian, too much an essentialist, too individualistic, too intellectually or cognitively-oriented [at the expense of practice, the body, and the emotions], too insensitive to history and culture, too devoted to such unattainable goals as "rigorous science" and "presuppositionlessness"), while not without merit, are largely based on reactions to his most famous works, those published during his lifetime. Almost all of these works are programmatic and introductory. They try to explain what phenomenology is, what it is for, and what its distinct subject matter is. But in his voluminous writings that he did not choose to publish during his lifetime (but which have been coming out continually since his death) he devotes himself far more to *doing* phenomenology than to introducing it and explaining it. In these writings he undertakes phenomenological investigations of such topics as time, the body, perception, and value. These writings paint a fuller, less one-sided picture of Husserl, and they lesson the force of the standard objections, for two reasons. First, the tendencies that draw criticism are much less pronounced in his applied phenomenological work than they are in his introductory and programmatic work. Secondly, and more importantly, the applied work is so rich in interesting, provocative, and fruitful insights as to render relatively inconsequential any disagreements one may have with him at the theoretical, meta-theoretical, or methodological level. To the extent that these works and this "new" Husserl are publicized, at least within philosophical circles, it seems possible that many philosophers who might otherwise not have given him a second (or first) look, now will do so.

Edmund Husserl and the Origins of Phenomenology: A Biographical Overview

Husserl (born in Prossnitz, Moravia, Austria, now part of the Czech Republic, on April 8, 1859) did not begin his academic career as a philosopher. He started out as a mathematician, studying under the renowned Karl Weierstrass, and earning a doctorate at the University of Vienna in that subject in 1883, with a dissertation on the calculus of variations, supervised by Leo Königsberger. He worked as Weierstrass's assistant from 1883 to1884.

During the years 1884 to 1886 Husserl attended Franz Brentano's lectures on philosophy. These lectures inspired him to devote the remainder of his life entirely to philosophy. (Almost fifty years later, in 1932, Husserl would remark, "Without Brentano I should not have written a single word of philosophy.")[5] Brentano presented philosophy as rigorously scientific, an idea that greatly appealed to Husserl, who went on to champion such a conception of philosophy in his own work.

Brentano was interested in understanding what is involved in knowing something. To know an object is to interact with it in such a way as not to change it. How does this work? Brentano noted that the object-as-experienced, which he called the "intentional object," is more evident to us than is the object itself. The intentional object belongs to me, and I am aware of it exactly as it is. It cannot conceal part of itself the way the external world can. Moreover, I am not only aware of the intentional object, but also aware of that awareness itself, all in one conscious act. (Otherwise, there would be an infinite regress—to know that I am perceiving an object I would need, in addition to the conscious act of perceiving the object, a second, reflective act of perceiving this act of perception; but to know this, I would need, in addition, a third act of perceiving that reflective act, and so on infinitely.) Husserl would go on to develop this idea of "intentionality" in his own way. It helped to inspire the very idea of phenomenology—the study of objects of experience, of the conscious acts of experiencing such objects, and of the correlativity of these two poles of experience.

As Husserl continued his studies of philosophy he was increasingly bothered by the absence of consensus in the field, and by the diversity and confusion of competing artificial theoretical constructions, each characterized by a profusion of technical terms and distinctions. This intensified Husserl's commitment to methodological rigor in philosophy, and especially to the two ideals of clarity and evidentialism—the grounding of all conclusions in the "givens" of experience.

Despite Husserl's decision to change his vocation from scientifically-oriented mathematician to philosopher, he retained throughout his life his interest in, and admiration for, the achievements of the sciences. At the same time, however, he found something lacking in the sciences in that they show no concern for their own

---

[5] As quoted in Barry Smith, *Austrian Philosophy* (Chicago: Open Court, 1994), 26–27.

foundations. They do not address questions about the nature of knowledge or of truth or rationality or evidence or logic. Rather, they are content to adopt prevailing conceptions of knowledge uncritically, so as to get on with work in their specific domain. It is philosophy that historically has taken up (as Husserl agreed that it properly should) the task of clarifying the all-encompassing criteria and standards of rationally defensible knowledge. But on the other hand, philosophy, unlike science, has no well worked-out method for achieving its goals. This is what Husserl attempted to provide with his developing Brentano-inspired project, which he came to call "phenomenology." As a first step, all scientific investigations must rely on conceptions of what are the essences of some of the things with which they deal—that is, what is the nature of the things, what qualities belong to them necessarily if they are to be the kind of things that they are, as opposed to those qualities that belong to them only accidentally and contingently. Knowledge of such matters cannot be arrived at through the methods of the sciences. Here again, Husserl saw a role for his developing idea of phenomenology.

Meanwhile, in 1886, Husserl, who was Jewish, converted to Christianity and was baptized into the Lutheran Church. In the following year he married Malvine Steinschneider. In 1892 Husserl became a father, as his daughter Elisabeth was born, followed in the next year by a son, Gerhart, and, two years later, by another son, Wolfgang. Husserl's marriage to Malvine lasted until his death in 1938, a period of over fifty years.

Husserl's first teaching position in philosophy was at Halle, where he began lecturing in 1887. In 1891 he produced his first book, *Philosophy of Arithmetic*, which for the most part presented his early, pre-phenomenological, thinking, and thus failed to express his new orientation.

His first phenomenological project, *Logical Investigations*, a large two-volume work, appeared in 1900-1901. It was well received, and attracted a good deal of attention, helping to establish Husserl as a significant new figure on the philosophical scene. Indeed, on the strength of it he was invited to take a position at Göttingen, where he proceeded to move in 1901. Sparked by *Logical Investigations*, a phenomenological movement in Germany quickly began to emerge, attracting such figures as Adolf Reinach, Alexander Pfänder, Johannes Daubert, and Moritz Geiger.

Husserl went on to devote his life almost exclusively to teaching, studying, and writing. During his years at Göttingen he produced *The Idea of Phenomenology* (1907), "Philosophy as Rigorous Science" (1911), and *Ideas Pertaining to a Pure Phenomenology and to a Phenomenological Philosophy, First Book* (henceforth "*Ideas I*") (1913), in addition to several smaller pieces, and numerous other works, some of them quite substantial, that have appeared only posthumously.

In 1913, in concert with several of his most distinguished students and followers, including Martin Heidegger, he founded the *Yearbook for Philosophy and Phenomenological Research*. Eleven books were eventually published in this series.

While Husserl's life during this period might appear rather quiet and uneventful, an impression that his dry writing style could only reinforce, he was in fact a philosopher of unusual passion, commitment, and intense moral concern, as is evidenced by the following remarks from a 1906 diary entry: "I was tormented by those incredibly strange realms: the world of the purely logical and the world of actual consciousness—or, as I would say now, that of the phenomenological and also the psychological. I had no idea how to unite them; and yet they had to interrelate and form an intrinsic unity" (PN, 490–91). Or again:

> Without getting clear on the general outlines of the sense, essence, methods and main points of a critique of reason, without having thought out, outlined, formulated and justified a general sketch of such a critique, I cannot live truly and sincerely. I have had enough of the torments of unclarity, of tottering back and forth in doubt. . . . I simply cannot go on without clarity. I will—I *must*—approach these sublime goals. . . . I am fighting for my life. . . . Only one thing will fulfill me: I must come to clarity! Otherwise I cannot live. I cannot endure life without believing that I shall attain it. (PN, 494)

Writing twenty-four years later, in 1930, his feelings evidently had not changed, as his reference then to "the despair of one who has the misfortune to be in love with philosophy" shows (AP, 52).

In 1916 Husserl's younger son, Wolfgang, was killed in action in World War I. (The following year his older son, Gerhard, was seriously injured in the war, but survived.)

Also in 1916 Husserl moved to Freiburg, as a full professor of philosophy. He was by this time famous in philosophical circles on the strength of the *Logical Investigations* and *Ideas I*. He was recognized as the founder of phenomenology, a substantial philosophical movement that had attracted a large number of impressive adherents. He remained at Freiburg until his retirement in 1928. While we now know this to have been an extraordinarily productive period in Husserl's career (he composed thousands of pages of interesting, original, and ultimately highly influential phenomenological analyses), none of this work met his high standards, and he chose to publish nothing during these years, with his next publication of new work, *Formal and Transcendental Logic*, not appearing until 1929. (*Phenomenology of Internal Time-Consciousness* was published in 1928, but it consisted of lectures and manuscripts dating from 1901 to 1911 that had only just been edited for publication.)

In 1923 Husserl was offered the chair of philosophy at Berlin, a strong sign of his eminence in German philosophical circles. A delegation from the University at Freiburg, which included the university president, prevailed on him to stay. One of the inducements was the offer of financing for a research assistant. Husserl chose Ludwig Landgrebe, and, subsequently, Eugen Fink.

Upon Husserl's retirement in 1928 he was succeeded, in accordance with his own expressed wishes, by Heidegger, who had recently published *Being and Time*.

An indication of Husserl's standing in the European philosophical world at the time of his retirement is that he was repeatedly invited to give lectures abroad. In April 1928 he presented a set of lectures in Amsterdam. Then, on February 23 and 25 of the following year, he delivered four lectures at the Sorbonne in Paris, the heart of philosophy in France, in the Amphithéâtre Descartes. Xavier Léon, of the Société Française de Philosophie, in his opening remarks at this event, called Husserl "the most eminent master in German philosophy." These lectures formed the basis for Husserl's *Cartesian Meditations*, published in 1931.

On January 23, 1933, seven days before Adolf Hitler became chancellor of Germany, the university arranged for a celebration of the golden anniversary of Husserl's doctorate. The Rector, some deans, and other high-level administrators participated in this event, and personally congratulated Husserl. But on April 14 Husserl was notified by Robert Wagner, Nazi state governor and party chief of Baden, that he (Husserl) was a "non-Aryan," and was therefore being formally dismissed from the university. In a July 1, 1933 letter to his friend, Gustav Albrecht, Husserl called this the greatest insult of his life, and expressed doubt that he would ever be able to get over it. Husserl's son, Gerhart, who held a teaching position in Kiel, was fired from his job for the same reason. Almost equally hurtful was the fact that Husserl and his family were being stripped of their identity as Germans, in spite of their service to the German nation during the First World War. (Both of his sons had served in the army, with the older son, Wolfgang, having been killed in battle. Husserl's daughter had also served as a nurse.) The final insult was to see Heidegger join the Nazis, become Rector, and go on to advocate for, and to implement, the Nazi vision: to make the university an authoritarian regime of absolute subservience to a supreme leader. On October 1, 1933 Heidegger was named *Führer* of the university. Ten days later, in a letter to the phenomenologist Roman Ingarden, Husserl wrote, "the old German university exists no more."

In a May 4, 1933 letter to Dietrich Mahnke, a former student of his teaching at Marburg, Husserl described his depression in the wake of the rise of the Nazis, and then commented:

> Finally, in my old age, I had to experience something I had not deemed possible: the erection of a spiritual ghetto, into which I and my truly worthy and high-minded children (together with all their issue) are to be driven. By a state law to take effect hereafter and forevermore, we are no longer to have the right to call ourselves *Germans*, the work of our intellects is no longer to be included in German cultural history. They are to live from now on solely *branded as "Jewish"* . . . as a poison that German minds are to protect themselves from, that has to be extirpated. . . . The future alone will judge which was the true Germany in 1933, and who were the true Germans—those who subscribe to the more or less materialistic-mythical racial prejudices of the day, or those Germans pure in heart and mind, heirs to the great Germans of the past whose tradition they revere and perpetuate.

Husserl went on to say that the worst thing of all in this entire horrific affair, the thing that caused him the greatest despair, was the role Heidegger played in it: "the worst because I had put my trust not only on his ability but on his character—which I still just cannot understand." He spoke of his disappointment at discovering

Heidegger's "anti-Semitism—even toward those among Jewish students and the faculty who were so enraptured by him," and even more so at the "grand finale ending this would-be friendship," Heidegger's public entry into the National Socialist Party on May 1, 1933 (three days prior to Husserl's letter to Mahnke). "What these last months and weeks brought struck the deepest roots of my being."

Since the Nazis now denied him any public platform in Germany, Husserl had to travel to Vienna, in May 1935, to deliver the lecture "Philosophy and the Crisis of European Humanity." In November he spent a week in Prague, giving a set of lectures on "The Crisis of European Sciences and Psychology," in addition to several other talks and informal discussions. Both trips were great successes for Husserl. It was, of course, impossible for him to publish these lectures in Germany, but an international yearbook called *Philosophia* agreed to publish an expanded and revised version of the Prague lectures. It appeared, in installments, in 1936. Husserl then incorporated this material into his final book project, which was published posthumously, and unfinished, in 1954 as *The Crisis of European Sciences and Transcendental Phenomenology*.

In September 1935 Husserl was stripped of his German citizenship. His license to teach was also taken away. In January 1936 he was removed from the official roster of lecturers at the University of Freiburg.

By the end of 1936 Husserl's son, Gerhart, and his son-in-law, Jacob Rosenberg (the husband of his daughter, Elisabeth) had left Germany to get away from the Nazis and start life anew in the United States. They were shortly followed by their families. Husserl himself had been offered positions abroad: at the University of Southern California in the US, and at Prague. Husserl carefully considered both offers, but ended up declining them, principally because, at his advanced age, he did not wish to interrupt his feverish research and writing program and to have to expend his energies, instead, on relocating and learning to navigate life in a new country, culture, and environment. Still, in a poignant letter to Ingarden (December 31, 1936), Husserl remarked, "We old ones remain behind alone; how we envy the children."

Husserl continued to receive prestigious invitations to lecture abroad. In late 1936 he was asked to address the International Philosophical Congress, scheduled to be held in Paris in August

1937. But the Imperial and Prussian Ministry for Science, Education, and the Formation of the People notified Husserl in June that he was being denied permission to participate. Other requests for permission to speak abroad, in response to other invitations, were simply ignored. Then, in late June 1937, Husserl was ordered for "racial reasons" to give up his apartment on the south side of Freiburg, where he had lived for twenty years, ever since arriving in Freiburg. He relocated to the east side of the city. He became seriously ill with pleurisy at this time, and was unable to continue his work. He died less than a year later, in Freiburg, on April 27, 1938. He was 79 years old. Only one Freiburg faculty member, the historian Gerhard Ritter, dared to attend his funeral.

The Nazi persecution of Husserl did not end with his death. His posthumously published *Experience and Judgment* could not be published in Germany, and so it was released, instead, only in Czechoslovakia. But then, when the Nazis annexed Czechoslovakia in March 1939, they destroyed all the copies remaining in Prague.

Shortly after Husserl's death a Franciscan priest, Herman Van Breda, traveled to Freiburg to work on a doctoral dissertation on Husserl's phenomenology. He then learned that the Nazis, as part of their scheme of wiping out all Jewish scholarship, planned to destroy Husserl's manuscripts. After consulting with Husserl's widow, Van Breda managed, with the help of several German nuns, to smuggle the documents out of Germany and transport them to a safe location, the University of Leuven, in Belgium. The conspirators hid the manuscripts in their luggage and delivered them to the Belgian ambassador in Berlin, who in turn sent them by diplomatic courier to the University of Leuven. The Husserl Archives were subsequently established there shortly after the end of World War II, and remain there today. (The Archives also contain Husserl's entire private research library, which Van Breda and his colleagues had taken the considerable trouble to transport to the university, thus preserving the extensive comments that Husserl had written in the margins of the books he had studied.) The rescuing of Husserl's manuscripts was a significant achievement, since they added up to over 40,000 pages—in shorthand! A project of publishing these documents is now well underway, with over forty volumes having been published to date. The regular, ongoing appearance of these "new" writings has helped to stimulate a revival of interest in Husserl's work.

Prospectus

In the remainder of this book I will offer an overview of that work, and attempt to trace its evolution, beginning with a discussion of Husserl's critique of "psychologism" in the *Logical Investigations*, the book in which he analyses the structures of the formal sciences of logic and mathematics, and inaugurates his project of phenomenology. I will then take up several of the central concepts, methods, and conclusions of that project as they emerge in the *Logical Investigations* and in *Ideas I* and other works of his middle period. These discussions, in turn, will lead to a consideration of the ideas of Husserl's last work, *The Crisis of European Sciences and Transcendental Phenomenology*, to be followed by a consideration of Husserl's contribution to ethics and to value theory, and a further clarification of Husserl's project by means of a defense of it against some important and often-stated objections that I believe to rest on misunderstandings. (My aim in these chapters is not to provide a substitute for Husserl's own texts, or to offer the definitive interpretation of them, but rather simply to give such help as a newcomer to phenomenology might need in order to benefit from reading his work directly.) This treatment of Husserl will be followed by a chapter offering briefer discussions of the work of four other important phenomenologists, together with suggestions for further reading.

1

Early Husserl

At the dawn of the twentieth century (1900-1901), Husserl's first phenomenological work, *Logical Investigations*, was published in two massive volumes, totaling over 1,000 pages. It was extraordinarily well received, winning praise from several of the most prominent German philosophers of the time, including Paul Natorp, Wilhelm Wundt, Heinrich Rickert, and Wilhem Dilthey, and establishing Husserl as a major philosopher—perhaps the leading contemporary German philosopher of logic. Though *Logical Investigations* went on to exert a wide, deep, and continuing influence on many currents of thought in continental Europe, the distinguished analytic philosopher Michael Dummett reports (in 2000—one hundred years after its publication) that it is still not widely known among English-speaking philosophers (P, xvii).

Though *Logical Investigations* is now primarily known as the work that introduced phenomenology to the world, it is not clear that this was Husserl's main purpose in writing it. Rather, it seems that an embryonic version of phenomenology began to develop organically out of his attempts to deal with the problems raised by that book, and that he only subsequently realized the potential of phenomenology for philosophy in general. This realization, in turn, provided Husserl with the task of his life—that of expanding, refining, and applying the phenomenological approach that he had first stumbled upon while trying to solve the problems he had chosen to address in his *Logical Investigations*.

The Attack on Psychologism

But what are those problems? While the book ends up tackling a wide variety of fundamental philosophical issues, its initial, guiding, overarching task is to explain the foundations of logic and mathematics. The difficulty of this task is enhanced by the unique status of logical and mathematical objects. For such objects obviously differ in their reality from physical things. One cannot observe with the senses, or conduct experiments on, numbers or logical laws. How can objective truths about such objects be established? In what is our knowledge of them founded?

Perhaps the most popular approach to these questions in the late nineteenth century, when Husserl was working on his *Logical Investigations*, was to hold that logical and mathematical truths are grounded in psychology. Such a stance followed directly from the naturalist world view that was then dominant, according to which all reality, in the final analysis, is physical. On this view, anything that appears to be nonphysical, including numbers and principles of logic, must, if they are to be granted any reality at all (so that there could be discoverable objective truths about them), be properties or effects of something physical. Since mathematical and logical objects are not physical, but rather objects of thought, they are therefore to be understood, on this view, as entities that owe their existence to the human mind, which, in turn, is an effect of physical things, such as the brain and central nervous system. Accordingly, logical laws are held to be reducible to psychological laws (specifically, laws that describe how we think, understand, make inferences, and judge), which are themselves ultimately reducible to physical laws.

By the time of Husserl's writing this widespread view had come to be called "psychologism" (though that term was much more frequently used by the doctrine's critics than by its defenders). Prominent psychologistic thinkers included (at least on Husserl's interpretation of their work), such figures as John Stuart Mill, Alexander Bain, Herbert Spencer, Wilhelm Wundt, Christoph von Sigwart, Benno Erdmann, Friedrich Albert Lange, Theodor Lipps, Ernst Mach, and Richard Avenarius. The major point of the "Prolegomena to Pure Logic" that took up the entirety of the first volume (in the original German edition) of Husserl's *Logical Investigations* was precisely to refute psychologism once and for all.

For in addition to regarding psychologism as utterly wrongheaded and demonstrably false, Husserl recognized that its acceptance would stand in the way of a proper understanding of and appreciation for the very different approach that he would be presenting in the six investigations of the second volume of his *Logical Investigations.*

It might be seen as ironic that Husserl would place so much importance on the refutation of psychologism, since it is widely held that he himself had defended a psychologistic position in his first book, *Philosophy of Arithmetic* (the only one he had published prior to the *Logical Investigations*). On this account, Husserl was converted to anti-psychologism by the harsh criticisms that Gottlob Frege (then an obscure mathematician, logician, and philosopher, but now celebrated as one of the founders of analytic philosophy) had directed against his *Philosophy of Arithmetic.*[1] There is some evidence to support this view. For example, W. R. Boyce Gibson reports that in a conversation held on June 24, 1928 Husserl, speaking of his *Philosophy of Arithmetic,* had said that "Frege's criticism was the only one [Husserl] was really grateful for. It hit the nail on the head."[2] And in the foreword to the *Logical Investigations,* while not specifically mentioning Frege, Husserl offers a quotation from Goethe by way of explaining the character of his own critique of psychologism: "There is nothing to which one is more severe than the errors that one has just abandoned" (LI 1, Foreword to First German Edition, 3).

But a growing body of literature argues that this standard view overestimates Frege's influence on Husserl and underestimates Husserl's originality.[3] Moreover, Husserl's own position with

---

[1] See Frege's "Review of Dr. E. Husserl's *Philosophy of Arithmetic,*" trans. E.W. Kluge, in *Readings on Edmund Husserl's Logical Investigations,* ed. J. N. Mohanty (The Hague: Martinus Nijhoff, 1977), 6–21.

[2] "Excerpts from a 1928 Freiburg Diary," *Journal of the British Society for Phenomenology* 2, no. 1 (January 1971): 66.

[3] See, for example, J. N. Mohanty, *Husserl and Frege* (Bloomington: Indiana University Press, 1982); Mohanty's "Husserl, Frege, and the Overcoming of Psychologism," in his *The Possibility of Transcendental Philosophy* (London: Martinus Nijhoff, 1985), 1–11; Dallas Willard, *Logic and the Objectivity of Knowledge* (Athens: Ohio University Press, 1984); Claire Ortiz Hill, *Word and Object in Husserl, Frege, and Russell* (Athens: Ohio University Press, 1991); and Claire Ortiz Hill and Guillermo Rosado Haddock, *Husserl or Frege? Meaning, Objectivity and Mathematics* (Chicago: Open Court, 2000).

regard to Frege's influence on the evolution of his views was more nuanced than the quotations cited in the preceding paragraph would suggest. Husserl never conceded that his theory as expressed in *Philosophy of Arithmetic* had been identical to the psychologism that Frege had rightly criticized. Nor did he think that his views were vulnerable to all of Frege's criticisms, or to those that Paul Natorp and Carl Stumpf had directed against other psychologistic thinkers. Nonetheless, his thinking did evolve in a decidedly anti-psychologistic direction, in part because he recognized that the critique of psychologism developed by Frege, Natorp, and Stumpf also exposed some mistakes that he himself had made.

In any case, according to Dummett, "while Frege's objections to psychologism had made little impact, that of Husserl's assault on it was overwhelming: the *Prolegomena* came close to killing off the influence of psychologism within German philosophy" (P, xvii). And I will argue that Husserl's arguments against psychologism can be applied with equal effectiveness against a variety of currently influential views.

But what are those arguments? Recall that, according to psychologism, logical laws are reducible to, and are explained by, psychological laws. For example, consider the following deductively valid argument:

1. A or B.

2. Not A

Therefore, B.

A psychologistic account of the validity of this argument might appeal to alleged natural psychological laws concerning our thought processes, claiming that this validity rests on the fact that anyone who considers the proposition "A or B," and who then conjoins it with the proposition "Not A," will derive from these two premises the conclusion "B."

One problem with such an analysis is that, as most teachers of logic know from painful experience, not everyone will, as a matter of empirical fact, derive the conclusion "B" from these two premises. Granted, it probably is true that most people, most of the time, think in accordance with well-established logical principles, and do so naturally, and often effortlessly. But it seems equally clear that almost everyone (and perhaps we don't need the "almost" here) thinks illogically some of the time, and that some people do so frequently. Indeed, for centuries logicians have been compiling lists of "logical fallacies," that is, mistakes in reasoning that are so common as to make it worthwhile to name, categorize, and study them, and to make a special effort to avoid falling prey to them in one's thinking. So the claim that logical laws reflect, express, or are straightforwardly derivable from, the way in which people in fact think, is simply mistaken.

Circularity

To their credit, some of the psychologistic thinkers Husserl criticizes anticipate this objection, and attempt to deal with it by modifying their theory. Instead of claiming that logical principles are reducible simply to "the psychological laws of human thought," without qualification, they instead maintain that logical laws are reducible only to those psychological laws that govern *correct* (or "proper" or "valid") thinking. But Husserl points out that this gives the game away. Psychology was supposed to explain, justify, and found the laws of logic. The problem is that if we must first consult the laws of logic in order to determine just which psychological principles of human thought pertain to *correct* thinking, and thus are capable of performing this foundational function, we are obviously engaging in circular reasoning.

Moreover, any empirical investigation into how people actually think will have to rely on logic. One will have to make logical inferences in order to arrive at conclusions based on the empirical data one will have gathered. So to try to base logic on anything empirical is to get things backward (or, at the very least, once again to argue in a circle). Psychology, like all empirical sciences, *presupposes* the validity of logic; so psychology cannot be used to *establish* the validity of logic.

A Priority

Yet another problem with attempting to reduce logic and mathematics to psychology is that our beliefs about psychological matters have the character, in common with all other beliefs that are derived from empirical generalizations, of being fallible, contingent, revisable in the light of further evidence, and uncertain. In all of these ways they stand in stark contrast to logical and mathematical truths, which are demonstrable, universal, necessary, and certain.

One reason for the tentative, provisional status of all claims based solely on empirical evidence is simply that we cannot ever observe all of the relevant evidence. For example, a common belief among seventeenth-century Europeans was that all swans are white. But no one at that time (or now, for that matter) had seen all swans, and the belief was not based on any conviction that all swans had been seen. Rather, it was based on a generalization from extensive, and exceptionless, experience. Every one of the hundreds or thousands of swans that one had personally seen had been white, and the same was true of all of the swans one had heard or read about in the reports of others. But, as it turns out, there were (and are) black swans in Australia. So the claim that "all swans are white" was (and is) false.

A related point is that sense-based observations of what is in fact the case rarely yield any insight into necessity—they fail to disclose anything about what *must be* the case. Observations and experiments can show that water happens to freeze at 32 degrees Fahrenheit, but we could easily imagine it freezing at 37 degrees, or at 23. That is why we have to look to find out; it is an empirical matter.

But logical and mathematical truths are not like this at all. 2 plus 2 doesn't just happen to equal 4; rather, it *must* do so, as a matter of necessity, and its failure to do so would be unthinkable. Similarly, we do not establish logical truths by first observing, for example, that in several thousand exceptionless cases in which A has been greater than B, and B has been greater than C, it has also happened to be the case that A is greater than C. Instead, here we have genuine insight. We can *see*, we can *grasp*, we can *understand*, that if A is greater than B, and B is greater than C, it *follows* that A must, absolutely, universally, necessarily, and without exception, be greater than C. We need not worry that we will encounter a counterexample in Australia.

If we count 25 cows in one pen, then count 25 more in another, then herd all of them into a larger pen, count them again, and find that there are now only 49 cows, we will seek an explanation. We will acknowledge that one possibility is that we miscounted in one or more of our three acts of counting. We will also consider the possibility that one cow that had been present during either one of the first two countings might, by the time of third, have been absent—it may have slowly wandered off. But we will not give any credence to the possibility that we have here simply observed a case in which 25 + 25 = 49, and thus obtained empirical evidence that 25 + 25 does not always equal 50.

So logical and mathematical truths hold a priori. Even if we might need to undergo certain experiences in order to be able to grasp these truths at first, once we have grasped them, we see that we do not need experience to confirm them, and that experience cannot possibly disconfirm them. They are prior to experience in the sense that we know, ahead of time, that they will obtain in any possible experience that we might have.

Psychological truths, by contrast, are a posteriori. To the extent that these truths are "known" at all, they can be known only after (posterior to) experience. If we wish to know how people in fact think, understand, make inferences, judge, and behave, we will have to do so on the basis of careful observation. We can imagine many possibilities, and we will have to look to see which of these are consistent with our experimental and observational findings. And another way in which the conclusions that we arrive at in this way are "after" experience, rather than prior to it, is that we cannot have absolute assurance ahead of time that they will hold in all future experiences. Because such conclusions are based on incomplete evidence, and fail to yield any insight into necessity, we must regard them as tentative, and remain alive to the possibility that future observations will indicate that they should be overthrown, or at least modified.

So logic and mathematics cannot possibly be reduced to psychology, since psychology cannot account for the universality, necessity, and a priority of logical and mathematical truths. If logical truths and mathematical truths were, in the final analysis, psychological truths, that is, truths about how we in fact happen to think, they would be contingent, tentative, and a posteriori. But they are not; so psychologism is false.

Similarly, the a priority of logical and mathematical truths, that is, their independence from anything empirical, entails that their validity does not even presuppose the *existence* of thoughts or beliefs, much less any particular conclusions about their contents.

Therefore, the psychologistic thesis, that such truths are explained by, and are reducible to, psychological laws concerning how humans happen to think (laws which would have to be discovered empirically, based upon the actual content of the thoughts and beliefs of real, existing persons), cannot possibly be correct.

An Explanatory Fallacy

Moreover, psychologism commits the fallacy of *obscurum per obscurius*. This is the fallacy of attempting to explain something obscure by means of something even more obscure. To put it another way, it is the mistake of offering an explanation that runs in the wrong direction. We need an explanation for an idea (or claim, or theory, or phenomenon, or what have you) only when we find it to be vague, or confused, or unfamiliar, or controversial, or resting on weak or conflicting evidence, or utterly unknown to us—in short, where there is some obstacle to our understanding it. A successful explanation will remove this obstacle. Understanding can be achieved when the vague and confused is explained in terms of the clear and precise, when the unfamiliar is illuminated by the familiar, when the controversial is grounded in the uncontroversial, when that which is based on weak evidence is bolstered by the addition of strong evidence, when the unknown is clarified by means of the known. If someone does not know who Jackson Pollock was, we can at least begin to provide some understanding by informing him or her that Pollock was a twentieth-century American painter, most noted for his large abstract canvases composed of dense, interlocking skeins of poured and spattered paint. Here the unfamiliar concept, "Jackson Pollock," is partially clarified by reference to concepts with which the recipient of this explanation is familiar. But suppose the explanation had been, instead, that "Pollock was a member of the 'New York School'—a colleague of De Kooning, Rothko, Kline, and Motherwell." This explanation would not be helpful, since anyone who did not know who Pollock was would likely also be unacquainted with the term "New York School," and with the other four painters mentioned, each of whom is somewhat less famous than Pollock. The explanation fails because it commits the fallacy of *obscurum per obscurius*—it attempts to explain the obscure by means of something even more obscure.

It is easy to see how psychologism commits the same fallacy. Many logical and mathematical truths are clear, precise, and demonstrable. They hold universally, are intuitively evident (that is, one can grasp, just by "looking" at them and thinking about them, that they are true, and, indeed, must necessarily be true), and are supported by all the evidence that is relevant to them. Most psychological theories, by contrast, are somewhat vague, and none of them are demonstrable. They hold only in general, and admit of exceptions. They are not intuitively evident, but rather rest on empirical evidence. And that evidence is not uniform, so they are upheld merely on the basis of a preponderance of evidence, which is to say, also, that they are maintained in the face of some counterevidence. So to explain logic and mathematics in terms of psychology is to explain the clear by the less clear, the precise by the approximate, the demonstrable by the merely empirical, the certain by the merely probable. It is to offer an explanation that runs in the wrong direction. It is to commit the fallacy of *obscurum per obscurius.*

Relativism

Yet another problem with psychologism is that it leads to relativism. The reason is that if logical laws are derived from the facts concerning how human beings happen to think, as psychologism maintains, it follows that a different psychology would lead to a different logic. Thus, since there is no reason to assume that the laws of human psychology are identical to those of animal psychology, or of the psychology of extraterrestrials (if there are any extraterrestrials), it would seem to follow that fundamental logical principles would have to be understood, on a psychologistic analysis, as holding only for human beings, and for any other beings who happen to think the way we do. Moreover, to the extent that people in different cultures think differently from one another, or even that different individuals within the same culture do so, this would apparently imply a further relativization of logic.

To see what this entails, concretely, consider the deductively valid argument form known as *modus ponens.* According to this rule of inference, the premises "a implies b" and "a" jointly entail the conclusion "b." The first premise states that if a is true, then b is as well. The second premise states that a is, in fact, true. The conclusion, then, is that b is true. To say that this argument form is deductively valid is to say that the truth of the premises would guarantee the truth of the conclusion. To put it another way, it would be impossible, and would entail a contradiction, for the premises to be true and the conclusion false. (One or both of the premises might turn out to be false, but that would affect the soundness of the argument, not its validity.) Now if psychologism were true, it would follow from the argument of the immediately preceding paragraph that *modus ponens* is not universally, or necessarily, deductively valid, but rather is so only for those who think in a certain way. Or, if that is too strong, the universal deductive validity of *modus ponens* would have to be understood as contingent and empirical, that is, as something that is established by the finding that everyone, in fact, happens to think in such a way as to render it so.

These relativistic implications of psychologism expose it to the objection that it, in common with other forms of relativism, is self-undermining. For on its own terms, psychologism cannot be the simple truth, but must rather, at best, merely be true relative to our contingent psychological make-up.

Of course, a defender of psychologism could claim otherwise, and insist that psychologism is objectively true, that is, that it captures the way things really are, and is determined by the real relations that obtain between the objects with which it is concerned (logical and mathematical principles, on the one hand, and the laws of human psychology, on the other), so that anyone who thought differently about it, and thus rejected it, would simply be mistaken. But that would be to defend psychologism by invoking precisely those ideas that psychologism is most concerned to reject and overthrow.

An Evidentiary Fallacy

The relativistic implications of psychologism suggest, further, that psychologistic thinkers commit an evidentiary fallacy, that of preferring the less evident over the more evident when the two conflict. Psychologism undermines basic logical principles, such as *modus ponens*, and mathematical truths, such as 2 + 2 = 4, by maintaining that these merely reflect the ways in which we happen to think, and thus are neither necessarily nor objectively true. But whatever one takes the evidence in favor of psychologism to be, surely that evidence is not as strong as is the evidence supporting *modus ponens* and 2 + 2 = 4.

For example, suppose someone defends psychologism with an argument containing three premises. Such an argument will be unsound if any one of its three premises is false, or if those premises (even if they are true) fail to entail psychologism. Now, however evident each of these premises might be, however likely they might appear to be true, it is highly doubtful that any one of them will be as evident, will appear quite as likely to be true, as is "2 + 2 = 4" or the conclusion that "b" follows from the premises "a implies b" and "a." Nor will the claim that the truth of psychologism follows from the truth of the three premises of the argument, no matter how evident *that* claim may be, likely be as evident as are basic mathematical and logical truths, such as the two just mentioned. But it would only be rational to accept as true the psychologistic undermining of *modus ponens*, or of "2 + 2 = 4," if the possibility that we were mistaken in thinking premise one to be true, the possibility that we were mistaken in thinking premise two to be true, the possibility that we were mistaken in thinking premise three to be true, *and* the possibility that we were mistaken in thinking it to be true that the truth of the three premises would entail the truth of psychologism, *when combined*, still failed to equal or surpass the possibility that we are mistaken in affirming the truth of *modus ponens*, or of "2 + 2 = 4." Since no argument for psychologism comes close to meeting this requirement, belief in psychologism stands exposed as irrational.

A defender of psychologism might reply that while *modus ponens* and "2 + 2 = 4" are indeed far more evident than are any of the arguments for psychologism, this is not a problem, since psychologism does not deny the *truth* of *modus ponens* or of "2 + 2 = 4," but rather only rejects their *objectivity*. What psychologism denies is that logical and mathematical truths are made true by the nature of, and relations among, logical and mathematical objects, quite apart from any contribution by human subjectivity (such as thinking). Rather, psychologism claims that what makes such truths true are precisely psychological laws pertaining to acts of thinking. It is therefore open to the defender of psychologism to argue that what is more evident than any of the arguments for psychologism is only the *truth* of certain logical and mathematical claims, which psychologism does not dispute, but precisely not that the explanation of, or foundation for, that truth is to be found in the objects with which the claims deal, rather than in the laws of human psychology.

But this argument does not seem very plausible. For one thing, when we note that A is greater than B, and that B is greater than C, what is then powerfully evident to us is that *A is greater than C*, rather than that we are psychologically so constituted as to *think* that it is. The content of what is evident to us here has to do exclusively with relations among objects of thought, that is, of ideas; considerations of psychological matters, or of our acts of thinking, make up no part of that content. Moreover, it is not clear that issues concerning the content of a claim, the truth of that claim, and the explanation of, or foundation of, that truth can be distinguished as sharply and kept as separate as the pro-psychologistic argument of the previous paragraph implies. For notice that, to the extent that I accept the psychologistic explanation of the evidentness of my logical and mathematical beliefs, this would likely alter the content of those beliefs. To believe that I am psychologically so constituted as to think that B is greater than C is, paradoxically, no longer to be quite so convinced that B *is* greater than C; it is to acknowledge, instead, that perhaps I merely *think* that it is.

It must be admitted, however, that this criticism of psychologism (that it commits the evidentiary fallacy of favoring the less evident over the more evident when the two conflict) is abstract, general, and lacking in specifics. While it might be worth pointing out that every part of any argument in favor of psychologism is likely to be less evident than are the basic principles of logic and mathematics, one still wants to know where, exactly, the pro-psychologistic argument goes wrong. What specific mistakes does it make?

Existence and Validity

One such mistake is that it conflates the two quite distinct issues of, on the one hand, explaining the *existence* of logical and mathematical principles, and, on the other, that of explaining their *validity*. To see this, suppose we grant, for the sake of argument, the naturalistic premise of the psychologistic thinkers, namely, that numbers and logical principles, being nonphysical, cannot exist without being thought about by minds capable of comprehending them. On this premise, numbers, and the concepts of addition and equality, are actualized, or brought into being, by acts of consciousness. But notice that it simply does not follow from this that the *truth* of the judgment that $2 + 2 = 4$ must similarly await, and be dependent on, an additional act of consciousness, which would affirm it. Rather, even if the existence of these mathematical and logical objects were dependent on acts of consciousness, this would be fully compatible with the possibility that it is precisely the nature of these objects themselves, once actualized, and not our thoughts about them, that determines what is true about them. And this possibility harmonizes with our strong sense that those who deny that $2 + 2 = 4$ are not simply thinking in a way that happens to be, in a purely statistical sense, highly unusual, but rather are making a mistake. While it is true that a thought can only exist if a consciousness actually thinks it, it is a fallacy to conclude from this that the validity of the thought depends on anything so contingent or empirical. No matter what anyone may happen to think (or refrain from thinking), $2 + 2 = 4$.

Is and Ought

A related mistake of the pro-psychologistic argument is that it runs together issues concerning what in fact *is* the case with quite different issues of normativity, that is, with issues of what *ought to be* the case. It is tempting, although on Husserl's view not precisely correct, to put the point this way: Empirical laws or generalizations, including psychological ones, are *descriptive*. Logical laws are *prescriptive*. So the latter cannot be reduced to the former. The laws of logic are not *descriptive* laws concerning how we *do* in fact think, but rather *prescriptive* laws concerning how we *should* think. They are laws that lay down the conditions for cogent thinking. If logic and mathematics were reducible to psychology, then $2 + 2$ would equal 4 only to the extent that human beings, as a matter of empirical fact, happen to think that way. Well, not everyone does think that way. And, more to the present point, those who do not think that way *should* do so, since $2 + 2$ *does* equal 4. (It would equal 4 even if everyone thought it didn't.)

While Husserl does indeed charge the pro-psychologistic argument with conflating the non-normative and the normative, he does not agree with the widespread belief, just mentioned, that logical principles are prescriptive, or that they lay down the rules for correct thinking. The reason is that he regards the subject matter of logic as having nothing to do with anyone's beliefs, opinions, or acts of thinking, any more than astronomy or geology or biology are concerned with such subject matter. Rather, just as each of these sciences is concerned with a certain domain of objects (that of stars, planets, comets, and the like, in the case of astronomy; rocks and solid earth, in the case of geology; and living organisms, in the case of biology), and attempts to discover truths about these objects, and about the relations among them, so is logic, on Husserl's view, devoted to the study of the properties, characteristics, and relations among a specific object domain (that of consistency, contradiction, implication, negation, and so forth), and precisely not to the study of what or how anyone happens to think, or even how they *should* think.

This point does not significantly undermine or even alter the objection just raised against the pro-psychologistic argument, however. The reason is that, even though logic, on Husserl's view, is not itself intrinsically normative (that is, it does not tell us how or what we should think), all that is needed to make it normative is to add to it the general normative principle that we should try to believe what is true, rather than what is false. Here again, the comparison to other sciences is instructive. Astronomy, geology, biology, physics, and chemistry are not about our thinking. Rather, they are about the natures, properties, and relations among objects in a specific domain. Moreover, these natures, properties, and relations must be inquired into and investigated. It is entirely possible to make mistakes in our thinking about them. Thus, if we adopt the normative principle that we should try to believe what is true, rather than what is false, when thinking about the objects studied by these sciences, it follows that any attempt to reduce these sciences to what we happen to think about the objects in their domain (so that astronomy would be the study, not of planets and stars, but rather of what we *think* about planets and stars), would be guilty of fallaciously conflating the descriptive issue of what we *do* think and the utterly distinct prescriptive/normative issue of what we *should* think. On Husserl's view, this is exactly what psychologism does. Logic and mathematics are concerned to study certain objects, not our thinking about those objects. And truths in these fields are determined by the natures of, and relations among, those objects. So psychologism, by reducing mathematics and logic to psychology, misidentifies the subject matter of mathematics and logic, and, insofar as we are concerned to believe what is true, also conflates descriptive and prescriptive issues with regard to the subject matter (human thinking) that it does address.

Consciousness and the Objects of Thought

Yet another psychologistic mistake is to misconstrue the nature of the relationship between consciousness and the objects of thought. The crucial error is the assumption that since what is thought about is *present to* consciousness, it must be understood to be *part of* consciousness. Such a conflation especially tempts those who maintain that mathematical and logical objects exist only by virtue of being thought about. The pro-psychologistic argument takes this premise to warrant the denial of independence and genuine objectivity to such objects, which are instead taken to be mere constitutive elements of consciousness. Indeed, many of the psychologists that Husserl criticizes even go so far as to conflate the *activities* of consciousness with the *objects focused on* by consciousness, referring to both simply as "contents of consciousness." But I can be aware of an elephant without the elephant somehow thereby becoming a part of me. And while being aware of things (like elephants) and having them appear to me are indeed constitutive elements of my consciousness, it doesn't follow that the elephant is. Finally, with regard to mathematical and logical objects, specifically, their independence and genuine objectivity is manifested in at least two ways: first, one can return one's attention to them again and again. If the mathematical or logical object somehow were identical to or contained within the subjective act of knowing, it would cease to be when the act of attending to it expired. Secondly, different subjects can attend to, and know, the same object, though the acts by which they do so are obviously different from one another. Mathematical and logical objects exist as identical unities throughout indefinitely many acts of focusing on them or thinking about them. The content "2 + 2 = 4" appears to be the same each time I think it, or whenever anyone thinks it. And logical laws are concerned exclusively with the content of beliefs, rather than with the individual contingent acts of believing them.

The Natural and the Ideal

The conflation of the act of thinking with the object thought about leads to another fallacious psychologistic conflation, the running together of natural, causal laws, on the one hand, and ideal, logical laws, on the other. To show that these are essentially and necessarily distinct, Husserl offers a thought experiment, in which we are to imagine "an ideal person, in whom *all* thinking proceeds as logical laws require." Husserl then points out that, while there may well be an explanation in terms of natural, psychological, causal laws as to why the individual acts of thinking undertaken by this person always coincide with logical norms, it is obvious that the natural laws and the logical laws in this assumed situation are not one and the same. "Causal laws, according to which thought must proceed in a manner which the ideal norms of logic might justify, are by no means identical to those norms. If a being were so constituted as never to be able to frame contradictory judgments in a unified train of thought, as never to be able to perform inferences which defy the syllogistic moods, this would not mean that the law of contradiction, the *Modus Barbara* etc., were laws of nature explanatory of this being's constitution." To put the point another way, there is one kind of explanation for why "B" follows from the conjunction of the premises "A or B" and "not-A," and quite a different kind of explanation for why any particular individual at any given time, or in any given act of thinking, *concludes* that it does. The first kind of explanation deals with the nature of the timeless and noncausal relationships between ideal objects, such as numbers and logical concepts, while the latter kind is concerned with causal events that take place at definite times and in specific places in nature. By running these two kinds of explanation together, or by reducing either one of them to the other, "the psychologistic logicians ignore the fundamental, essential, never-to-be-bridged gulf between ideal and real laws, between normative and causal regulation, between logical and real necessity, between logical and real grounds" (LI 1, Prolegomena, §22, 50).

Partly as a result of Husserl's powerful critique, psychologism is rarely defended today. But his antipsychologistic arguments are nonetheless important, for at least two reasons. First, I want to suggest that Husserl's arguments provide just what is needed to expose and to diagnose the mistakes of a great number of influential contemporary views. Secondly, Husserl's critique of psychologism motivates, and sets the stage for, his turn toward phenomenology.

Psychologism and Postmodernism

To begin with the first of these reasons, notice that, just as psychologism had attempted to explain mathematics and logic in terms of psychology, so do many recent and current thinkers who are labeled "postmodern" attempt to explain truth claims of all kinds in sociological and/or historical terms. The influential philosopher Richard Rorty, for example, has consistently maintained that objective truth is closed off to us, and that we would therefore be better off jettisoning such a notion in favor of something more accessible to us. Accordingly, he has, at various times, recommended that we conceive of "truth" as equivalent to "the judgment of our cultural peers,"[4] "the upshot of free and open encounters,"[5] or "what it is useful for us to believe,"[6] as opposed to understanding it to refer to an accurate statement of the way things really are. But Rorty's proposed reduction of objective truth claims (including claims in logic) to matters of cultural consensus or pragmatic usefulness suffers from many of the very defects that Husserl had already diagnosed in the psychologistic proposal of reducing logic and mathematics to psychology.

For example, notice that questions about what "our culture" (however that is defined) happens to believe, about whether those

---

[4] See, for example, "John Searle on Realism and Relativism," in *Truth and Progress* (New York, Cambridge University Press, 1998), 71–72; *Philosophy and the Mirror of Nature* (Princeton, NJ: Princeton University Press, 1980), 335; "Hilary Putnam and the Relativist Menace," in *Truth and Progress*, 53; and "Cosmopolitanism Without Emancipation," in *Objectivity, Relativism, and Truth* (New York: Cambridge University Press, 1991), 220.

[5] See, for example, *Contingency, Irony, and Solidarity* (New York: Cambridge University Press, 1989), 52; and "Science as Solidarity," in *Objectivity, Relativism, and Truth*, 38.

[6] See, for example, "Intellectual Historians and Pragmatist Philosophy," in *A Pragmatist's Progress? Richard Rorty and American Intellectual History*, ed. John Pettegrew (Lanham, MD: Rowman & Littlefield, 2000), 208; "Something to Steer By," *London Review of Books* (June 20, 1966): 7; "Introduction" to *Truth and Progress*, 1; and "Rorty v. Searle, At Last: A Debate," *Logos* 2, no. 3 (Summer 1999): 62.

beliefs amount to a consensus, about the process by which any such consensus was achieved, and about whether the beliefs in question are useful to some purpose, are, like psychological questions about how human beings think, empirical in character. One must gather and consult evidence, and then evaluate that evidence logically, if one is to arrive at an accurate answer to them. But if one must presuppose the validity of logic in order to determine, say, what our culture happens to believe, then what our culture happens to believe cannot, without circularity, be used to establish the validity of logic.

Similarly, because of the empirical basis of conclusions about cultural consensuses and about what is useful to believe, such conclusions must be regarded as contingent, fallible, and revisable in the light of possible future evidence, in short, as failing to achieve the necessity and a priority that characterizes logical truths. And this stark difference between logical truths, on the one hand, and truths about consensuses or utility, on the other, entails the inadequacy of any attempt to reduce the former to (or to replace the former with) the latter.

Furthermore, Rorty's proposals appear to suffer from the same sort of self-undermining incoherence that Husserl had detected in psychologism. If we are to reduce "truth" to "the judgment of our cultural peers," for example, then we will have to figure out just what *is* the judgment of our cultural peers. So if we want to know what the truth is about X, where X could be anything at all (a matter of science, history, mathematics, geography, or what have you), we must first discover the truth about what our cultural peers *think* about X. But if all truths, including those concerning the identity of the content of beliefs, is to be reduced to "the judgment of our cultural peers," then the only way to determine what is the judgment of my cultural peers is to consult the judgment of my cultural peers on the topic of the identity of the content of the judgment of my cultural peers. And this, in turn, could only be determined by finding out what is the judgment of my cultural peers on *it*, and so on infinitely. We could escape this infinite regress by taking the position that we can and should seek the objective truth about what our cultural peers believe, rather than settling for the (possibly erroneous) *judgment* of our cultural peers on this topic, but this would amount to an utter abandonment of the claim that we should replace the quest for objective truth with an appeal to the judgment of our cultural peers. Or we could continue to press that claim while covertly continuing to make use of the idea of objective truth in attempting to determine just what it is that our cultural peers believe. But that would be incoherent. Or we could escape the contradiction by claiming that the objective truth is available to us only with respect to the issue of what our cultural peers believe, and not with respect to any other issue, whether logical, mathematical, historical, scientific, or what have you. But surely such a claim is arbitrary and implausible.

The proposal that we reduce truth to "what is useful for us to believe" fares no better. For, once again, how are we to determine which beliefs are useful? To make the problem easier, let us assume that we know what outcomes we are seeking: we want to rid ourselves of a persistent cough, to make the faucet stop dripping, to arrive at our destination safely and on time, and to win our tennis match against our rival. Now, which beliefs will be most useful in terms of facilitating the achievement of these outcomes? Well, if objective truth is closed off to us, and is to be replaced by "what is useful for us to believe," then the question of the truth of beliefs concerning the utility of beliefs is itself to be determined by what is useful for us to believe. So "X is true" means "it is useful to believe X," which, in turn, means that "it is useful to believe that it is useful to believe X," which, in turn, means that "it is useful to believe that it is useful to believe that it is useful to believe X," and so on infinitely. And once again, this infinite regress can only be avoided by an appeal to objective truth regarding claims as to what is or is not useful to believe that would either be inconsistent (if such an appeal is made while one is continuing to maintain that objective truth is unattainable, and should always be replaced with the notion of what is useful for us to believe), or arbitrary and implausible (if the claim is that the issue of what is useful to believe is the only one about which objective truth is available to us and should be sought).

Moreover, Rorty's proposals, no less than the psychologistic theories that Husserl had discussed, appear to commit the fallacy of *obscurum per obscurius.* To see this, consider an exchange between Piotr Gutowski and Rorty that took place at a scholarly conference. Gutowski offered the claim that it is an objective fact (in the sense that anyone who thought otherwise would simply be wrong) that there was not at that very moment a big green giraffe, just behind Rorty, "that is trying to eat the violet leaves growing on his head." Rorty replied as follows:

> Now about giraffes: I want to urge that if you have the distinction between the idiosyncratic and the intersubjective, or the relatively idiosyncratic and the relatively intersubjective, that is the only distinction you need to take care of real versus imaginary giraffes. You do not need a further distinction between the made and the found or the subjective and the objective. You do not need a distinction between reality and appearance, or between inside and outside, but only one between what you can get a consensus about and what you cannot.[7]

The problem I want to raise is this. If it is possible to find out that there really is a consensus about the presence, or lack thereof, of a real giraffe, then why isn't it also possible, even without such knowledge of a consensus, to find out whether or not there really is a giraffe present? Or, to put it another way, if there is a problem in finding out directly that a giraffe really is or is not present, why does this problem not also carry over to the project of finding out whether or not there really is a consensus about the presence or nonpresence of a giraffe? Why are consensuses easier to know about than giraffes? If they aren't, then what is to be gained, from a practical standpoint, by defining "truth" or "reality" in terms of consensus? It is as if Rorty were claiming that society's norms and judgments are unproblematically available to us, when nothing else is. But why would anyone think that it is easier to see, for example, that society *judges* giraffes to be taller than ants than it is to see that giraffes *are* taller than ants? If anything, this gets things backwards. I would argue that the category "the way things are" is, over a wide range of cases, significantly *more* obvious and accessible to us than is the category "what our culture thinks." Is it a *more* clear and obvious truth that we *think* that giraffes are taller than ants than that giraffes *are* taller than ants? I am quite certain of the latter truth from my own observation, but I have never heard anyone else address their own thoughts on the relative heights of giraffes and ants, let alone discuss their impressions of

---

[7] The exchange between Gutowski and Rorty is to be found in *Debating the State of Philosophy*, ed. Józef Niznik and John T. Sanders (Westport, CT: Praeger, 1996). The quotations from Gutowski and Rorty are from pages 111 and 114–15, respectively.

public opinion on the issue. Similar remarks apply to many elementary moral, mathematical, and logical truths. For example, I submit that each of the following claims is more evidently true than are any statements about what people believe about them: "Anything that is red must be extended in space." "If it is true that I am either at home or at the library right now, and if it is also true that I am not at home right now, then it must be true that I am at the library right now." "The pitch level at which a spoken utterance is delivered is often irrelevant to its meaning." "9 + 7 = 16." "Very few human beings can run a mile in fewer than four minutes." "Some fish can swim." "Some human beings can make sounds come out of a flute." "Most people spend most of their time closer to the surface of the Earth than to the surface of the Sun." "Sacrificing everything else so that one can devote all of one's time and energy to the collection of match sticks is not the best possible way to live one's life." "Kindness is intrinsically better than cruelty." "Some birds are red." "Ignorance and cowardice tend to be bad things." "Michael Jordan was a very good basketball player." "It is not necessary, in order for a painting to be good, that it depict ballet dancers in full flight." "Some people are older than others." "A political system that causes all of its citizens to starve to death is a bad one." One could go on and on forever. Because these claims are more evident than are any claims about what people happen to believe about them, Rorty's attempt to explain them in terms of cultural consensus, like the psychologistic attempt to explain basic logical and mathematical truths in terms of psychology, commits the fallacy of *obscurum per obscurius*.

I would point out, moreover, that this problem remains no matter how one understands such phrases as "reality" or "the way things are." For example, if we understand them in some jacked-up, metaphysical sense, to be expressed with upper-case lettering as Reality-as-it-Really-Is, beyond language or thought or anything human, then, while it is understandable that we might want to deny that we know whether or not a giraffe is "really" present, so should we deny that we know whether or not we "really" have achieved a consensus on the matter. (For notice that knowledge of consensus seems to require knowledge of other minds and their thoughts, and it is unclear why anyone would think that our knowledge of the existence of other minds is any less problematic than is our knowledge of the existence of an independent physical

world.) If, on the other hand, we understand them in a more humdrum sense, merely as meaning that things typically are the way
they are no matter what we might think about them, and that
some of our thoughts about them are made wrong by the way the
things are, then, while it is easy to see how we might be able to
gather evidence fully sufficient to entitle us to claim to "know"
that we have achieved a consensus on giraffes, so is it clear that we
might be able to claim to "know" some things about giraffes, even
in the absence of any consensus about, or knowledge of consensus
about, such matters. Of course, one could use the jacked-up sense
of "reality" when saying that we don't know what giraffes are
"really" like, while simultaneously using the humdrum sense of
"reality" when saying that we can nevertheless cope by knowing
what our culture's consensus view of giraffes is, but what would be
the sense or purpose of this double standard?

Similar remarks apply to Rorty's attempt to reduce claims of
objective truth to appeals to "our culture's epistemic norms," or
to "the upshot of free and open encounters." For, once again,
what problem is solved by saying that we can turn away from
attempts to determine the objective truth about the relative height
of giraffes and ants and instead settle for calling the "truth" on this
matter whatever is so dictated by consulting our culture's epistemic norms? To put it simply: if we can't find out about the size
of animals, then neither can we find out about our culture's epistemic norms; and if we can find out about our culture's epistemic
norms, then so can we find out about the size of animals. There
are criteria and standards of "knowledge" in terms of which we can
have knowledge of neither, and others in terms of which we can
have knowledge of both. But I know of no plausible criteria or
standards whereby we can't know the "reality" or "the way things
are" or "the objective truth" about the greater height of giraffes
relative to that of ants but can know the "reality" or "the way
things are" or "the objective truth" about our culture's epistemic
norms in terms of which we judge giraffes to be taller than ants.

The same problems recur when we focus on Rorty's efforts to
understand "truth" in terms of "the upshot of free and open
encounters." In order to know whether or not giraffes are taller
than ants we must first know, on this proposal, (a) whether or not
there is a consensus that giraffes are taller than ants, and (b) if
there is, whether or not the communication that produced that

consensus was free, open, and undistorted. But isn't it obvious that it is easier to determine whether or not giraffes are taller than ants than it is to determine either (a) or (b)? Or, to put it another way, wouldn't any skeptical doubts about our ability to determine even something so obvious as that giraffes are taller than ants also be more than sufficient to wipe out any hope of being able to know about the outcome, and degree of openness, of any process of public communication? So what problem is solved by saying that what it means to know, or to hold as true, that giraffes are taller than ants is to know that there is a consensus, formed as a result of free and open communication, that giraffes are taller than ants? Once again, the Rortian, objective truth-denying theory commits the fallacy of *obscurum per obscurius*.

These problems recur, once again, when Rorty proposes that we analyze "truth" pragmatically, in terms of what it is useful for us to believe. For insofar as Rorty's move to pragmatism is motivated by doubts about our ability to know how things really are, the problem remains unsolved. For any grounds we might have for doubting that we can know whether or not giraffes "really" are taller than ants would easily carry over to our efforts to find out whether or not it "really" is useful to believe that giraffes are taller than ants. On the other hand, any standard of "knowledge" sufficiently relaxed as to allow us to "know" that it is useful to believe that giraffes are taller than ants would also be lax enough to enable us to "know," irrespective of the issue of the utility of belief, that giraffes are taller than ants. Since it is not clearer, more evident, or easier to know, that it is useful to believe that giraffes are taller than ants than that, simply, giraffes are taller than ants, the attempt to explain the latter in terms of the former commits the fallacy of *obscurum per obscurius*.[8]

Rorty is far from unique, however, in engaging in fallacious reasoning of this sort. Thousands of other contemporary thinkers, many of them quite influential, make the same mistakes that Husserl had diagnosed over a century ago in his critique of psychologism. For example, the noted Belgian political theorist, Chantal

---

[8] The preceding five paragraphs are adapted from pages 371–73 and 376–77 of my "Rorty on Objectivity and Truth," in *The Philosophy of Richard Rorty*, ed. Randall E. Auxier and Lewis Edwin Hahn (Chicago: Open Court, 2010), 367–90. Rorty's reply to my essay is to be found in the same volume, pages 391–93.

Mouffe, while admitting that "it is always possible to distinguish between the just and the unjust" and "the legitimate and the illegitimate," nonetheless insists that "this can only be done from within a given tradition, with the help of standards that this tradition provides; in fact, there is no point of view external to all tradition from which one can offer a universal judgment."[9] But if the claim that "in fact, there is no point of view external to all tradition from which one can offer a universal judgment" is, as it clearly appears to be, a straightforwardly universal judgment, it simply contradicts itself. Similarly, if distinctions between the legitimate and the illegitimate can be made "only from within a given tradition," then it is clear that the *judgment* that it is illegitimate to claim to offer a universal judgment transcending any particular tradition must itself be understood as arising from within a particular tradition, which it cannot transcend.

Similarly, Barry W. Sarchett, in an article defending "the postmodern turn," writes that this turn "requires that we pay as much attention to who is speaking and who is not authorized to speak as we do to what is being spoken. It requires a sense therefore that all knowledge and values depend on power differentials. . . . When people talk about what is true or false, good or bad, the postmodern response is to pose more questions: better or worse for whom? In what context? For what purposes?"[10] But if Sarchett is claiming that these postmodern insights are true, or at least are superior to a point of view that would deny them, his own position entails that this truth or superior value depends upon "power differentials," that these postmodern insights achieve their truth or superiority only for *some* people, in *some* contexts, and for *some* purposes, and that, in evaluating these claims in support of "the postmodern turn," we are to pay as much attention to the fact that it is Barry Sarchett who is issuing them as to the content of the assertions themselves.

The problem, in short, is that in the very act of issuing their assertions these postmodern deniers of objective truth unwittingly contradict themselves. But, as Husserl correctly anticipated, they claim

---

    [8] "Radical Democracy: Modern or Postmodern?," trans. Paul Holdengräber, in *Universal Abandon?*, ed. Andrew Ross (Minneapolis: University of Minnesota Press, 1988), 37.

    [10] "What's All the Fuss about This Postmodernist Stuff?," in *Campus Wars*, ed. John Arthur and Amy Shapiro (Boulder, CO: Westview Press, 1995), 24.

to be unimpressed by this objection. As Husserl puts it, the subjectivist "will not bow to the ordinary objection that in setting up his theory he is making a claim to be convincing to others, a claim presupposing that very objectivity of truth which his thesis denies. He will naturally reply: My theory expresses my standpoint, what is true for me, and need be true for no one else" (LI 1, §35, 78).

It is easy to find examples of contemporary thinkers who make exactly this move. For example, consider the claim, widely endorsed in some circles, that "scientific theories are mere reflections of the social interests of those who produce and promote them." Noted literary theorist Barbara Herrnstein Smith attempts to argue against the charge that such a claim is self-refuting by maintaining that "the charge fails if the supposed self-refuter disavows the 'mere,' and the presumably self-*excepting* claim is revealed as (or transformed into) an explicitly and flagrantly self-*exemplifying* one: 'You charge my theory of the social interests of all theories with reflecting social interests? But *of course* it does: it could hardly prosper otherwise!"[11]

Note the high price that Smith, and others with similar views, must pay if they are to attempt to evade the charge of self-referential inconsistency in this way. For the claim that scientific theories are reflections (mere or otherwise) of the social interests of those who produce and promote them has usually been put forth in order to debunk science's alleged pretensions to achieving objective knowledge about the world. But surely this debunking only carries weight if it can itself lay claim to such pretensions. Why should we take it seriously if it is not true, and cannot even *claim* to be true? Were it to turn out to be *true* that scientific theories utterly fail to deliver objective knowledge about the world, and that they instead stand unmasked and exposed as reflections of the social interests of those who produce and promote them, that would be interesting and revelatory indeed. But now we learn from Smith that the claim that scientific theories are reflections of the social interests of those who produce and promote them is *itself* to be understood to be a reflection of the social interests of those who produce and promote *it*. In that case, why should we care? Surely everyone already knows that there are many people

---

[11] *Belief and Resistance* (Cambridge, MA: Harvard University Press, 1997), 76.

who try to elevate themselves socially by attempting to knock down those who, like scientists, currently enjoy greater prestige and respect. Moreover, while Smith, and other opponents of objective truth, often make this move at or near the end of a presentation, in an attempt to answer the self-refutation objection all at once in one move, it is important to go back over the texts of such writers again, so that every sentence and every claim can be reinterpreted in the light of the concessions that they have had to make in order to avoid self-refutation. Every premise, every bit of data, every inference that Smith presents in support of her theses must be read this way: "It is a reflection of my social interests to maintain that . . . " Sentences which had initially seemed bold and daring, tend, when they are read in this way, quickly to be drained of all interest.

So another approach is needed, one that is not vulnerable to the objections that plague both psychologism and some versions of postmodernism. Husserl's critique of psychologism points the way toward what such an alternative approach might look like. Indeed, several of the central features of Husserl's project of phenomenology either find their first expression in, or else flow directly from, his refutation of psychologism.

Bracketing

For example, consider Husserl's technique, implicit in the *Logical Investigations* and fully realized only in subsequent works, of "bracketing" questions concerning the nonexperiential existence of objects of experience. It is easy to see how such a procedure might have been inspired by wrestling with logical and mathematical problems, and by noticing the spectacular failure of psychologism to deal with them satisfactorily. For notice that, while it is unclear what kind of independent existence, if any, should be granted to numbers and logical concepts, they clearly nonetheless exist as objects of thought, are richly meaningful as such, and somehow achieve sufficient independence from our thinking about them as to be fully capable of rendering some of our statements about them false. Moreover, as Husserl's critique of psychologism shows, a good way to make a complete mess of logic and mathematics is to begin with a theory about the nature of the existence of mathematical and logical entities, and then to attempt to ground logical and mathematical truths in that theory. But since such entities, as experienced, even in the absence of a theory about what kind of existence they may have, are already meaningful, and are able to determine which of our claims about them are true and which ones false, the way appears to be clear to investigate them as such, and simply to set aside questions about their independent existence. It is but a short step from this to the realization that similar reasoning holds for objects of experience generally. Like numbers and logical concepts, their meanings, and truths concerning them, are fully accessible to us quite apart from any worries about their ontological status (that is, the kind or degree of existence they may have). Consequently, in Husserl's subsequent works he advocates that such worries be bracketed, so that objects of experience, that is, phenomena, might be studied on their own terms, as such.

Intentionality

Similarly, Husserl's emphasis on, and radicalization of, the concept of "intentionality," which he had learned from his great teacher, Franz Brentano, stems, in part, from his understanding of the failure of psychologism. Brentano had argued that it is the distinguishing feature of all mental "acts," for example, acts of thinking, perceiving, remembering, doubting, questioning, loving, and hating, that they "take" (that is, "have," or "point to," or "intend") an object. To perceive is to perceive *something*; and there is no remembering without something remembered, nor hating without something hated. Moreover, Brentano had recognized that the relation uniting intentional act to intentional object is to be distinguished from a causal relation. To see a cup, to notice that it is on the table, and to grasp that, since it is taller than the salt shaker, so must it also be taller than anything that is shorter than the salt shaker, is not to *cause* the cup to exist, or to be on the table, or to be larger or smaller than anything else. Nor is it to move the cup, or heat it up, or break it into a dozen pieces, or to enter into any other kind of causal relationship with it. While there undoubtedly is a causal explanation for my ability to see, to compare, and to grasp or understand things, my acts of seeing and grasping do not themselves act causally on the objects seen or understood. In short, the intentional act of "having" an object is utterly different

from any kind of act by means of which I might causally interact
with that object.

But since Brentano's main interest in intentionality had been
confined to the issue of finding an accurate and reliable criterion
by which the realm of the mental might be distinguished from that
of the physical, he had taken little notice of the idea that the object
of any conscious act (that is, the "intentional object," or phenomenon) could be studied on its own, or with reference to the conscious act (that is, the "intentional act") that is directed toward it
and which discloses it, without reference to issues concerning its
independent existence. This had been left to Husserl, who would
go on, not only to regard intentionality as crucial to his investigation of consciousness, but also to see that numbers and logical
concepts (and, eventually, everything that is experienced) could
profitably be investigated as intentional objects. It is this insight, in
turn, which has allowed Husserl to avoid the problems that psychologism had brought on to itself by attempting to ground the
existence of numbers and logical concepts in human psychology.
The problem is not merely that psychologism had failed to bracket
questions concerning the ontological status of mathematical and
logical entities, but also that, in connecting those entities to the
conscious acts of human beings, it had recognized only one kind
of connection, namely, that of causality. Numbers, according to
psychologism, exist *because* we think of them; certain logical principles are valid *because* we happen to think in accordance with
them. But, as we have seen, this leads to paradoxes that are avoided
if the connection binding our acts of thinking about logical and
mathematical objects to those objects themselves is understood to
be intentional, rather than causal.

Eidetic Reduction

A third feature of Husserl's phenomenology that flows from his
engagement with logic and mathematics, and from his critique of
psychologism, is his technique of "eidetic reduction." "Eidos," in
classical Greek, means "essence." So Husserl's "eidetic reduction"
refers to a procedure of bracketing, or setting aside, the contingent
particulars, or irrelevant details, that are attached to a given object,
and of focusing, instead, on its essential principles—the features of
a thing that make it be that kind of thing, and without which it

could not be that kind of thing. For example, what makes a yellow thing yellow is its color; its size and shape are utterly irrelevant. Conversely, what makes a square thing square is its shape, with its color and size receding into insignificance.

Husserl's work on mathematical and logical issues facilitates this orientation toward essences, since mathematics and logic are eidetic disciplines. They deal exclusively with abstract, ideal, essential entities. The truth of the statement that $2 + 2 = 4$ holds whether we are dealing with pairs of dogs, or of rocks, or of carrots. (To perform the eidetic reduction on the statement that "2 dogs plus 2 dogs = 4 dogs" would be to render it, simply, as "$2 + 2 = 4$.") It makes no difference to the truths about circles what color the circle is, or what thickness the line is that describes it, or whether that line is painted, drawn in chalk, or constructed out of plastic. (Indeed, when reasoning about circles, it is necessary not only to disregard such inessential contingencies, but also to correct for the distortions they introduce—no drawn circle can ever be perfectly circular, though the contemplated and understood circle that the drawn circle "points" to can be). And the logical truth that "B" follows from the truth of the two premises "If A, then B" and "A," holds no matter what content is represented by "A" and by "B."

So one does not need to perform the eidetic reduction on "2," "circle," or "*modus ponens.*" These are already eidetic entities. And several of the fallacies of psychologism are directly traceable to its failure to recognize this fact. But one of the innovations of Husserl's phenomenology is to show that anything whatsoever can be "reduced" to its eidetic dimension. One way of doing so is simply to regard it, by means of selective focusing, as an *example* of something. Thus, a particular dog might be seen as an instance of the category "dog," or as a particular breed of dog, or as a mammal, or as a vertebrate, or as an animal, or as a living thing, or as a hairy thing, or as a brown thing, or as a thing that can feel pain, or as an instance of a specific size, shape, or mass, or as something visible, or as something existing at the present time, and so on infinitely. Indeed, performing the eidetic reduction in this way is essential to the process of coming to understand anything whatsoever, whether it be a person, a tool, a work of art, or what have you, with which we were previously unfamiliar. Our understanding of this entity in its full particularity must proceed by means of general, abstract, essential categories with which we are already familiar. For example, in coming to understand a person whom one has just met, one might begin by seeing him or her as a man, woman, boy, or girl; as old, young, or middle-aged; as quiet or outgoing; as funny or serious; as a representative of a specific job or profession; as a member of a socioeconomic class; as an exemplar of various characteristics of personality that one has encountered before, and so forth, until gradually, over time, one acquires a (perhaps still rudimentary) sense of this person as a gestalt, that is, as a whole, as a unique essence. Similarly, our ability to understand works of literature, in which we are introduced to characters we have never met, and who have done things we have never done, stems, in large part, from the successful use we make of the eidetic reduction. If I have never had the specific experiences that have brought these characters joy or fear or despair, I can still at least partially understand their experiences because I, too, have known joy and fear and despair.

This is important because the contingent details of our lives are unique and specific to us. Thus, if we are to understand each other, and the world we share, it will have to be in terms of general, essential principles that are widely accessible. The study of mathematics and logic shows that such understanding is possible, at least in those object domains. But the point of the eidetic reduction is that eidetic inquiry can be undertaken in any object domain, because all objects exemplify multiple eidetic structures. There is a kind of *logic* to joy, fear, and despair, to temporality, intersubjectivity, and embodiment, to art, history, and science, to work, play, and death, and so forth. The point of phenomenology is to describe and to clarify these essential structures of experience.

Phenomenology thus differs from psychology in that phenomenology deals with essences, which are universal and necessary, while psychology, in common with all other empirical sciences, deals with facts, which are particular and contingent. Phenomenology is an eidetic science.

Critique of Scientism

Husserl's attack on psychologism also leads, in his subsequent phenomenological work, to a full-scale critique of scientism—the doctrine that everything knowable can be explained in scientific terms, and should be investigated using empirical methods. Husserl's criticism is not directed against science itself. (Recall, in this connection, that his ambition is for his phenomenological philosophy to qualify as a "rigorous science.") But on his view science is not everything; and, in particular, it is not "first philosophy." Rather, it presupposes theses on the nature of reality that it does not attempt to justify, and thus it cannot serve as a foundational starting point for knowledge. Similarly, logical principles, such as the principle of noncontradiction, are presupposed by all of the sciences, and therefore are superior to, and foundational to, them.

Husserl's critique of psychologism illustrates the point that it is a mistake to confuse philosophical questions with empirical scientific ones, as if the methods of the latter were adequate to the task of addressing the former. This lesson still needs to be learned. Most of Husserl's arguments against psychologism could, with very minor adjustments, be advanced with equal power against more recent attempts to reduce truth claims in various object domains to explanations, rooted in some scientific theory (whether biological, sociological, economic, or neurological), of why we *think* the way we do in those domains.[12]

Objective Truth

A related implication of Husserl's arguments against psychologism is that the idea of objective truth is foundational to all inquiry. To say that truth is "objective" is to say that true statements are true irrespective of what anyone thinks about them. For example, the earth has a definite shape, and the statement that accurately describes that shape is true, no matter what anyone might think about it, so that it is possible, in principle, for everyone to be wrong (which may have happened if, at one time, everyone thought that the earth is flat). The truth is discovered or recognized, not created or constructed. Those who deny this contradict themselves, since they either explicitly or implicitly defend as objectively true their own preferred alternative (whether relativist, subjectivist, or constructivist) to objective truth.

---

[12] One example of such attempts is Edward O. Wilson's much-discussed suggestion that "the time has come for ethics to be removed temporarily from the hands of the philosophers and biologicized" (*Sociobiology* [Cambridge, MA: Harvard University Press, 1975], 562).

Psychologism obviously fails to give correct analyses of objectivity, truth, and knowledge; and Husserl's observation of this, achieved during the course of his investigations into the foundations of logic in the *Logical Investigations*, motivates his lifelong concern for these matters. His aim, above all else, is to understand what knowledge truly is, and how to go about attaining it.

Intuition

Finally, Husserl's engagement with numbers, logical concepts, and essences of all kinds helps to explain one other notable feature of his phenomenology, namely, its appeal to intuition. For Husserl is a kind of empiricist. His project is to ground all knowledge claims rigorously in lived experience. This project obviously includes knowledge claims about numbers, logical entities, and essences, as these are fully capable of yielding evidence, and of putting constraints on our acts of forming or maintaining beliefs about them. But since they are nonphysical, they pose a problem for Husserl's empiricist program—we cannot perceive them with the senses. In what sense, then, can we experience them? How do we access them? Husserl's answer is that we can confront them intuitively.

Etymologically, "intuition" means "seeing into." For Husserl, it refers simply to the act of attending to something that is present to us. He defines it as any "fulfilling act whatever," that is, any act in which "something appears as 'actual,' as 'self-given'" (LI 2, Investigation VI, §45, 280–81). To intuit something is to inspect it directly, as opposed to learning about it on the basis of indirect evidence or argument. So conceived, perception, that is, the direct sensory confrontation with physical objects, is a species of intuition, but one that is not available for mathematical or logical objects. To apprehend these, or any other essences, one needs insight, or "eidetic intuition."

While one might suspect that such "intuition" must be something mystical or exotic, Husserl insists that is nothing of that sort. Consider, for example, how it is that we know the difference between the essences of sound and color. According to Husserl, we know this through pure, unmediated, intuition (PRS, 111). But surely there is nothing occult or arcane about this. Rather, as is often the case with intuition, here we are dealing with the obvious and the mundane.

As Husserl explains,

> Intuiting essences conceals no more difficulties or "mystical" secrets than does perception. When we bring "color" to full intuitive clarity, to givenness for ourselves, then the datum is an "essence"; and when we likewise in pure intuition—looking, say, at one perception after another—bring to givenness for ourselves what "perception" is, perception in itself (this identical character of any number of flowing singular perceptions), then we have intuitively grasped the essence of perception (PRS, 110–11). . . . The whole thing . . . depends on one's seeing and making one's own the truth that just as immediately as one can hear a sound, so one can intuit an "essence"—the essence "sound," the essence "appearance of thing," the essence "apparition," the essence "pictorial representation," the essence "judgment" or "will," etc.—and in the intuition one can make an essential judgment. (PRS, 115)

So we know the essences of things intuitively. We are well practiced at the intuitive grasping of essences, since objects are always given to us in experience as essences, at least insofar as they present themselves as meaningful (that is, as "red," or "large," or "fruit," or "apple," and so forth). The essence of on object is invariant in all of the different perspectival presentations of it; it is the element that unifies those different presentations as all referring to the same object (or meaning). (This essence is also available to different observers, grounding a refutation of relativism.)

We can identify a number of different things as red only because we know what "red" is—we know its essence. We don't infer that something is red based on other considerations, evidence, or argument. Rather, we grasp its redness directly, that is, intuitively. All experience involves such intuitive grasping, since seeing is seeing-as. Moreover, while meaning can be achieved through conscious acts alone, truth, on Husserl's view, requires intuition—a movement from empty to fulfilled meaning-intentions. I can invent or imagine or consider any number of hypotheses, but I cannot know which of them are true without evidence and insight. And while some of my conclusions might be based on argument and inference, these, if they are to be sound, must be grounded in intuition, that is, in what is directly "seen" to be the case. In this way, according to Husserl, all genuine knowledge is founded on immediate evidence and intuition.

Meaning

On that basis Husserl attempts, in his *Logical Investigations,* to provide a phenomenological description and clarification of the basic concepts of logic. Of these, the most fundamental is the concept of meaning. As Husserl explains, "pure logic, wherever it deals with concepts, judgments, or syllogisms, is exclusively concerned with the *ideal* unities that we here call 'meanings'" (LI 1, Investigation I, §29, 224). In this way Husserl sets himself in opposition to the many recent and contemporary analytic logicians who think that logic is primarily concerned with the realm of language, not that of meaning.

Since the investigation of meaning only became a major philosophical topic in the early years of the twentieth century, Husserl's work in this area, along with that of Frege, Alexius Meinong, Bertrand Russell, and G. E. Moore, may justly be regarded as pioneering. Husserl is unique, however, in that his approach to this issue is phenomenological. His method is simply to describe what goes on in our lived experience of meanings. For that reason, he does not force his theory of meaning to conform to some epistemological theory (that is, a theory of knowledge), such as one that would tie meaning to public verifiability.

Notice, for example, that it is a clear datum of experience that some things present themselves to us under the headings of "good" or "bad," or "better" or "worse." Moreover, such presentations certainly appear to us as powerfully meaningful, despite any doubts we may have about our ability to prove them to others. Therefore, the theory that publicly unverifiable claims are meaningless flies in the face of the evidence of lived experience. (And indeed, when such a view has been defended, it has been on the basis of considerations other than fidelity to the data of lived experience.)

Similarly, while many philosophers have attempted to restrict meaning exclusively to the domain of language (perhaps because language is public, and thus allegedly lends itself to objectivity and verifiability more readily than does private, unarticulated, experience), Husserl insists, once again on the basis of the data of experience, that meaning is not always presented linguistically. To the contrary, meaning is often "given" as prior to language, as it is, for example, in the common experience of having to struggle to put into words the gist of some meaning that one has encountered.

In any case, nearly every major aspect of Husserl's project in the *Logical Investigations* pushes him in the direction of grappling with meaning. The procedure of bracketing questions concerning the independent *existence* of the objects of experience naturally reorients the inquirer toward the question of the *meaning* of those objects *as* they are experienced. The investigation of intentionality brings out the point that we experience objects as meaningful, with the meanings varying, in part, based on the selective focusing acts of consciousness (so that a dog is encountered, variously, as a German Shepherd, as a pet, as an animal, as a threat, as something brown, and so forth). The eidetic reduction, in turn, involves a turn toward meaning, as one ignores the irrelevant, contingent aspects of an object, and instead studies essential principles: what does it *mean* to be a "pet" or an "animal" or a "threat"? Finally, the laws or rules pertaining to meaning appear to be nonempirical, and to deal with entities that do not exist in any ordinary or obvious sense. In this way, the study of meaning is similar to the study of mathematical and logical objects, and of the principles governing them— in short, the subject matter of the *Logical Investigations.*

Essential Distinctions

In order to bring clarity to the topic of meaning, the first order of business is to distinguish several related but distinct notions that otherwise might be conflated or even confused with one another. For example, Husserl distinguishes signs from expressions. All expressions are signs, but the reverse is not true. Smoke is a sign of fire, in the sense that it *indicates* fire; but smoke does not *express* fire, or *stand for* it, in the way the word "fire" does. Genuine expressions must therefore be distinguished from indications. An indication is something whose existence or presence motivates a belief in something else. For example, slurred speech and a wobbly gait may indicate intoxication, just as clouds of a certain kind may indicate that rain is coming. But these are not expressions, because their function is not to express meaning, unlike ordinary speech and writing.

Further complicating matters is the fact that expressions, no less than such nonlinguistic signs as smoke, clouds, or a wobbly gait, also carry out the function of indicating something. So one must distinguish between meaning and indication even when dealing with genuine expressions. For example, if I say that the coffee is cold, you will usually infer, unless you have some special reason to think that I am joking or lying, that I *believe* that the coffee is cold. But the statement that the coffee is cold *means* something about the coffee, not about my beliefs, even though my utterance may *indicate* something about them. (And what the statement *refers* to is something else again, namely, the state of affairs in which the coffee is cold.) Husserl gives the example of my saying sincerely that "the three perpendiculars of a triangle intersect in a point," and points out that, while my saying so is based on the fact that I judge so, and while anyone who hears and understands me will probably *infer* that I judge so (with the result that in my making this statement I therefore *intimate* something about myself and my beliefs), it would nonetheless be a mistake to confuse any of this with the actual *meaning* of my statement, that is, with what it *asserts*:

> What this statement states is the *same* whoever may assert it, and on whatever occasion and in whatever circumstances he may assert it, and this same thing stated is precisely this, *that the three perpendiculars of a triangle intersect in a point*, no more and no less. . . . What we assert . . . involves nothing subjective. My act of judging is a transient experience, but what the statement states, the content . . . neither arises nor passes away. It is an identity in the strict sense, one and the same geometrical truth. (LI 1, Investigation I, §11, 195)

Proof that meaning and indication are distinct can be found by considering what is involved in meaningful expressions in "uncommunicated, interior mental life" (LI 1, Investigation I, §8, 190). For when I think in words without attempting to communicate them to others, I rarely, if ever, am attempting to indicate to myself something about my thoughts or attitudes. Rather, insofar as I am concerned with words at all (unless I am interested in the sheer physical sound of them when they are spoken, or in their appearance when written), I am engaged with their meaning—a meaning that remains the same whether I attempt to communicate it to someone else or merely think it myself. (And of course, in my interior mental life I frequently think in words that I neither speak nor write.) Moreover, since I can use language in thinking all by myself, communication and indication (or intimation) are not essential to the use of linguistic expressions, although meaningfulness is. (And note that this is so even if the original and primary purpose of language is to communicate with others.)

The meaning of an expression must also be distinguished from the object to which it refers: "Each expression not merely says something, but says it *of* something: it not only has a meaning, but refers to certain *objects*. . . . But the object never coincides with the meaning. . . . [This] distinction means the same as the distinction between what is meant or said, on the one hand, and what is spoken of, by means of the expression, on the other" (LI 1, Investigation I, §12, 197).

This distinction is perhaps best illustrated by cases in which multiple phrases which clearly differ in meaning nonetheless all refer to the same object. For example, while the meaning of "the fortieth president of the United States" obviously differs from that of "the star of *Bedtime for Bonzo*," both refer to the same entity, Ronald Reagan.

Since meanings are distinct from the objects to which they refer, the study of the former can be separated from an inquiry into the latter. In particular, the investigation of meanings can be conducted without reference to the issue of the independent existence of the objects bearing them. After all, "the 497th president of the United States" does not exist, and may never exist, but this does not stop the concept from being meaningful.

Moreover (and this is a finding one might anticipate on the basis of Husserl's critique of psychologism), meanings must also be distinguished from the conscious acts by and through which such meanings are disclosed. Suppose, for example, that I want to know what color a certain car is, and so I make a point of finding the answer by looking at the car. Upon doing so I see, and conclude, that the car is blue. While my conviction that "the car is blue" depends in this case on my focusing on the color of the car (as opposed, say, to its size or shape), and on my seeing that it is blue, these actions (and, for that matter, my mental states in believing that the car is blue and in communicating that information to others) are not identical to, and must be distinguished from, the meaning content itself, namely, that "the car is blue."

While this point may appear obvious and trivial, it stands in opposition to a popular line of thought according to which meaning is to be understood psychologically. On this view, meaning is not part of the furniture of the world, but rather emerges only when conscious agents focus their attention on the world in certain ways, ask questions of it, and undertake projects with respect to it. For example, the meaning of a tree will vary depending on whether one wants to seek shade, pick apples, study botany, or make a landscape painting. In itself, on this view, the tree has no specific meaning.

Husserl's point, however, is that even if meanings emerge only as a result of conscious acts, it does not follow, nor is it true, that the meanings are therefore *reducible* to those acts. Logically, the fact that A is a necessary condition for B does not entail that B is reducible to A, or identical with it. And phenomenologically, it is a clear datum of experience that the conscious acts of focusing, seeing (or intuiting), and judging are distinguishable from the meanings that these acts disclose.

Such meanings must also be distinguished from the physical marks or sounds that (typically by arbitrary convention) point to them. The marks or sounds exist in time and space; the meanings to which they point do not. Meanings are nonphysical, atemporal, and ideal.

Moreover, with regard to expressions (as opposed to the meanings conveyed by them), one must, further, distinguish the physical aspect (the sounds of speech and the visible marks of writing) from the meaning-endowing aspect. For sounds and marks to convey meaning, they must be taken up in a certain way. The listener or reader must, in a sense, "look past," and take no interest in, the physicality of the sound or mark (the timbre and pitch of the sound, the shape of the mark), and instead approach it from the standpoint of its signification—what it is attempting to express. It is thus up to the hearer or reader to bring to life what would otherwise be lifeless sounds or marks. Meaning is ideal, and cannot be reduced to anything physically real, such as the sounds of speech or the physical marks of writing. The raw acoustic or visual content of an utterance requires a meaning-giving act on the part of the hearer or reader in order for a meaning to be grasped.

So, in summary, Husserl carefully distinguishes among (1) meaning, (2) the expression that expresses that meaning, (3) the mental acts of the speaker who writes or utters that expression, and (4) the object to which the expression refers. Husserl claims, further, that these elements are present in all meaningful expressions. *Every* expression means something, refers to something, and intimates or manifests something. And in the case of written or spoken expressions, Husserl further distinguishes each of these elements from (5) the expression's physical sound or mark and (6) the conscious act that endows that sound or mark with meaning. Thus, one can distinguish among (1) the meaning, "Bill is taller than Jim," (2) the utterance, whether spoken or written, "Bill is taller than Jim," (3) the speaker's or writer's belief that Bill is taller than Jim, (4) the objective state of affairs that Bill is taller than Jim, (5) the sound of the spoken words or look of the written ones in the utterance, "Bill is taller than Jim," and (6) the conscious act that transforms those sounds or marks into conveyors of meaning.

With regard to (6), Husserl draws yet another distinction, that between acts that *bestow* or *confer* meaning and those that *fulfill* meaning. The former, that is, meaning-conferring acts (also called "meaning-intentions" or "empty" or "merely signitive" acts), are those conscious actions by which a sound or a physical mark is construed as an expression, as something that conveys meaning. Meaning-fulfilling, or "intuitive," acts, by contrast, are those in which the meaning intention is intuitively confirmed or illustrated. If you tell me that it is raining outside, I can understand your meaning even if I do not know whether or not your claim is true. Part of what is involved in the act of comprehending your meaning is understanding, at least in a vague and tentative way, what it would mean to "see" or "intuit," whether perceptually or by means of a direct, nonperceptual "grasping," that your claim is true. To understand your claim that it is raining outside is, at least in part, to read you as saying that I would see water falling from the sky if I were to look at the window, and that I would get wet if I were to walk outside. Were I then to undertake these actions, and to see and feel the falling raindrops, this "evidence" (Husserl's term for what is directly, intuitively "seen") would fulfill what had originally been an "empty" meaning-intention.

As J. N. Findlay explains,

> The fulfillment of a meaning is a state in which that meaning may be said to be (wholly or partially) carried out, exhibited, illustrated, embodied or actually given . . . Such fulfillment is in some sense a necessary correlative of meaning: a meaningful use of terms must in some

sense prepare for, do duty for, look or strive towards a state in which *what* it means will be completely shown or worked out. This is true even in the case of self-contradictory or not finitely exhaustible meanings: it is in *attempting* to carry them out that we become aware of their self-contradictory or not finitely exhaustible character. Mere meaning, therefore, *presses* toward an appropriate fulfillment, and is incomplete till that fulfillment is achieved.[13]

Thus, an empty intention of signification can be understood even when the object to which it refers is absent. But such an intention nonetheless points to a fulfillment that can only come from the intuitive presentation of the object. So meaning, and the successful communication of meaning, does not depend on perception or intuition. This explains why false, and even self-contradictory, expressions are meaningful. When a statement is false, the meaning-intention corresponding to it cannot, *in fact*, be fulfilled. When a statement is self-contradictory, the meaning-intention corresponding to it cannot, *in principle*, be fulfilled (and we might be able to know this a priori). So, on Husserl's view, it is false that self-contradictory statements are meaningless. To the contrary, it is only because they are meaningful that we are able to know that there is no possibility of their ever being intuitively confirmed.

Ideality

Husserl claims that meanings are ideal. What does this mean? Ideal objects are atemporal. They do not come into or pass out of existence or undergo any other kind of change. Moreover, they are universals, in the sense that they are in principle capable of having instances. "Red," "large," and "dog" are examples of universals. They have instances, since there are many red things and large things, and many individual dogs, even though "red" "large" and "dog" are not themselves real entities that run around on their own in the world. Real objects, such as individual red things, large things, and dogs, exist in time, do come into and pass out of existence, and are capable of undergoing changes. They are not universals, but individuals; they cannot have instances.

---

[13] "Some Reflections on Meaning," in Findlay's *Language, Mind, and Value* (Atlantic Highlands, NJ: Humanities Press, 1963), 212.

The act of judging that 2 + 2 = 4 is "a fleeting experience, originating and passing away." This marks it as something real. But *the meaning content*, "2 + 2 = 4," "does not originate and pass away" (LI 1, Investigation I, §11, 195, translation modified). This marks it as ideal. Moreover, this ideal thing, this meaning, is universal, in the sense that it stands in the same relation to each individual act of thinking or expressing that content as "redness" stands to each of the many instances of red things.

Meanings maintain their identity throughout varying contexts. They can be successfully communicated from one person to another. A person (or, for that matter, different people) can return again and again to the same meanings. For example, the meaning of "2 + 2 = 4" remains constant throughout the many different individual acts, undertaken by different persons, at different places and times, of stating, writing, reading, or otherwise attending to and understanding that meaning. These characteristics—identity, communicability, and repeatability—indicate ideality.

If two people say, at two different times and in two different places, that "Obama won the election," it is the same sign that is used, even though there may be many differences in the sound of the two utterances—for example, differences in pitch, timbre, and accent. And the meaning of the two utterances is also identical. This shows that both the sign and its meaning are ideal. They do not exist in space and time, and are in that sense not real. "A proposition or a number is not a real event in the universe, thus not something which exists here and there . . . exercising real causality. That holds only of the written number and of the spoken proposition, spoken now or some other time. But the written or spoken expression of a number or of a proposition is not the Pythagorean [theorem] itself or the number 4 itself . . ." (PP, §3a, 15).

We access ideal meanings eidetically, that is, by disregarding what is contingent, particular, and inessential (such as the clear or raspy sound quality of a spoken utterance, or the thickness of the lines in a printed message), in favor of what is general and essential. All of our experience, to some degree, requires such eidetic focusing. Our experience would be an incoherent jumble of utterly new, singular, and consequently unrecognizable and incomprehensible, bits of information were it not processed and organized eidetically, by means of ideal meanings. Science, insofar as it is based on experience, would be impossible as well.

Husserl's reasoning on this issue echoes that of the ancient Greek philosopher Plato, who had been disturbed by the challenge laid down by his brilliant predecessor, Heraclitus. According to Heraclitus, one cannot set foot in the same river twice, because by the time one reintroduces one's foot into a river, after having withdrawn it, the river, with its rushing waters and swimming wildlife, will have changed. For Heraclitus, the river is a metaphor for all reality: everything is in flux; nothing is constant, stable, or permanent; everything is constantly changing. But if that is true, how can there be knowledge of anything? If everything is in flux, it would seem to follow that nothing stands still long enough for us to obtain genuine knowledge about it. We would always have to live in fear that the conclusions we had drawn in the early stages of any inquiry might, by the time we finish our investigation and turn our attention to other issues, no longer be valid.

In response to this challenge Plato had drawn a distinction between objects of the senses (that is, physical objects) and objects of thought ("forms" or "ideas"). According to Plato, while Heraclitus is right about the former, he is wrong about the latter. While physical objects, accessed by the senses, do indeed come into and pass out of existence, and undergo constant changes while they do exist, the world of ideas, that is, a world of universals, accessed by the mind, is a realm of stability. So, while a person who had been my friend might change and become my enemy, this does not alter the permanent, unchanging nature of "friendship" itself, or of "enmity." The natures of these universals are not altered by this event, and neither are the enduring truths that pertain to them, such as the truth that friendship, all else equal, is *better* than enmity. Indeed, it is precisely because this event "instantiates" such truths that it is, in the empirical world of individual things perceived by the senses, a bad thing.

Husserl agrees with Plato in holding that it is by means of ideal and atemporal universal meanings that we successfully refer to temporal, nonideal things, events, and states of affairs in the world. Knowledge, language, and communication would be impossible if meanings did not retain a stable identity throughout the shifting contexts in which they are used. Thus, the existence of knowledge, language, and successful interpersonal communication suggests the ideality and stability of meaning.

But Husserl is not a Platonist in the sense of thinking that ideal objects exist in some mysterious otherworldly realm of their own, exerting a causal influence on nonideal objects (as in the idea or form "Red" causing red things to be red). Nor does he agree with Plato that ideal objects are more real than are objects of the senses. To the contrary, for Husserl, the ideal is precisely to be *contrasted* with the real. Indeed, he asserts that "the sphere of *real* objects . . . is in fact no other than the sphere of *objects of possible sense perception*" (LI 2, Investigation VI, §43, 278). So what is the nature of the connection, as he sees it, between ideal universal meanings, on the one hand, and the world of contingent, particular experienced things, on the other? The difficulty in answering this question is intensified by his insistence on the independence of ideal meanings and truths from the "real world" of "actual things": "There are purely ideal truths which assert nothing about the world, nothing about what is real. . . . The truth that 2 + 3 = 5 stands all by itself as a pure truth whether there is a world, and this world with these actual things, or not. . . . The same holds for the law of noncontradiction and other such principles. Purely ideal truths are 'a priori' and are discerned as truths in the unconditioned necessity of their universality." But he immediately goes on to explain that while ideal truths do not in any way *depend* on anything real or factual, they do, nonetheless *apply*, universally, to everything real that falls under the scope of their concepts:

> Though ideal objects do not refer to actual facts, in their sense they refer implicitly to *possible facts*—ideally possible, ideally conceivable. In pure arithmetic no counted things or events of the factual world are presupposed; but every number does have a universal extension. All conceivable groups, all that can be in any way imagined, are included in the idea "3," to the extent that they are enumerable as 3. Accordingly, every arithmetical proposition and all arithmetic is a priori applicable to every conceivable group and consequently, for instance, to every group which in fact actually exists. . . . To every ideal object there belongs inseparably an ideal extension, the idea of a totality of conceivable single instances, and together with it a general validity, which is not restricted by the presupposition of factual singularities, factual data. This is just what unconditioned universal validity means. "Before" the givenness of a fact and a world of facts (a priori) we can be unconditionally certain of this, that whatever we assert as logicians, arithmeticians and so forth, must be applicable to anything

and everything that may be encountered as the corresponding factual reality. (PP, §3a, 16, translation modified)

So it is very far from Husserl's view to hold that ideal meanings and truths apply only to an ideal realm, having no application to the real world of the objects of everyday experience. To the contrary, he maintains that ideal meanings and truths apply universally to everything that corresponds to them in "factual reality." (This connection between the ideal and the real is not causal, but rather consists of shared meaning and truth.) Just as the abstract, ideal, a priori truth, "2 + 2 = 4," applies to rocks, pencils, people, bananas, or anything else in the real world of everyday experience that can be counted or conceptualized numerically, so do truths about "friendship" and "enmity" apply to anyone who is or could be a friend or an enemy; and truths about "health," "sickness," "justice," "time," "work," "color," "space," "nutrition," "size," and so on endlessly, apply to anything in one's experience that falls under these headings (or instantiates these ideas)—*but only to the extent that it does so.* (As Heraclitus had pointed out, objects in the world tend constantly to change. Moreover, such objects instantiate many ideal meanings simultaneously [what has color also has size and shape], and contain many other features that are irrelevant to whatever feature is at issue. All of these factors greatly complicate, and render messy and imprecise, many of the judgments that one makes about real objects in the world.)

Husserl's agreement with Plato is manifested in his statement that "the ideal objectivities with which the logician deals" exist "in themselves," in the sense that "they are what they are whether or not they are counted, thought, judged, known—every mathematical proposition and every number." But on the other hand, his disagreement becomes clear when he goes on to insist that these ideal objects "become objects of consciousness and become knowable in subjective psychic lived experiences," and even that we are "compelled to say" that numbers are "produced in counting" and the truth "subjectively formed in the act of judging." The conjunction of these two findings concerning ideal objects establishes for Husserl "a great task never before seriously considered," namely, "to make of this unique *correlation* between *ideal objects* of the purely logical sphere and subjectively psychic lived experience as forming activity a theme for research." He points out, for example, that if I repeatedly undertake certain activities, such as counting or drawing inferences, I repeatedly produce "identically the same pure number, identically the same truth, etc. But to speak about this in vague and empty generality does not yield any scientific knowledge." So he calls for a detailed and specific investigation into the nature of the "hidden psychic experiences" which "are correlated to" the idealities in question, and which evidently must run their course in a "determinately appropriate" way so that "the subject can be conscious of and have evident knowledge of these idealities as objects." He calls this inquiry "the proper theme of the *Logical Investigations* and, in corresponding amplification, of all phenomenology" (PP, §3b, 17–18, translation modified). This amplification of which Husserl speaks stems from his realization that "the same problems which had arisen" in connection with "logical and mathematical idealities" in the *Logical Investigations* evidently also "had to be posed for all objectivities" and "real objects of knowledge" (PP, §3b, 20).

Universals

As we have seen, Husserl's account of meaning leads him directly into the ancient philosophical problem (or, more accurately, the cluster of related problems) of universals and particulars. Since the things that we encounter in our experience are particular (an individual horse, but never "horse" itself; a particular green thing, but not "green" in general; a specific round thing, but not "round" or "roundness" as a stand-alone entity; and so forth), what is the status of universals, such as "horse," "green," and "round"? Are these real? Do they exist? How do we acquire knowledge about them? And what is the relationship between universals and the particular things that instantiate them?

In order to clarify these issues, Husserl begins, once again, by drawing distinctions. He distinguishes among (1) a red object, (2) the redness in that object, and (3) "red" as a universal. He often uses the term "species" with regard to (3). Thus, when he speaks of "the species red" he is referring to "red" as an ideal entity, something that does not run around by itself in our experience, but rather is instantiated only in particulars, such as red tomatoes, fire trucks, or flowers. Such instances of species in concrete particulars—item (2) in the three-fold distinction just mentioned—he calls "moments."

Husserl's position is that the red object (1) is real. It comes into and passes out of existence, exists in space and time, undergoes changes, and interacts causally with other objects. The species red (3) is an ideal object. It does not come into or pass out of existence (the simultaneous annihilation of all red things would not destroy it); nor does it exist in space and time, undergo changes, or interact causally with other objects. The red-moment (2) is real. (Note, for example, that a thing that had been a different color might turn red, with that redness then, in turn, fading away. So the redness in a thing can come into and pass out of existence, undergo changes, and so forth.) But at the same time the red-moment is also an instance of something ideal, the species red.

Husserl goes on to argue that "the basic foundations of pure logic and epistemology" can be assured only "by defending the intrinsic right of specific (or ideal) objects to be granted objective status alongside of individual (or real) objects" (LI 1, 238). But how can something that is not "real" be granted "objective status." Well, notice that it is objectively true that 2 + 2 = 4. The point of the adjective, "objectively," here is to say that this truth is made true by the nature of the objects it concerns (that is, "2," "4," "addition," and "equality"), rather than by something subjective (our, or someone's, taste, or desire, or preference, or opinion, for example). Thus, while numbers are ideal, rather than real (we don't encounter the number 2 walking down the street), nonetheless they have the power to render some of our statements about them true and others false. For Husserl, this makes them objects, even though they are not real: "Numbers, propositions, truths, proofs, theories, form in their ideal objectivity a self-contained realm of objects—not things, not realities such as stones or horses, but objects nonetheless. . . . 'Object' in the most universal logical sense means nothing else than anything at all about which meaningful and true statements can be made" (PP, 15, §3a, translation modified).

Husserl's name for this position, which grants objective status to ideal objects, and which refuses the psychologistic strategy of "explaining them away" in terms of the laws of human psychology, is "idealism." He hastens to add, however, that he is not endorsing idealism as "a metaphysical doctrine." He is not claiming, for example, that reality consists only of minds and ideas, and that what are commonly understood to be physical objects should be reinterpreted accordingly. Rather, he clarifies that the "idealism" he endorses is merely "a theory of knowledge which recognizes the 'ideal' as a condition for the possibility of objective knowledge in general" (LI 1, Investigation II, Introduction, 238).

With regard to our knowledge of universals, Husserl says that this is accomplished through "abstraction." But, once again, he quickly explains that he does not mean by this term what others (most notably, the British empiricists, such as Locke, Berkeley, Hume, and Mill) do. Thus, Husserl rejects the claim that we come to know universals by noticing that a number of individual objects resemble each other in some way, and then, perhaps gradually and gropingly, identifying and isolating the common feature, and then fixing it conceptually. Rather, in "abstraction," in the sense that Husserl endorses, "we directly apprehend the Specific Unity *Redness* on the basis of a singular intuition of something red. We look to its moment of red, but we perform a peculiar act, whose intention is directed to the 'Idea', the 'universal'. Abstraction in the sense of this act is wholly different from the mere attention to, or emphasis on, the moment of red" (LI 1, Investigation II, §42, 312). It is simply a datum of experience that just "as universal objects differ from singular ones, so, too, do our acts of apprehending them. We do something wholly different if, looking at an intuited concretum, we refer to its sensed redness, the individual feature it has here and now, and if, on the other hand, we refer to the Species Redness, as when we say that Redness is a Color" (LI 1, Prolegomena, §39, 86). In other words, it is a phenomenological fact that the experience of intending or meaning something general is qualitatively dissimilar to the experience of intending or meaning something particular. We do not arrive at universal concepts by generalizing about and abstracting from a sequence of individual experiences (for example, arriving at the abstract, general, or universal concept "yellow" by first noticing what several yellow things have in common.) Rather, it is only because of eidetic intuition—our ability to grasp an essence by perceiving it directly (perhaps with the help of imaginative variation)—that we are able to group otherwise dissimilar things (taxi cabs, dandelions, and lemons) under the same heading ("yellow") in the first place. In other words, Husserl argues that the British empiricists argue in a circle on this issue. For example, Locke contends that we arrive at the general idea "red" by looking at several red things, disregarding all the ways they differ, and in that way, managing to focus on the one respect in which they are similar. But Husserl points out that the notion of "similarity" relied on here will only work if one already comprehends the essence "red," the very thing that this disregarding and focusing exercise was supposed to explain. He also rejects the British empiricist position that general ideas have a mere psychological existence and basis. While that position has the merit of recognizing the importance of consciousness, it fails to acknowledge the objectivity of universals and essences.

While Plato's position is definitely not vulnerable to that objection, Husserl finds it to be defective in a different way, in that it fails to recognize ideal individuals, that is, eidetic singularities. For Plato, individuals instantiate or imitate essences (Forms or Ideas). Each individual horse, for example, differs in many respects from every other individual horse, even though each instantiates the Form "Horse." For Husserl, by contrast, there are some individuals that are themselves essences, and not merely instances of some more generic essence. The relation "underneath" is an example. If the plate is underneath the toast, and the table is underneath the plate, the relation between the plate and the toast is in that respect *identical* to that holding between the table and the plate.

Husserl's chief grounds for granting objectivity and existence (albeit ideal) to independent universals, detached from the particular things that instantiate them (in other words, to "species," as opposed merely to "moments") are phenomenological. It is, once again, a clear datum of experience that we often think about, talk about, and in some sense *encounter* such entities as we move through our lives. In these experiences our attention is directed to these universals themselves (justice, anger, redness, quantity), rather than to particular individuals (a just resolution of a specific dispute, an angry driver, a red tomato, a stack of eleven books) or to "moments" (the justice in this resolution, the anger of this driver, the redness of this tomato, the "elevenness" of this stack of books). Moreover, these universals, understood phenomenologically, that is, strictly as objects of experience, are fully capable of ruling out as false some of our beliefs or statements about them. Further, though ideal, they are "given" in experience as having a status that contrasts starkly with those objects of thought that present themselves as fictitious, purely imaginary, or logically absurd. And all of this can be accounted for without assuming that universals have a spatiotemporal existence, or that they exist in some shadowy, otherworldly realm, or that they are mere contingent products of the human mind, subject to the vicissitudes of human psychology.

Those who have resisted granting any kind of objectivity or existence to universals have often done so on the basis of the claim that it is unhelpful, and therefore unnecessarily cumbersome and unwieldy, to clutter up the landscape with so many entities, when one can explain everything perfectly satisfactorily without granting existence to anything other than individual things. But in Husserl's critique of the British empiricists he makes the case that this is untrue—numerous issues that can be dealt with quite satisfactorily and straightforwardly given the independent objectivity of universals instead generate enormous difficulties and complications when the task is to anchor all true statements in the antics of particular individual things. (Notice, for example, that without universals no meaningful statement could be successfully communicated.) Of course, this by itself does not prove the objectivity of universals. Many intellectual puzzles could be solved by arbitrarily making up and positing something that would solve the problem. (Why does the light come on when I open my refrigerator door? There is a little man in there who flips the light switch.) But the case is quite different when the object needed to solve the problem is not an invention, a product of imagination, but rather something regularly encountered in everyday experience. And Husserl's claim is that, as a clear and obvious matter of fact, we do experience universals regularly, and "grasp" them immediately, although we do so through eidetic intuition, rather than by means of sense experience.

Moreover, this experience of universals further underscores Husserl's theory of the ideality of meaning—the thesis that the objective meaning-contents of intentional acts differ radically in kind both from those acts themselves and from the real, individual things in the world to which those meanings refer. For no two real events in the world, that is, events that begin, take time, and then end, can ever be identical to one another. Nor can any such event be repeated. The reason is the one identified by Heraclitus. Everything in the "real" world (as Husserl would define it) is in a constant state of flux. And for the same reason, no two individual things in the world can ever be the same as one another, or "repeated." (If a painter were to make a painting, destroy it, and then make an "identical" copy, the new work would not, strictly speaking, be "identical" to or "the same" as, the original.) So when I perceive (or remember or imagine) an object, such as the tree in my backyard, neither my conscious act of focusing on the tree, nor the tree itself, understood as a real, individual object in the world, is identical to anything else, or repeatable.

And yet, identity and repeatability are the norm when it comes to the realm of experienced meanings. Here I am, sitting at the *same* desk, in the *same* room, banging away on the *same* computer, working on the *same* book, as I was yesterday, and the day before that. Similarly, insofar as I encounter objects in my experience under the heading of meanings—this is round, or red, or quiet, or unjust, or fascinating, or incomprehensible—I encounter them as, at least in that respect, identical to other experienced objects-as-meanings. Thus, the realm of sameness and repeatability, which is to say, the realm of universals, is also the realm of the meant. A thing can be the same only for a consciousness that can focus on it in a certain way, and retain that focus throughout the unceasing shifts of temporal existence (fluctuations which that same consciousness either ignores or dismisses as irrelevant). The physical world does not tell us how to divide itself up into discrete objects, or how to conceptualize the divided parts as meaningful. Thus, to see two numerically and temporally distinct things as "the same" requires selective focusing and conceptualizing—acts of consciousness that are not determined by the physical world. As James M. Edie points out, "sameness can be recognized only on the level of the ideal correlates of mental acts. It is a 'transcendental' structure of our dealings with the world *as experienced*; it is a structure not of the real but of our experience of the real."[14]

Parts and Wholes

Husserl's analysis of universals, and of the relationship between universals and the individual particular things that instantiate them, leads him to a detailed consideration of the relationship between a whole and its parts. His discussion of this issue falls

---

[14] "What Is Phenomenology?," in Edie's *Edmund Husserl's Phenomenology: A Critical Commentary* (Bloomington: Indiana University Press, 1987), 12.

under the heading of work in "formal ontology"—an attempt to work out an a priori theory of objects. Just as formal logic applies equally to all areas of inquiry, in that its rules do not depend on the specific natures of the issues or concepts dealt with in different subject domains, so does formal ontology lay down a priori rules and principles that apply equally to all kinds of objects. Whereas formal logic is concerned with general and universal *meaning categories* (subject, predicate, proposition, premise, conclusion, and so forth), formal ontology deals with *object categories* of similar generality and universality (object, property, part, whole, state of affairs, existence, individual and species, unity, number, magnitude, and so on).

Husserl further distinguishes formal ontology from regional ontology. Such concepts as something, object, quality, relation, connection, plurality, number, order, whole, part, and magnitude are abstract and formal—they deal, in general, with any kind of object or thing. By contrast, such concepts as tree, house, color, tone, space, sensation, feeling, thought, and shape are material—they deal with particular kinds of things and their (often) unique and specific properties. The former group of concepts belongs to the domain of formal ontology, the latter to that of regional ontology (they concern some particular region of material beings).

Husserl begins his analysis of parts and wholes by distinguishing between two different kinds of parts: pieces and moments. Pieces can exist independently, apart from the whole of which they are a part. For example, a page can be detached from a book and present itself as an independent thing—a page. Similarly, the steering wheel of a car, a member of a basketball team, and the rind from a watermelon can be separated from the car, the team, and the watermelon, respectively, and be understood as separate, independent entities. All of these things, though perhaps originally parts of wholes, are also capable of being wholes themselves.

Moments, by contrast, are parts of wholes that cannot be detached in this way. The color blue cannot exist on its own as an independent thing, but rather must be spread over some surface taking up some space. (Husserl says of the color of a piece of paper that "its essence, its pure Species, predestines it to partial being: a color *in general and purely as such* can exist only as a 'moment' in a colored thing" [LI 2, Investigation III, §7, 12].) Similarly, the pitch, loudness, and timbre of a sound cannot be separated from that sound; a smile cannot be separated from the face that smiles; and movement cannot be separated from the thing that moves. Consequently, moments, unlike pieces, cannot become wholes.

With these distinctions in place, Husserl is able to offer a new analysis of an issue that Immanuel Kant had famously introduced, that of accounting for "synthetic a priori" truths. On Kant's view, there is no special problem about *analytic* a priori truths. A priori truths are true necessarily and universally. Their truth does not depend on any particular state of affairs; rather, they hold in any conceivable circumstance. Thus, we can know in advance of any particular experience that such truths will hold good with regard to whatever is disclosed in that experience. They are, in that sense, "a priori," or prior to experience. Analytic statements, as Kant defines them, are those in which the predicate is already contained (perhaps covertly) within the subject, as in the statement, "all bachelors are unmarried." Since the term "bachelor," in the relevant sense, means "unmarried man," the statement reduces to "all unmarried men are unmarried," a rendering which makes clear the fact that the predicate is already contained within the subject. It is easy to see that analytic statements, so defined, are true a priori. Anyone who chose to conduct an empirical investigation of the truth or falsity of the claim that all bachelors are unmarried, would, in so doing, betray a complete misunderstanding of the meaning of that claim. For what would it mean to discover, say, that three percent of bachelors are, in fact, married? Such a finding is ruled out in advance of experience (a priori) since anyone who would be found to be married would also be found, by definition, not to be a bachelor. Thus, analytic statements achieve a priori truth, but only at the cost of vacuity—they merely unpack the implications of the meanings of words and tell us nothing about the world.

Synthetic statements, by contrast, do give us information about the world. A synthetic statement, on Kant's definition, is simply one that is not analytic—its predicate is not already contained within its subject. Rather, with a synthetic statement, two distinct ideas are conjoined, as in the statement, "most bachelors are younger than forty years of age." Note that there is nothing in the definition of "bachelors" which guarantees the truth or falsity of this claim. Moreover, it is a dubious candidate for a universal and necessary truth. For, even if it were to turn out to be true, this would have to be determined by some sort of empirical investigation. Thus, this synthetic statement cannot be classified as a priori. Rather, its status is a posteriori. It cannot be known, prior to experience, to hold for any possible experience that we might have. To the contrary, its validity can be assessed only after (posterior to) the deliverance of the evidence of experience.

The significance of the concept of synthetic a priori truths is that, if such truths exist, they would combine the strengths of analytic a priori and synthetic a posteriori truths, while jettisoning their weaknesses and limitations. Synthetic a priori truths would achieve the universality and necessity of analytic a priori truths, and the informative character of synthetic a posteriori truths, but without the triviality of the former or the contingency and uncertainty of the latter. But *are* there any such truths? Many have denied this, contending that the analytic a priori/synthetic a posteriori disjunction is exhaustive.

Husserl begins his approach to this issue by offering a different account of the essential distinction between analytic and synthetic statements. Instead of locating the difference in the issue of the presence or absence of the predicate within the subject in a statement, Husserl suggests that greater clarity can be achieved by distinguishing between questions that deal broadly, formally, abstractly with objects in general, and questions that concern the material differences between different kinds of objects. On Husserl's account, analytical a priori disciplines, laws, and necessities apply to the former domain, with synthetic a priori ones applying to the latter.

So analytically necessary (or analytic a priori) statements are those whose truth has nothing to do with the material properties of the objects with which they deal, or with anything that is peculiar to them, or with anything that is factual, or with the issue of whether or not any particular thing exists. If such statements do contain references to particular things, it must be the case that such references could be replaced with references to any other particular things without this in any way affecting the truth of the statements in question. "2 dogs + 2 dogs = 4 dogs" is analytically necessary, because "dogs" could be replaced with "books," "trees," "ideas," "rocks," or anything else, and remain true. "In an analytic proposition it must be possible, without altering the proposition's logical form, to replace all material which has con-

tent, with an empty formal *Something*, and to eliminate every assertion of existence by giving all one's judgments the form of universal, unconditional laws" (LI 2, Investigation III, §12, 21). So, for
Husserl, the universality and necessity of analytic a priori truths is
formal, rather than material.

Synthetic a priori truths, by contrast, have to do with the specific material characteristics of the kinds of objects with which they
deal. One of Husserl's examples is the statement that "anything
colored is extended in space." This is a universal and necessary
truth. It is unthinkable that anything could be colored without
being extended in space, and we know, in advance, that anything
colored that we will encounter will be extended in space. Thus, the
statement that "anything colored is extended in space" is a priori.
But it is synthetic. It depends on the (material) essences of color
and space. So its universality and necessity, like that of all other
synthetic a priori truths, on Husserl's analysis, is material, rather
than formal. (Notice, however, that the statement in question also
qualifies as synthetic by Kant's criteria, since the concept of
"color" does not in any sense include the idea of "extension," in
the way that the concept "bachelor" includes the idea of being
"unmarried.")

But the formal/material distinction is not the only one that
Husserl uses in his analysis of synthetic a priori truths. He also
relies (and again, this is in contrast to Kant) on his whole/part and
pieces/moments distinctions. The statement that anything colored
is extended in space, for example, is an instance of a synthetic a priori law concerning the relations between moments and wholes. We
know, in advance of any particular experience, that every sound we
will hear will be at some definite pitch and loudness, that every
smile we see will be expressed by a face, and that every color we
encounter will be extended in space. While much of what we know
consists of a posteriori knowledge, learned from experience,
Husserl insists that such learning takes place within the context of
an a priori framework that makes it possible.

One final distinction that is important in this connection marks
the difference between something that "founds" and something
that "is founded" in it (or dependent on it). As Husserl draws this
distinction, A is founded on B if A cannot appear without B—that
is, A's existence requires the existence of B. For example, color is
founded in extension, memory is founded in perception, and intu-

itive fulfillment is founded in a meaning intention (that is, a meaning-conferring, or signitive, act).

Husserl's theory of founding and dependence applies always to species, or else to individuals insofar as they instantiate species. Accordingly, the laws of founding and dependence that he describes (and also laws of compatibility or incompatibility) are ideal, and thus a priori (universal and necessary). So if two attributes or qualities are united in an object (if, for example, the object is both blue and rectangular), this is because of necessary a priori laws of either dependence or compatibility between the unified parts at the level of species. Blueness and rectangularity are compatible; but blueness and redness are not (or at least they are not in the same way—when a thing is both blue and red, that is because different parts of it are differently colored). It is a synthetic a priori truth that the same part of a thing, the exact same spot, cannot be both blue and red at once.

Two points about this must be emphasized. First, such truths concerning the dependence (that something blue must be extended in space), compatibility (that a blue thing could be, but is not required to be, rectangular), or incompatibility or necessary exclusion (that a blue spot cannot simultaneously be red) of species cannot be arrived at simply by analyzing the relevant concepts. They are not tautologies, truths of definition, or Kantian analytic truths. Rather, they are truths concerning the material essences of these different species. It is because of what blue, extension, rectangularity, and red *are* that they enter into the various relationships of dependence, compatibility, or incompatibility into which they do, in fact, enter.

Secondly, our knowledge of such truths is not a posteriori. It does not depend on hypothesis, observation, and inductive generalization. If it did, our conclusions concerning these matters would be tentative, provisional, subject to modification in the light of further observation, based on nothing more than the fact that all of the blue things we have seen thus far have been extended in space, and have not been red. But clearly our conclusions are based on something more than this, namely, insight into the essences of these things. We can *grasp, see, understand,* that red and blue exclude one another, and that both require extension in space. That is why we know in advance of any experience (a priori) that we will never encounter a colored thing that is not extended in space, or a thing that is both red and blue in the same spot. Our knowledge of this is not inductive, but *intuitive*.

Pure Logical Grammar

A further application of Husserl's analysis of parts and wholes is to be found in his theory of pure logical grammar. The task of this theory is to work out the principles governing the ways in which meanings can be combined so as to form new meanings. A well-formed proposition is a meaningful whole that is made up of parts (such as individual words, and, in some cases, prefixes and suffixes) that are also themselves meaningful. But not just any combination of meaningful parts will form a meaningful whole. (This is an instance of Husserl's general finding that "all combinations whatever are subject to pure laws," so that "in no sphere is it possible to combine items of any and every kind by way of any and every form: the sphere of items sets a priori limits to the number of combinatorial forms, and prescribes the general laws for filling them in" [LI 2, Investigation IV, §10, 62].) Husserl's analysis attempts to establish that the laws regulating the forming of meaningful wholes out of meaningful parts, that is, the laws of pure logical grammar, are formal, a priori constraints on meaningful thought, just as the formal, a priori principles of logic regulate and constrain the drawing of logical inferences.

When words are combined in such a way as to violate the formal, a priori laws of pure logical grammar, they fail to comprise an understandable meaning, and the result is nonsense, as in the utterance "The is or and." Husserl emphasizes that the meaninglessness of such utterances is not attributable to something subjective, such as a "mere factual incapacity" on our part, or some "compulsion of our mental make-up," but rather is "objective" and "ideal," "rooted in the pure essence of the meaning-realm," and graspable "with apodictic self-evidence" (LI 2, Investigation IV, §10, 62).

But Husserl also insists that nonsense must not be confused with "countersense." In the case of a countersense, the combination of meanings in the utterance in question violates no formal rules. Instead, the problem is material. Incompatible meanings are combined in such a way that we can know, a priori, that no object corresponding to the combined meaning can possibly exist. The concept of a "round square" is thus an example of a countersense. It is absurd, rather than nonsensical. Far from being meaningless, it is precisely the richly meaningful nature of the concept "round square" that allows us to see, with luminous clarity, that we are in principle precluded from ever encountering an entity that would instantiate it. Our knowledge of the impossibility of the existence of a round square is intuitive. It is rooted in our insight into the material essences of roundness and squareness.

Here, as elsewhere, Husserl criticizes his contemporaries (and, by implication, ours) for persistently confusing the a priori and empirical realms, and, more specifically, for extending the latter beyond its proper limits while simultaneously betraying an unfounded prejudice against the former:

> The foundations of speech are not only to be found in physiology, psychology and the history of culture, but also in the *a priori*. The latter deals with the essential meaning-forms and their *a priori* laws of compounding or modification, and no speech is conceivable that is not in part essentially determined by this *a priori*. Every investigator of language operates with notions stemming from this field, whether he is clear on the matter or not. (LI 2, Investigation IV, §14, 74)

While we are usually less interested in these a priori laws governing meaningfulness than we are in the twin questions of whether or not a given utterance avoids self-contradiction (and obeys other laws of formal logic), and, if it does, the question of whether or not it is true, these issues, nonetheless, are logically posterior to the question of whether or not the utterance is meaningful. And according to Husserl this question, in turn, can only be settled by reference to a priori laws of essence governing the combining of parts into wholes.

Intentionality Again

But Husserl's project of attempting to understand knowledge, truth, and objectivity ultimately leads him, in the *Logical Investigations*, to the study of consciousness. For it is only by being conscious of something that we can know it. Still, in the light of Husserl's critique of psychologism, it is clear that the foundations of logic and epistemology (theory of knowledge) that he is seeking are not to be found in empirical psychology, or in any other empirical discipline. So in studying consciousness Husserl focuses not on its causal preconditions but on its noncausal relations with its objects. He does not consider consciousness as a thing or a substance, but rather as an "intentional" relation toward transcendent objects. Consciousness, and specifically consciousness as intentionality, provides Husserl with the noncausal foundations he is seeking for logic and epistemology. Accordingly, intentionality comes to serve as the main theme of his phenomenology. Indeed, at the very outset of the *Logical Investigations*, Husserl announces his intention to investigate a topic that will go on to occupy him throughout nearly all of his subsequent work, namely, "the relationship . . . between the subjectivity of knowing and the objectivity of the content known" (LI 1, Foreword to First German Edition, 2).

"Intentionality" refers to the directedness or "aboutness" of conscious acts. Conscious experiences are distinguished by their object-directedness. One loves, fears, sees, judges, hears, thinks, fantasizes, doubts, expects, recalls, and so forth, and each of these acts takes an object. One sees a tree, fears a snarling dog, imagines a far-away planet, and judges a state of affairs. Intentionality, then, is the unique characteristic of conscious experiences. It is the characteristic of being related to, oriented or directed toward, an object in such a way as to "have" the object, in the sense of being presented with it. Conscious acts aim at, are about, are directed toward, "intend," some object. Moreover, this correlativity of the conscious act and its object is a feature of *all* conscious experiences. Consciousness is not first something in itself, which can later enter into a relationship with something else. Rather, consciousness is *essentially* relational, and always takes an object. "In perception something is perceived, in imagination, something imagined, in a statement something stated, in love something loved, in hate hated, in desire desired etc." (LI 2, Investigation V, §10, 95). Our being as conscious agents is intentional. Consciousness is, in principle and necessarily, self-transcending and directed toward objects that are different from itself.

The intentional relation between a conscious act and its object is unique, and unlike any causal, or purely physical, relation. No purely physical phenomenon exhibits anything like the relationship between the act of judging and the thing judged, or between love and the thing loved, or between imagining and the thing imagined, and so forth. The connection between consciousness and its objects is one of meanings and of rational justifications, as opposed to one of natural causality. Nonconscious objects are not related to one another in this way. To explain a belief in terms of meanings, concepts, purposes, reasons, evidence, and argument, is not to explain it in terms of psychological laws (or any other kind of mechanistic causality), nor is the former reducible to the latter. Causal explanation and rational justification are two utterly distinct kinds of things.

Through a conscious act one is aware of an object, one experiences it, even if the object in question is ideal or imaginary. It is obviously possible to think about absent, fictional, or nonexistent things. Such things can be intentional objects. Consider the status of mathematical objects—numbers, such as "4" and "7," and geometrical shapes, such as "circle" and "square." These concepts are not arbitrary. Though they are abstractions, and must be realized through conscious acts, they are not inventions. They are objective, and it is possible to make genuine discoveries about them that have universal validity. Mathematical objects provide a kind of model for intentional objects generally. An object is whatever is aimed at by an intentional act. We are subjects only insofar as we are ceaselessly intentionally directed toward objects of all kinds. We are engaged with a world of objects.

Husserl's handling of the problem of nonexistent objects brings into focus one of the ways in which his account of intentionality improves on that of his teacher, Brentano, from whom he had first learned about intentionality. Brentano's solution to the problem (on the one hand, it doesn't seem right to deny them *any* kind of existence, since we seem, after all, to be thinking about *something* when we think about unicorns, but, on the other hand, they don't seem to exist out there in the world) had been to say that intentional objects have "mental in-existence," meaning that they are contained within consciousness. On his view, every mental state contains its objects within itself. The problem is that we see many kinds of objects, most notably objects of perception, in profile. Thus, on Brentano's view we would either have to say that the intentional object is nothing but the façade that we see (which is phenomenologically, or descriptively, false), or, if we prefer to remain faithful to the fact that it is an object that we intend, not a profile, then the doctrine that the intentional object is immanent to consciousness would entail that we experience all sides of the object at once (which, again, is manifestly false). Husserl's account of intentionality allows him to make an advance on the empiricists, since they can't make sense of the fact that it is objects, rather than immediately-present sense data, toward which we are directed. His advance on Brentano, by contrast, consists in the fact that he, unlike Brentano, can account for the fact that there is more (indeed, infinitely more) to the extramental objects that we intend than is given in any perception (or any finite series of perceptions) of them. Such objects are transcendent to, rather than immanent in, our consciousness of them. This is a datum of experience. Objects present themselves to us as going beyond our experience of them.

A further implication of the intentionality of consciousness is that consciousness is highly active. There are always many objects in my perceptual field to which I could direct my attention, and even more should I instead choose to undertake a project of recollection or imagination, rather than one of perception. Consciousness is always selective in its intentional activities—we focus on this, to the exclusion of that. What one sees (or hears or imagines or hates or doubts, etc.) depends in part on how one focuses, and thus brings part of the perceptual and conceptual manifold to the foreground while relegating the rest to the background. We perceive a figure on a ground, and our activity is indicated by the fact that the world does not organize itself in this way for us.

Consciousness is active and interpretive from the outset in at least two other ways as well. First, we "see" more than is literally present. Objects in our perceptual field are always given in profile. The image that strikes our optic nerve is of the front of the object, but not the back, of the top, but not the bottom, of one side, but not the other. Nonetheless, what I "see" is a house, not the front, or top, or side of a house. From the very beginning I bring to bear on my act of perceiving a house my background knowledge about houses. It is not the case that I first see a façade of a house and then subsequently draw the inference that it has a backside.

We do not first encounter neutral or formless or raw sense data, which we then assemble into objects through acts of consciousness. Rather, what we encounter, right from the outset, is a world of objects—independent, real, already meaningful, objects. We do not assemble perceptions of shape, color, texture, taste, smell, and sound into objects. Rather, through intentional acts we aim at objects. Though these objects do, admittedly, provide us with sense data, we are typically unaware of such data, noticing them only on those relatively rare occasions when, through acts of abstraction, we shift our attention away from the objects with which we are typically engaged and instead deliberately focus on them. For in my experience generally "I do not see color-sensations but colored things, I do not hear tone-sensations but the singer's song, etc. etc." (LI 2, Investigation V, §11, 99). Experience does not come in bits of color and sound. We live in a world of barking dogs, weeping disgraced televangelists, and rainbows.

Secondly, we see (or remember, or imagine, or in some other way intend) objects always under the color of some categories and not others. Indeed, no object can emerge in our experience as meaningful except insofar as we focus on it selectively in such a way as to bring out that meaning, so that we see an apple, variously, as a "small thing," a "red thing," an "edible thing," a "fruit," an "apple," and so forth.

Essential Distinctions

In analyzing intentionality one can distinguish among (1) the conscious act, (2) its semantic content or meaning, and (3) its object. With regard to (1), Husserl further distinguishes the "quality" of the act from its "matter." The quality of an act is its "general act-character" as being "merely presentative, judgmental, desiderative, etc.," with the matter being what *is* presented, judged, desired, and so forth (LI 2, Investigation V, §20, 119). It is one thing to perceive x, and quite another to imagine it, or doubt it, or fear it. These distinctions have to do with the quality of the act. Quality and matter can be combined in a limitless variety of ways. Each quality can take on different matters, just as each matter can be combined with different qualities. "The two assertions '2 x 2 = 4' and 'Ibsen is the principal founder of modern dramatic realism', are both, *qua* assertions, of one kind; each is qualified as an assertion, and their common feature is their *judgment-quality*. The one, however, judges one content and the other another content. To distinguish such 'contents' from other notions of 'content' we shall speak here of the *matter* . . . of judgments" (LI 2, Investigation V, §20, 119).

Similarly, though now moving in the opposite direction:

> Content in the sense of 'matter' is a component of the concrete act-experience, which it may share with acts of quite different quality. It comes out most clearly if we set up a series of identical utterances, where the act-qualities change, while the matter remains identical. All this is not hard to provide. . . . A man who frames the presentation 'There are intelligent beings on Mars' frames the same presentation as the man who asserts 'There are intelligent beings on Mars', and the same as the man who asks 'Are there intelligent beings on Mars?', or the man who wishes 'If only there are intelligent beings on Mars!' etc. etc. . . . What do we mean by the 'same content'? . . . One and the same state of affairs is presented in the presentation, put as valid in the judgment, wished for in the wish, asked about in the question. (LI 2, Investigation V, §20, 120)

The distinction between content and object is based on the observation that the same object can yield different contents, depending on the description under which, or the perspective from which, it is intended. Thus, to recall a recently-mentioned example, one and the same object, a particular apple, can be experienced as meaningful in an almost limitless variety of ways, as a "small thing," a "red thing," an "edible thing," a "fruit," an "apple," and so forth, as a result of the equally varied number of ways in which we might focus on it. This consideration shows that meaning and object are not identical. As Husserl puts it, "the matter . . . [is] *that element in an act which first gives it reference to an object, and reference so wholly definite that it not merely fixes the object meant in a general way, but also the precise way in which it is meant.* The matter—to carry clearness a little further—is that peculiar side of an act's phenomenological content that not only determines *that* it grasps the object but also *as what* it grasps it (LI 2, Investigation V, §20, 121).

With reference to the distinctions Husserl draws in his analysis of parts and wholes, notice that quality and matter are moments, rather than pieces, of an intentional act. There is no act of perceiving, wishing, or doubting without something perceived, wished for, or doubted; and there is no intentional object that is not intended by some kind of act or another (whether perceived, wished for, doubted, and so on). "Act-quality is undoubtedly *an abstract aspect of acts*, unthinkable apart from all matter. . . . The same holds of matter. A matter that was not matter for presentation, nor for judgment, nor for . . . etc. etc., would be . . . unthinkable" (LI 2, Investigation V, §20, 122).

Husserl calls the unity of an intentional act's quality and matter its "intentional essence" or "semantic essence." This essence is repeatable and shareable. So if I at two different times ask the same question (for example, "are there intelligent beings on Mars?"), or if two different people ask that same question at the same time or at different times, the meaning of these different intentional acts is identical in each case. But this does not mean that these different acts or experiences are the same in every conceivable way. Rather, one presentation might be fuller, more vivid, or in some other way more intense than another, without this in any way entailing even the slightest variation in meaning.

A final distinction concerns the mode of givenness of the intentional object. Consider two acts of judging that "it is raining outside right now." In these two acts both the quality and the matter are the same. But suppose that in one case I am inside in a windowless room when I make this judgment, and in the other case I am outside getting drenched. In the former case my intention is empty, or merely signitive, while in the latter it is fulfilled, or intuitive.

Knowledge

This example also illustrates Husserl's analysis of knowledge. To know that "it is raining outside right now" is to have one's meaning-intention that "it is raining outside right now" intuitively fulfilled.

Husserl begins his analysis by arguing, once again, that meaning does not in any simple or straightforward way reside in the world or its objects, but must rather emerge through distinctive acts of consciousness. Nor is meaning identical to, or reducible to, what we perceive, since (a) one and the same perception can give rise to a variety of meanings (and judgments), and (b) one and the same meaning (and judgment) can be founded on different perceptions. Husserl gives this example:

> I have just looked out into the garden and now give expression to my percept in the words: 'There flies a blackbird!' *What is here the act in which my meaning resides?* I think we may say . . . that it does not reside in perception, at least not in perception alone. . . . For we could

base quite different statements on the *same percept*, and thereby
unfold *quite different senses*. I could, e.g., have remarked: 'That is
black!', 'That is a black bird!', 'There flies that black bird!', 'There it
soars!', and so forth. And conversely, the sound of my words and their
sense might have remained the same, though my percept varied in a
number of ways. Every chance alteration of the perceiver's relative
position alters his percept, and different persons, who perceive the
same object simultaneously, never have exactly the same percepts. (LI
2, Investigation VI, §4, 195)

Moreover, a listener who hears my words, but who neither looks
out into the garden to see what I am seeing nor even reenacts it
imaginatively, may still understand my meaning quite well. A merely
signitive and an intuitive act can have the same meaning. If I see a
dead raccoon by the side of the road, and thus say, "there is a dead
raccoon by the side of the road," this means the same thing as it
does when it is repeated by someone else to whom I have made a
report. Such a person might well understand this utterance even if
he or she neither sees what I saw perceptually, nor even bothers to
picture it imaginatively. In this case, the meaning-intention remains
empty, but no less meaningful than my fulfilled meaning-intention.
My meaning is communicated, and thus shared, even though I do
not convey my perceptual experience, that is, my intuition, to my
interlocutor. Thus, meaning must arise from "a type of act free from
the limitations of the perception or the imagination which so often
fail us" (LI 2, Investigation VI, §4, 196).

But to grasp, to understand, to be able to make sense of, a
statement or claim, is very far from the same thing as knowing it
to be true. For knowledge requires evidence.

Evidence

Evidence is "*the experience of the agreement* between meaning and
what is itself present, meant, between the actual *sense of an assertion* and the self-given *state of affairs*" (LI 1, Prolegomena, §51,
121). When "self-evidence" is achieved, "the object is not merely
meant, but in the strictest sense *given*, and given as it is meant, and
made one with our meaning reference" (LI 2, Investigation VI,
§38, 263). Husserl is here making use, once again, of his distinction between empty, unfulfilled, merely signitive intentions, on the
one hand, and intuitive fulfillment, on the other. "Evidence" is the

experience of the self-givenness of something in complete intuitive fullnesss. Or again, evidence is the intuitive "giving" of the thing itself (or the state of affairs). The thing or state of affairs is "present" to consciousness, which "sees" or "grasps" it.

Knowledge thus arises from the bringing together of two kinds of experience: the intentional and the intuitive (or evidential). The latter is the empirical part; the former, in a way, is the rational, or conceptual, part. Objectifying acts are either intuitive or signitive, depending on whether the object is intuited directly or intended symbolically. In a signitive act an object is thought in an "empty" way. Signs, such as words or symbols, refer to an object, but that object is not given intuitively. It is not "present" for us to "see" in any way. In an intuitive act, by contrast, the intended object is present for us to see. Intuition is nonsignitive. One encounters the "thing" (whether a physical object, an abstract universal, or a state of affairs) itself, and not a sign for it.

The connection between signitive meaning-intentions and their intuitive fulfillment holds, moreover, in connection with issues of meaning, no less than for issues of evidence, truth, and knowledge. For Husserl maintains that we can only fully understand a meaning-intention if we know, in principle, how to verify it, which is to say that we know how to determine its truth value. Even nonexistent and impossible (because self-contradictory) objects are understood in this way. Part of what it means to understand the meaning content "round-square" is to recognize the a priori impossibility of acquiring evidence (intuitive meaning-fulfillment) of a round square. A real object, for Husserl, is one that is intuitively given. To say that centaurs and round-squares are not real is to say that our merely signitive intentions of them are not fulfilled. Because many of our signitive intentions are not (and, in some cases, cannot) be fulfilled, it follows that "the realm of meaning is . . . much wider than that of intuition" (LI 2, Investigation VI, §63, 312).

Note that Husserl is in this sense an objectivist: truth value is determined by states of affairs, not by our thoughts, attitudes, tastes, agreements, or the like. He insists that we can *experience* truth. The reason is that we can experience actual states of affairs, and not merely representations of them.

Evidence is not to be confused with subjective conviction, however, or a feeling of certainty and infallibility. We know that people can feel that way about all sorts of crazy falsehoods. Indeed, people can feel that way about anything, so such a conception of evidence would lead to relativism. Evidence is public, and the experiential part of it is fallible. It is always open to criticism and correction. But this correction must come about as a result of better and stronger evidence. The correction for faulty seeing is better seeing.

Intuitions do not yield knowledge unless they fulfill a meaning-intention, or thought. But the thought need not always come first. One might intuit something without knowing it, because one lacks the corresponding thought, which might be arrived at later.

There are degrees of intuitive fulfillment. A picture might provide some degree of fulfillment, but typically not the degree that a perceptual encounter with the intended object that such a picture depicts would. Also, one presentation might differ from another in clarity and vividness. So one presentation might better fulfill a signitive meaning-intention than another, just as (to use Husserl's own analogy), a finished painting perhaps better presents a likeness than does a drawing, which is, in turn, superior in this regard to a rough sketch, which might still to some degree present the likeness intuitively in a way that is not the case when one's thinking is utterly confined to words or symbols.

A thing can be "given" in experience in many ways, and with widely varying degrees of evidence. In most experiences evidence is given only "inadequately." An object is given inadequately when it is given incompletely and one-sidedly. Typically, such experiences contain "unfulfilled" elements, as when I see a house from the front and expect it to have sides and a back, which I am at the moment unable to see. Evidence is "adequate" when there are no longer any unfulfilled meaning elements. Self-evidence is "apodictic" when the denial of what the evidence shows is absolutely unthinkable. (We have apodictic evidence that one can't shoot a 17 in a regulation round of golf.) But if the evidence merely generates a conviction beyond all reasonable doubts, it is "assertoric."

Perceptual evidence is never adequate, that is, complete, since objects are given in perception only in profile. Nor can objects that are perceived with the senses ever present themselves with apodictic evidence, because their nonbeing is always conceivable. But this does not mean that perceptual evidence is worthless. Rather, it entails only that such strength as perceptual evidence can achieve is necessarily less than that of full adequacy or apodicticity. Different standards of evidence are appropriate for different subject domains. Evidence concerning matters of fact cannot reach the highest levels of strength attainable in connection with essential principles. Knowledge based on the evidence of the senses cannot yield the insight that is attainable in mathematics and logic. But even within the domain of sensory experience, intuitive fulfillment is not an all-or-nothing matter. Here, too, there are different degrees of fulfillment, entailing different degrees of evidence. How many profiles have I intuitively seen? How clearly have I seen them? There are distinctions of range, clarity, vividness, and precision, among others, which must be taken into account.

Profiles

We see objects always partially, always in profile, and yet they are given in experience as having other sides that are not currently visible. The object is a unity of the inexhaustibly many different ways it can be perceived. In one sense, we never see the object itself, since we cannot see all of these perspectives at once, but rather see only a profile. But from the standpoint of phenomenological description, it is not accurate to say that we see a profile. Rather, we see the object itself in the very act of seeing its profile. We see the object, right from the start, without additional acts of perception or conception, as a whole, complete object, that is, as a unity, as comprising sides that we cannot now see. Every perceptual act points beyond what is given in that perception, and anticipates what would be given in further perceptions of the same object. We can move about the object, seeing different aspects of it, investigating it in different ways, but there is no way, in principle, ever to complete this task. Perception is thus an "infinite task."

"Retention" and anticipation are important here. As I move about an object, or in some other way scrutinize several of its aspects sequentially, one at a time, I retain in my stream of conscious experience the aspects or profiles I have already seen, and synthesize those with the ones I am seeing now and with those I anticipate seeing (as in the back side of the house which I am now viewing from the front). The consistency and coherence of these profiles (also called "adumbrations") confirms the object's unity, just as inconsistency can falsify our assumption of the objective unity of the thing. The object is the ideal unity of the combination of all of the infinite possible appearances of it. The Kantian idea of a thing in itself, that is, a thing outside of, or underlying, the phenomenal field entirely—for example, a thing outside of space and time—is an absurdity.

All of this is eidetically necessary. The idea that a perceived object could be given in all its aspects all at once, or be seen from no particular perspective, proves, upon examination, unthinkable and absurd. The object is *given* as having other sides that are presently inaccessible. Our knowledge of these unseen sides is never perfect, even when dealing with very familiar objects, but neither is it ever absolutely nothing. What is presented is always sufficiently determinative as to rule out some possibilities as to what will be revealed when the object is examined from other standpoints, and to suggest others as "open possibilities." We will expect what is currently unseen to be compatible with what is currently seen, and also to cohere with what we know about the perceived object from earlier encounters with it. (Or, if we have had no such encounters, our expectations will be constrained, though to a lesser degree, by knowledge we have gleaned from experiences with objects that are similar to it in ways that are relevant to the expectation in question.) Thus,

> Indeterminateness is never absolute or complete. Complete indeterminateness is non-sense; the indeterminateness is always delimited in this or that way. I may not know exactly what sort of form the back side has, yet it precisely has some form; the body is a body. I may not know how matters stand with the color, the roughness or smoothness, the warmth or coldness, yet it pertains to the very sense of the apprehension of a thing that the thing possess a certain color, a certain surface determination, etc. (TS, 49–50)

So, while there is always an empty aspect to perception, because I see things only in profile, this emptiness is not absolute. I have some idea what to expect from the sides that I cannot currently see. What I do see suggests certain possible fulfilling were I to turn my attention to the presently unseen sides. This presence/absence/expectation-of-possible-fulfillment structure is to be found in all intentional experience. The interplay of presence and absence is part of what is involved in "having an object."

These analyses make clear some of the ways in which Husserlian phenomenology differs from rival views, such as classical empiricism, sense data theory, and relativism. In opposition to the British empiricists, Husserl claims that it is an essential feature of perception that it "enables us to go beyond the 'image' which alone [according to the empiricists] is present in consciousness, and to relate to it *as* an image to a certain extraconscious object. . . . Relation to its [transcendent] object is part and parcel of the phenomenological essence of consciousness" (LI 2, Investigation V, Appendix to §11 and §20, 125–26). Similarly, because the empiricists are committed to the claim that we see only an image, and precisely not anything that is not present to our senses, they cannot account for the clear datum of experience that, though we see an object only in profile, what we "see" is not a façade, but rather a three-dimensional object seen from one side. In perception what is present to us are not uninterrupted images or bits of sense data, but rather data that are right from the start perceived as images of some object or other. Perception is generally intentionally directed toward objects rather than toward images of them or perspectives on them.

The "not seen" aspect of perception also helps Husserl to overcome a kind of immanentism. The object is obviously not "in" consciousness, since it is given as having limitless content that is not currently accessible to, much less "in," consciousness. We typically have intentions toward an object that can only subsequently be fulfilled.

Finally, the fact that objects of perception are always seen in profile—we see a part of the whole, and not the whole itself—is relevant to the critique of relativism. Relativism tends to see perceived differences as reflecting different whole closed systems, rather than as different aspects of a larger, more complex whole.

Intuition Again

It is crucial to grasp that, according to Husserl, "experience" cannot legitimately be limited to sense experience. Intuition, which in Husserl's sense means "looking at something first-hand," is an act that brings the object itself to us in person, in "originary givenness." Sensory perception can do that, but so can intellection. Intuition thus includes both sensory perception, as in seeing a physical object, and insight into essences, as when one "sees" that a colored thing must be extended in space. We can "intuit" (or "perceive" or "see" or "grasp") as "objects" states of affairs and other non-sensuous structures. For such things clearly are sometimes "given" in experience. "In common parlance, therefore, *aggregates, indefinite pluralities, totalities, numbers, disjunctions, predicates . . ., states of affairs,* all count as 'objects', while the acts through which they seem to be given count as 'percepts'" (LI 2, Investigation VI, §45, 281).

An intuition is an intentional act that is constrained by what is given to it. (Signitive thinking, by contrast, deals with pure meanings in the abstract, quite apart from any perceptual constraint.) Intuitions make reality claims and yield evidence about the world. Insight isn't the same thing as strong, or even unshakable, subjective conviction. It is impossible to have insight into, to grasp intuitively, the "truth" that $2 + 2 = 5$. If A is truly given, and thus genuinely evident, then no one can experience the absurdity of A. Genuine insights cannot conflict. (On the other hand, while this is analytically true, the point is of little practical help. When two people, each claiming insight, disagree, we may know, analytically, that at least one of the claims to insight is wrong—but that won't tell us which one.)

While appeals to intuition are frequently ridiculed, for the most part intuition involves nothing remotely fancy or controversial. It amounts to little more than an ability to think abstractly, and to realize, for example, that sounds are not colors, that colors must be extended in space, and that it is impossible to see a physical object from all sides at once. How do we know these things? Surely it is not by first observing that these patterns have held uniformly in all of our previous experiences, and then postulating, on that basis, that they will continue to hold in all future experiences. That may very well be the basis on which we know that bread nourishes us, that fire burns us, and that water freezes at 32 degrees Fahrenheit. But then, notice (1) that we have no insight into these matters, and (2) that we can easily imagine them being otherwise than they are. There is no conceptual or other intellectual difficulty whatsoever about understanding the possibility that bread might poison us, rather than nourish us, that fire might make us feel cold, or that water might freeze at 39 degrees Fahrenheit (or 37, or 43, or 51). We simply find, by observation, that these other possibilities are not, in fact, actualized in our experience. But we have insight into—we can *see*, *grasp*, and *understand*—that sounds not only are not in fact colors, but could not possibly be colors (the idea that they could be is unthinkable); that colors must, of necessity, be extended in space, and that it is impossible to see a physical object from all sides at once. These insights are examples of the achievements of intuition. There is nothing occult or mystical about intuition. It has nothing to do with hunches or inspired guesses. Rather, it consists of grasping directly, rather than by means of the intermediary of reasons, what is clearly present in experience—what is directly evident.

Categorial Intuition

Husserl claims that our lived experience is far richer than is the "experience" that the classical British empiricists describe. In addition to objects accessible to the senses, we can directly experience abstractions, essences, universals, and states of affairs. Accordingly, Husserl distinguishes between sensuous intuition and categorial intuition. The former has to do with what is given to the senses, the latter with insight into generic structures of experience that could in principle be fulfilled by an indefinitely large number of cases of sensuous intuition. To see that an apple has a specific size, shape, and color is an example of categorial intuition. To experience an individual thing of any kind is to receive a "clue" regarding which activities of consciousness are necessary for an understanding of the essence of that kind of thing.

It is one thing to intuit, by means of sense perception, a specific physical object. But how can one intuit a truth concerning something general, or universal? How can one intuit, not a truth about the red thing in front of me, but rather truths about red things in general, or about "red" as a universal? It is in this context that Husserl introduces the notion of "categorial intuition," or, as he will later call it, "eidetic intuition": "The intuited object is not here itself the thing meant, but serves only as an elucidatory example of our true general meaning." In this case we are oriented toward "what is universal, [which] is merely documented in intuition" (LI 2, Investigation VI, §41, 275).

Categorial acts include acts of conjoining, distinguishing, and counting. A categorial act is not an act of sense, but rather is intellectual, and its object is not a physical object, but an ideal object. A proposition is an example. "We do not merely say 'I see this paper, an inkpot, several books', and so on, but also 'I see that the paper has been written on, that there is a bronze inkpot standing here, that several books are lying open', and so on" (LI 2, Investigation VI, §40, 271).

I can see that the grass is green. I do not have to see, separately, the grass and the greenness, and then, by some sort of nonintuitive intellectual act, put it together that the grass is green. Rather, I can literally *see that* the grass is green. The same is true of conjunction. I can see that there are tables and chairs together. I don't have to see the chairs and tables separately, and then, in a separate, nonintuitive act, insert the conjunction. Instead, I can see the "andness" of the tables and chairs. Similarly, I can see conditionals (if I hit that glass with a hammer it will break) and disjunctions (either I will eat before class or I'll feel hungry toward the end of it). In this context, recall from the "Introduction" Sartre's description of encountering Pierre's absence from the café. In full agreement with Husserl, and for the same phenomenological reasons (those of descriptive fidelity to the data of experience), Sartre claims that he can *see* Pierre's absence—he can intuit it, encounter it; it is given, it is present, all in contrast to abstract judgments one might make, after the fact, about any number of other people who were also not present at the café. Their absences were not seen, not intuited.

Through categorial intuition one can directly encounter abstract, ideal, nonphysical things. One can do the same with states of affairs. Such intuitions fulfill complex or categorial intentions. We can intend universals and essences. We can also intend every kind of combining of ideas, and, indeed, every kind of predication. Such intentions involve more than sense perception, since, although I can see and touch a dog, see and touch hair, and see the color brown, I cannot literally see (in the sense of sense perception) that the dog has brown hair. This is a state of affairs that does not take a position in physical space. To apprehend and understand it requires intellection. That the dog has brown hair can be given intuitively. This involves categorial intuition, and not merely sensuous intuition. (Typically, as in this case, part of the work of categorical intuition is to grasp the part/whole relations among objects, as in recognizing that the dog's hair is part of the dog, and that "brown" is part of the dog's hair.)

Notice that, while both the dog and its brown hair (and, for that matter, the brownness *of* its hair) are "real," in Husserl's sense (they come into and pass out of existence, undergo changes, and are accessible by the senses), the state of affairs, or fact, that the dog has brown hair is not in that same sense a "real" object. Nonetheless, it is obviously objective in that it is nothing at all like a mere fiction or thought, and, even more importantly, since it is something external to our subjectivity that has the power to make our thoughts or judgments about it true or false. Thus, categorical intuition can disclose objectivities that sense perception alone is powerless to make manifest.

"Sensuous or real objects can . . . be characterized as *objects of the lowest level of possible intuition*, categorical or ideal objects as *objects of higher levels*." The latter, in contrast to the former, are "*constituted* in relational, connective, or otherwise articulated acts, *acts founded on other acts which bring other objects to perception*" (LI 2, Investigation VI, §46, 282). Low level acts of perception are foundational to "new acts of conjunction, of disjunction, . . . of generalization, [and] of . . . relational and connective knowledge" (LI 2, Investigation VI, §46, 282). "In such founded acts we have the categorial element in intuition and knowledge, in them assertive thought . . . finds fulfillment; the possibility of complete accord with such acts determines the truth, the rightness, of an assertion" (LI 2, Investigation VI, §46, 283).

We enjoy a great deal of freedom in our categorial thinking. For example, Husserl says that we have "abundant freedom" to "*unite* or *not to unite*," and "to connect and relate, to generalize and subsume etc." He adds that

> There are many arbitrary ways to divide up a sensuously unified group into part-groups: we may at will arrange these diversely divisible part-groups, and effect same-level connections among them, we can also build connections of the second, third . . . order upon one another. Many possibilities of categorial shaping therefore arise on the foundation of the same sensuous stuff. Just so, we can compare any item from one and the same sense-complex with any other of its members, or distinguish it from them. We can make either of them the subject-term, or, by arbitrary conversion, the object-term of some relation in

question. We can put these relations into relation with one another, connect them collectively, classify them etc. (LI 2, Investigation VI, §62, 309, translation modified).

Nonetheless, "this *freedom of categorial union and formation . . .* has its *law-governed limits.*" Were this not the case, we would not be able to "speak of categorial perception and intuition." For if we are genuinely *seeing* something, the thing we are seeing places limits on how we see it. Husserl gives the example of the part-whole relation, pointing out that we are not free to see the part as the whole or the whole as the part. I cannot, for example, actually perceive the book as a part of one of its pages. Similarly,

> It is also not open to us to treat [the part-whole] relation as one of total identity or of total exclusion etc. [For example, I cannot see the book as identical to one of its pages, or as excluding the having of pages.] We can no doubt 'think' any relation between any set of terms, and any form whatever on the basis of any matter—think them, that is, in the sense of merely meaning them. But we cannot really carry out 'foundings' on every foundation: we cannot *see* sensuous stuff in any categorical form we like, let alone *perceive* it thus, and above all not perceive it *adequately.*" (LI 2, Investigation VI, §62, 309)

Synthetic categorial acts can be distinguished from ideative categorial acts. The former involve putting together elements ascertained by means of lower-level intuitive acts, as when one intends or intuits, as a higher-level object, the state of affairs that the cat is on the mat, on the basis of intuiting "the cat" and "the mat." The judgment that the cat is on the mat is founded on these elements. "The cat" and "the mat," having been objectified by means of sense perception, are then taken up by categorial intuition, and synthesized under a categorial form (one having to do with the relative physical positions of two objects), so that a new object, the cat's *being on* the mat, is disclosed.

Ideative, or eidetic, acts, by contrast, involve grasping the essence or universal by abstracting from the individual, as when one thinks of kindness as such by taking as a point of departure for the ideative process one particular act or a few particular acts of kindness.

Truth

Husserl defines each of the related terms "evidence," "knowledge," and "truth" in terms of an agreement between what is meant and what is intuitively given in experience. How, then, do the meanings of these terms differ? While Husserl offers a number of fine distinctions for each term, the basic differentiation runs as follows. There are degrees of evidence, that is, degrees of intuitive verification of meaning-intentions, and a sufficiently high degree must be reached before the verifying intuition can properly be deemed "knowledge." And while knowledge presupposes a knower, "truth," for Husserl is ideal. This explains why it is possible for there to be truths that no one knows. No one knows, for example, what I had for breakfast on May 17, 1971 (I don't remember, and there are no records of such trivia), or whether or not there is life on a specific planet in a distant galaxy. But surely there are truths pertaining to these questions—I ate this, rather than that, making the statement that I ate *this* true, and the statement that I ate *that* false. And either there is life on that planet or there isn't, with the belief or statement that matches whatever is the case being thereby true, and the contrary belief or statement false. All of this makes sense, on Husserl's account, because we understand what sort of evidence would, in principle, establish these truths, irrespective of whether or not such evidence is (or ever will be) actually available, or whether or not anyone has ever formulated a belief in connection with these questions. What is true is what *can*, in principle, intuitively fulfill a meaning-intention. Truth, and, for that matter, validity, objectivity, and their opposites, "do not pertain to an assertion as a particular temporal experience, but to the assertion *in specie*, to the pure, self-identical assertion 2 x 2 = 4 etc." (LI 1, Prolegomena, §51, 121).

Husserl's account puts a new twist on the correspondence theory of truth. On that classical theory, "truth" is understood in terms of a correspondence between, or a matching up of, a thought (or belief or statement), on the one hand, and reality-as-it-is-in-itself, on the other. Such a theory gives rise to skeptical doubts, as one might wonder how we can escape the constraints of our own finitude and subjectivity so as to compare our beliefs against a realm that lies entirely outside of that subjectivity. But on Husserl's conception, truth has to do with a correspondence

between what is intended in two different acts (a meaningful judgment, on the one hand, and a perception or an intuition of fulfilling
evidentiary contents, on the other), rather than a correspondence
between consciousness and an object that is utterly independent of
consciousness. There is no bridging of two distinct ontological
domains.

While such a move will neither answer, nor in any other way satisfy, the skeptic, Husserl's purpose is phenomenological. That
there are truths, and that we can sometimes know them, is a palpable datum of experience. The phenomenologist's primary task is
to describe, and to elucidate, such experiential data, rather than
defend them against those who would reject or explain them away
on the basis of some grand theory. (In any case, Husserl provides
an ample critique of skepticism as part of his refutation of psychologism in the Prolegomena to the *Logical Investigations*.)

It is a distinctive feature of Husserl's account of truth that he
does not regard it as primarily linguistic, or as concerned with
propositions and judgments. Rather, truth is experiential. We perceive an object or a state of affairs, which we recognize as identical
to a meaning-intention, which it fulfills. This "experience of truth"
is primary, and foundational to propositional truth.

Husserl's phenomenological account of truth does not restrict
its scope to any particular subject matter. Many philosophers follow Kant in deciding ahead of time, based on general, theoretical
arguments, what can be known and what cannot—what sorts of
questions are, in principle, accessible to us, and what sorts are not.
But Husserl takes the position that concepts, theories, and claims
of all kinds must be judged on a case-by-case basis. Do they do full
justice to the phenomena they attempt to comprehend? Are they
themselves fully intuitively evident? If so, they pass muster. This
applies to moral, aesthetic, and political theories no less than mathematical, logical, or scientific ones.

Freedom from Presuppositions

One of the most widely criticized aspects of Husserl's thought is
his oft-repeated claim that philosophy should be "presuppositionless." Charles Hartshorne understands this claim to mean that "we
should inhibit all presuppositions, such as that we are in a world
along with a host of other experiencing creatures and with some

things seemingly without experience. We should bracket these beliefs and simply say what our experience for itself is and what, with absolute evidence, it discloses." Hartshorne criticizes this position as follows:

> When I first heard Husserl saying all this, I thought him naïve. Intellectual history strongly suggests that we are bound to have presuppositions, that they are not made harmless by blanket declarations of their dismissal or bracketing and that it is better to make the most relevant ones explicit from the start. We also have good reason to think that observation, to be effective, needs to be motivated by the desire to answer definite questions or test definite theories. The question, "What are the data of direct experience?" is much too vague.[15]

Both of Hartshorne's objections can be clearly illustrated in connection with a famous incident in the history of science: the discovery of the planet Neptune. In 1846 astronomers noticed that the orbital path of Uranus was deviating slightly from what Newton's gravitational theory implied that it should be. Did this prove Newton wrong? An alternative possibility, which occurred to astronomer Urbain Le Verrier, was that there might be a hitherto unknown major planet in a certain location in the solar system. The existence of such a planet, which would, in accordance with Newton's theory, be expected to exert a degree of gravitational pull on Uranus, could account for Uranus's otherwise surprising movements. On the night of September 23-24, 1846, at the Berlin Observatory, Johann Gottfried Galle's telescopic observations, undertaken on the basis of Le Verrier's calculations, confirmed the existence of the planet now known as Neptune. Far from refuting Newton, this incident, in which the theory successfully predicted, and led to the discovery of, something that would otherwise not have been anticipated, supplied dramatic confirming evidence for Newton's gravitational theory.

This episode illustrates Hartshorne's first objection, that "we are bound to have presuppositions," because it shows that we cannot test one thing without making assumptions about (that is,

---

[15] "An Anglo-American Phenomenology: Method and Some Results," in *Pragmatism Considers Phenomenology*, ed. Robert S. Corrington et al. (Washington, D.C.: Center for Advanced Research in Phenomenology & University Press of America, 1987), 59.

presupposing) other things. In order to test the theory that the attraction of bodies to one another is a measurable and predictable function of their masses and distance from one another, one has to do so on the basis of some belief about the locations and masses of the relevant bodies. One cannot test everything at once, because no test can be informative unless the background assumptions that are relevant to the test are correct. To be sure, one could test those background assumptions, but only by making the background assumptions that are necessary to *those* tests, and so on infinitely.

The incident also illustrates Hartshorne's second objection, that "observation, to be effective, needs to be motivated by the desire to answer definite questions or test definite theories." Indiscriminate, aimless looking and describing is unlikely to lead to anything as valuable as the formulation of Newton's gravitational theory, the testing of that theory, or the discovery of Neptune. For anything like that to happen, one's observations typically have to be guided by some sense of what is important, or relevant, or interesting. A crime detective who simply "looks" at a crime scene, but who knows nothing about what to look for, is highly unlikely to solve the case. The same holds for scientists and philosophers. Observations are maximally informative when they speak either in favor of or in opposition to some hypothesis or theory.

It is not clear, however, that Hartshorne (or other critics who advance similar objections) are interpreting Husserl's call for pre-suppositionlessness correctly. Consider, for example, the very first reference to presuppositionlessness in Husserl's writings: "An epistemological investigation that can seriously claim to be scientific must . . . satisfy the *principle of freedom from presuppositions*. This principle, we think, only seeks to express the strict exclusion of all statements not permitting a comprehensive *phenomenological* realization" (LI 1, Introduction to volume II, part I of the German Editions, §7, 177).

Notice that this formulation does not call for the elimination of all assumptions, or even merely those that have not been phenomenologically confirmed. Rather, it calls *only* for the rejection of those "*not permitting* a comprehensive phenomenological realization." So a presuppositionless philosophy, for Husserl, is one that rigorously excludes any assertion that cannot be justified phenomenologically, that is, intuitively. This does not rule out the careful use of provisional, or hypothetical, assumptions. For example, one might begin with some logical concepts and principles that one has inherited historically. But the point is that these must then be attended to explicitly. Are they intuitively evident? If they are not—if, for example, they are untestable postulations, articles of faith, or mere verbalisms that cannot be brought to "givenness" in experience—they are to be discarded. So when Husserl says that he intends phenomenology to be a "presuppositionless" philosophy, he does not mean that it should literally be a philosophy devoid of presuppositions, but rather that it should be a philosophy that would go out of its way to take nothing for granted, to try to bring to light all of its assumptions, to thematize them, and then either to bracket those assumptions explicitly or, where possible, to subject them to phenomenological investigation, that is, to ground them in the evidence of lived experience.

Another criticism of Husserl on this issue is that it is not psychologically possible to exclude, disregard, or bracket all of one's presuppositions, in part because it is impossible to be aware of all of them. But even if it is impossible to identify and subsequently exclude *everything*, it does often appear to be possible to disregard *specific, clearly identified things*. For example, in evaluating college applicants it would be possible to focus on their scores on standardized tests and disregard their grades (or vice versa) even if one were aware of the information to be excluded. Similarly, in Husserl's calls for presuppositionlessness, he is not shy about specifying exactly what kinds of things he wants to set aside. For example, immediately after issuing his initial statement about freedom from presuppositions, he clarifies his meaning by calling for something similar to what he would subsequently term "the phenomenological reduction":

> We must keep apart from the pure theory of knowledge questions concerning the justifiability of accepting 'mental' and 'physical' realities which transcend consciousness, . . . questions whether it is justifiable or sensible to oppose a second, even more emphatically 'transcendent' world, to the phenomenal nature with which science is correlated, and other similar questions. The question as to the existence and nature of 'the external world' is a metaphysical question. (LI 1, Introduction to volume II, part I of the German Editions, §7, 177–78)

In further explaining what he means by the principle of presuppositionlessness, Husserl announces that his *Logical Investigations* aspire, specifically, to "freedom from metaphysical, scientific and psychological presuppositions" (LI 1, Introduction to volume II, part I of the German Editions, §7, 179). The reason is that the aim of phenomenology, according to Husserl,

> is not to *explain* knowledge in the psychological or psychophysical sense as a *factual* occurrence in objective nature, but to *shed light* on the *Idea* of knowledge in its constitutive elements and laws. It does not try to follow up the real connections of coexistence and succession with which actual acts of knowledge are interwoven, but to understand the *ideal* sense of the *specific* connections in which the objectivity of knowledge may be documented. It endeavors to raise to clearness the pure forms and laws of knowledge by tracing knowledge back to an adequate fulfillment in intuition. . . . From the beginning, as at all later stages, its scientific statements involve not the slightest reference to real existence: no metaphysical, scientific and, above all, no psychological assertions can therefore occur among its premises. (LI 1, Introduction to volume II, part I of the German Editions, §7, 178)

In this way, phenomenology is like mathematics, which also makes no reference to real existence, and, if Husserl's antipsychologistic arguments are correct, is completely independent of psychology. The specific presuppositions to be avoided are metaphysical and scientific. Husserl wishes to place the focus on what is given in experience, not on what one takes to be scientifically or metaphysically necessary to explain those experiences or their content. Phenomenology is thus concerned with conscious acts, experiences, and objects, rather than with, say, the neurological basis for consciousness.

But the idea that philosophy, and specifically phenomenology, demands the exclusion of certain subject matters (namely, metaphysics, natural science, and psychology) is not the only reason for Husserl's interest in the ideal of presuppositionlessness. His motivation, in part, is also similar to that of Descartes—the realization that while philosophy over the centuries has succeeded in producing a number of dazzling concepts, theories, and systems, the problem is that these have come to take on a life of their own, hardening into dogmas, and obscuring, rather than illuminating, the vital questions that had initially sparked philosophical questioning. These constructions therefore need to be brushed aside so that we might once again turn to "the things themselves," as opposed to our fancy theories about them, just as they reveal themselves to us in our experience. Husserl's proposal is that, as far as possible, descriptions should respond to the demands of the things themselves, rather than to those of existing theories, categories, concepts, vocabularies, or assumptions.

In this connection, note the difference between attending to a linguistic expression, on the one hand, and a perceptual object, on the other. In the former case, the physical characteristics of the objects which provoke our attention to meanings (the sounds of the words, the shapes of the marks on paper) are arbitrary and conventional, and uninteresting in themselves. We look past them to get to the intended meaning. (This is what makes a multiplicity of languages possible.) The case is otherwise with perceptual objects. While we see them only in profile, there is nothing arbitrary about them. Only these shapes can indicate "elephant." One and the same object, such as some marks on paper, can be taken up either signitively or intuitively, the former if we are interested in their linguistic meaning, the latter if we attend to them as physical objects (as when we appreciate their shape aesthetically, something we could do even if the words are in a language we do not understand, or even if the marks are not of letters in our alphabet). A proposition can also be taken up either signitively (attending to what it means) or intuitively (seeing that it is the case, that it is true). These are two different acts. Thinking and seeing are not the same thing. Husserl's idea is that seeing, intuition, is original, primary, and justifying. We see something, and then use linguistic markers to remind us of what we have seen. But the problem is that before long we find that we are dealing exclusively with the linguistic markers, and we forget the rich intuitive content of which they stand as mere markers. The intuitive foundation of thought gives way to a technical skill in associating and manipulating symbols. The symbol, which originally expressed something seen and grasped, becomes part of a system of rules, so that they function in a manner similar to chess pieces in chess (an analogy Husserl uses in (LI 1, Investigation I, §20, 210–11). They become part of a system of rules, and thus take on a "games-meaning" that eventually begins to drown out their original intuitive sense. Husserl says the same thing about arithmetical signs, which become embedded in the rules of the "game" of calculation. Thus, a large part of the goal of the *Logical Investigations* is to rediscover the sense and justification of logic and mathematics—a sense and justification that has been lost, in spite of the fact that both disciplines flourish at the level of technology. "The outcome of our investigation of this point will be the delineation of a new, purely theoretical science, the all-important foundation for any technology of scientific knowledge, and its having the character of an *a priori*, purely demonstrative [that is, intuitive] science" (LI 1, Prolegomena, §3, 14). And in a very late work, "The Origin of Geometry," included as Appendix VI in the *Crisis*, Husserl claims that "in every individual life from childhood up to maturity, the originally intuitive life which creates its originally self-evident structures through activities on the basis of sense-experience very quickly and in increasing measure falls victim to the seduction of language. Greater and greater segments of this life lapse into a kind of talking and reading that is dominated purely by association. . . ."

Thus, Husserl's famous imperative—"Back to the things themselves!"—can be understood only against the background of understanding that we tend to get lost in the world of words, concepts, symbols, and the like that we use to represent to ourselves the objects of experience. We become so content to think about and to manipulate these markers that we completely forget about, and thus fail to consult, the things that those markers are intended to represent. Worse yet, we begin to confuse the things with their representations. It is against these mistakes and confusions that Husserl's slogan protests.

"Things" are to be contrasted with verbalisms and mental constructions. We can intuitively confront, make present to us, the former, but not the latter.

So even though we cannot really bracket all of our prejudices and assumptions, perhaps we can figure out what are some of the most basic and obfuscatory of them. Some of these taken-for-granted postulations, these "sediments" of tradition, of language, and of theoretical speculation, turn out to be so widespread as to be considered basic elements of "common sense." Others comprise part of our cultural heritage, while still others are products of the history of philosophy. In any case, Husserl's call for presuppositionlessness entails that we make a specific effort to identify and to bracket them.

That call can also be understood in at least two other ways. The first has to do with the distinction between contingent truths, on the one hand, and truths that are universal and necessary, on the other. A contingent truth is one that depends, for its truth, on what the world happens to be like. To know such a truth, we typically have to know quite a few other things as well, as the example of the discovery of Neptune illustrates. But a universal and necessary truth, such as "2 + 2 = 4," is true no matter what the world is like, and no matter what is happening in it. Knowledge of such a truth is prresuppositionless in the sense that one need not make any assumptions about the world in order to know that it is true. Husserl's call for presuppositionlessness is part of his project of bracketing whatever is contingent, so that only that which self-evidently must be true remains. This necessary and essential residue is that which can then be presupposed in all other forms of rational inquiry (including nonphenomenological ones.)

Another approach to the understanding of presuppositionlessness is by means of thinking about intuition. Intuition is the direct "seeing" of something, whether perceptually or by rational "grasping," so that one knows the truth of a claim by directly inspecting it, rather than through the intermediary of reasons. One argument for granting validity to intuition is that knowledge appears otherwise to be impossible. The argument for this runs as follows. If one denies that anything can be known directly, and insists, instead, that all genuine knowledge claims be backed with reasons, the result, in every case, is an infinite regress. If I claim to know A, then I must have a supporting reason, B. But then, I can't know B unless I have a supporting reason, C, and so on forever. So if I have any knowledge at all, which appears to be the case, then it must be that I can escape this infinite regress only by knowing some things directly, that is, intuitively. The ideal of presuppositionlessness, then, can refer to the project of attempting to describe and to catalogue these intuitive truths—that is, those that do not depend on reasons beyond themselves. Because they do not rest on anything other than themselves, it follows that they do not rest on anything presupposed. Such truths also tend to be universal and necessary, and to be of such a basic nature as to be foundational to truths of the more ordinary sort, those that are conditional, and are known by inference. These universal and necessary, presupposionless, a priori, primitive, foundational truths comprise the subject matter of phenomenology.

2

Middle Husserl

One philosophical topic that is not extensively addressed in the *Logical Investigations* is time. This is a serious omission since, on Husserl's view, time-consciousness is the most important phenomenological problem (OPCIT, Supplementary Text No. 50, "The Modification Proper to Primary Memory," 346).[1] Husserl began to work on this issue in earnest in 1901, the year in which the second volume of the *Logical Investigations* was published, delivered a series of lectures on it in 1904-1905, and remained preoccupied by it for several years. His lectures and manuscripts on time-consciousness from the years 1901–1911 were finally published as a book, *The Phenomenology of Internal Time-Consciousness*, in 1928. Though Heidegger was formally credited with having edited these lectures and manuscripts, a credit that most of the contemporary scholarly literature takes at face value, it appears that the bulk of the work was actually done by Husserl's research assistant, Edith Stein,[2] and one of her successors, Eugen Fink.[3]

---

[1] He also declares it to be the most *difficult* phenomenological problem (OPCIT, Supplementary Text No. 39, "Time in Perception," 286).

[2] John B. Brough, "The Phenomenology of Internal Time-Consciousness," in *Husserl: Shorter Works*, ed. Peter McCormick and Frederick A. Elliston (Notre Dame, IN: University of Notre Dame Press, 1981), 271.

[3] Ronald Bruzina, *Edmund Husserl & Eugen Fink* (New Haven, CT: Yale University Press, 2004), 15–16.

The Phenomenology of Internal
Time-Consciousness

Husserl's focus is not on objective time, as measured by clocks, but rather on lived, or experienced, time. For example, in perception, objects present themselves as enduring, as succeeding one another, or as existing simultaneously with one another. We do not typically experience time in a strictly linear, one-directional way. If I am playing tennis, for example, while my focus is most often on what is happening right now, I will throughout the match have many occasions for thinking about the past (what has been working for me, and what has not; what strengths that I must try to neutralize has my opponent's game up till now revealed, and what has been shown about weaknesses that I might be able to exploit) and about the future (what should I try next). Typically we fly back and forth among these different temporal modes.

Accordingly, Husserl rejects the commonsense view that, since the past is no longer (it is gone), and the future is not yet, we can only be perceptively aware of the present, Rather, he holds that the present is always in dynamic relation to both the past and future. The past and future are part of the horizon of the present.

He arrives at this conclusion by working through the puzzle of how to account for the consciousness of objects that are not fully present all at once, but rather unfold over time. How does one perceive a melody, or a speech, or a movie? The fact that we clearly are able to do so, that, in fact, we often quite effortlessly perceive succession and duration when we attend to objects of all sorts, suggests to Husserl that consciousness gives us perceptual access to more than what is strictly present at any given precise instant, and that the stream of consciousness is not a series of unconnected events. He rejects the proposal that as we perceive the present we also simultaneously remember what has just happened and imagine what will happen. He does so for phenomenological reasons. The experience of remembering or imagining a melody is qualitatively quite different from that of hearing one, even though listening to a melody clearly involves attending to much more than the sounds that are occurring at each instant of the experience. Husserl's solution is to suggest that perception is essentially temporally structured. What he calls "primal presentation," that is, attention to what is strictly occurring at a given instant, is always accompanied by both "retention" (consciousness of the just-elapsed phase of the object, coupled with an awareness of the continuity of that phase with what is occurring now) and "protention" (an unreflective anticipation of what may be about to happen, together with a sense of its continuity with what is given in primal presentation.)

It is important to notice that retentions and protentions are typically not focused on or put into words. Suppose someone gives me oral instructions on how to perform some task. Suppose, further, that I am keenly interested in performing the task well, and consequently have no difficulty focusing intensely on the instructions. Suppose, finally, that the oral presentation of the instructions takes some time (90 seconds, let's say), and that the instructions include no filler, but rather consist entirely of essential information. Surely when I am 50 seconds into hearing these instructions I am no longer hearing the words uttered during the first 10 seconds, and it may very well be that I no longer remember them. But if I am a good listener it may be that I nonetheless understand them even now, not by grasping them explicitly as a discreet unit and then synthesizing them with what is being currently said, but rather by constituting them as a unity with what is being said now (and with what remains to be said). What I am hearing now makes sense only in the light of what I have already implicitly understood by what I have already heard, insofar as what I have already heard prepared me to anticipate that the contents to come will fit under a certain category with a certain definite range. (Having heard, "to get to the bathroom, go down this hallway; it is the first room on the . . . ," I am prepared to hear "left" or "right," but not "rhinoceros.")

Or again, think of what happens when watching a movie. In order to follow the action, one must learn a great deal on the fly: this guy has a violent temper, and can be dangerous; these two are in cahoots against that one; this one is in love with that one, but is too shy to say so, and so forth. But notice that you don't take time out from watching what is happening now in order to formulate these conclusions to yourself. Rather, you learn one thing in passing insofar as it makes sense of the next thing, which in turn gives you an expectation of what the next thing will be. While these many awarenesses unfold over time, they are experienced in the mode of perception, not memory or imagination, and they disclose an object of substantial temporal duration, not a series of discreet presents. As more and more time goes by, experiences that once were retained with great clarity and differentiation may become somewhat mushed together and confused, even though one retains something of the gist of what could be learned from those experiences, since that gist in each case became attached to what came next in the stream of experience. And what is now gone is not utterly extinguished. Rather, it leaves behind deposits or "sediments," necessitating, Husserl came to realize, a historical turn in the conceptualizing of phenomenology, as "genetic phenomenology," rather then static phenomenology.

One piece of evidence that retention and protention are part of perception, and are to be distinguished from recollection and imagination of the future, is that while one can deliberately, voluntarily, decide to recall something from the past or to imagine what some future experience will be like (or, for that matter, to terminate these projects and return one's attention and focus to matters of present concern), retention and protention are involuntary and necessary constituents of all perceptual acts whatever. It is impossible to choose to perceive something by means of separate, discrete observations of what is given in a succession of instants. Attention to what is given in perceptual experience shows that it always involves retention and protention. Eidetic analysis shows that it always must be so—this is part of the essence of perception.

Further evidence for this conclusion is provided by the phenomenon of surprise, or more precisely, the fact that surprise is always possible. This shows that anticipation, that is, protention, is part of every experience. I will be surprised if I open a door and find on the other side, not a floor or solid ground on which to step, but an abyss; or if I see a batter in baseball, after hitting the ball, run toward third base; or if the beautiful rock I have been admiring suddenly runs away from me. This is because, as Husserl puts it, there is always, as an essential ingredient of any kind of experience, a "horizon of anticipation." Sometimes that anticipation is for something quite specific, as is the case when I have invited a particular guest to visit me at 8 o'clock and my doorbell rings at exactly that time. In that situation the appearance of anyone else at my doorstep would provoke some degree of surprise. But in the more typical case my expectation is merely that a certain *kind* of event, something within a certain *range* or category, will happen. If our experiences did not include this element of "protention" they would lack connection and coherence. My successive perceptions of the first, second, and third notes of a melody would seem separate and discrete, without the connective tissue provided by protention and retention.

And the same is true of my successive perceptions of the front, side, and back of a house. For when I move around a static physical object, such as a house, I see it from several different angles. These individual perceptual experiences do not present themselves as unique, each separate and distinct from the others. Still less do they suggest that they are providing me access to different objects. Nor do I experience them as fragmentary and disjointed. Rather I encounter them as synthetically integrated, each continuous with the others, and as giving me, in a seamless, coherent manner, an ever increasing stock of information about the object of my focused attention, the house. This process of synthesizing the information contained in these perceived "profiles" unfolds over time. We see the object *as* an object, that is, as something that transcends all of the individual acts of perceiving it, only insofar as we perceive it as an identity that endures across the different acts that disclose it, and across the different profiles by which it is disclosed. But this happens, in turn, only because of the essential temporality of consciousness. Without such time-consciousness, the constitution of an object, as a unity that is sustained against the manifold of its appearances, would be impossible. So Husserl's analysis of the perception of objects that unfold over time carries over to objects that appear to remain static and unchanging. Time-consciousness is an essential condition of the possibility of any consciousness of any perceptual object at all. The constitution of objects of all kinds in perceptual experience always involves continuously progressing syntheses of retentions, protentions, and primal presentations. Without time-consciousness, we would experience nothing but an incomprehensible series of fleeting, unrelated, sensations. (To be sure, some intentional objects are not temporal. The equation "$2 + 2 = 4$" does not belong to any time [or place, for that matter]. But the act of thinking it does take time.)

Husserl's analysis of time-consciousness has exerted a strong influence on Heidegger, Sartre, Merleau-Ponty, and many other major continental thinkers. (It is no accident that Heidegger's *magnum opus* is called *Being and Time*.) But in recent years it has also attracted the interest of neuroscientists, leading to the creation of a new hybrid discipline, neurophenomenology. Evan Thompson explains the domain of this new discipline:

> Consider our experience of time. . . . Our sense of the present moment as both simultaneously opening into the immediate future and slipping away into the immediate past depends on the formal structure of our consciousness of time. The present moment manifests as a zone or span of actuality, instead of as an instantaneous flash, thanks to the way our consciousness is structured. . . . The present moment also manifests this way because of the nonlinear dynamics of brain activity. Weaving together these two types of analysis, the phenomenological and neurobiological, in order to bridge the gap between subjective experience and biology, defines the aim of neurophenomenology.[4]

Ideas I

While it is in the *Logical Investigations* that Husserl first begins to develop the idea of phenomenology, the point of that book is not so much to introduce phenomenology as to *use* it in addressing problems in the philosophical foundations of mathematics and logic. The first full-scale work in which he attempts a thorough and systematic explanation of his project of phenomenology is *Ideas I*, published in 1913.

It is almost impossible to exaggerate the degree of influence this book has exerted. It has been carefully studied, and mined for insights, by nearly every significant twentieth-century philosopher of continental Europe, and by many other important figures in other disciplines in the humanities and social sciences.

But it is also a controversial book, far more so than the *Logical Investigations*. Many of the admirers of the earlier work have objected to Husserl's abandonment (as they see it) of the realism implicit in his call for a return to "the things themselves," and his turn, instead to "transcendental idealism" (to be discussed subsequently).

---

[4] *Mind in Life* (Cambridge, MA: Harvard University Press, 2007), 15.

The Eidetic Reduction

Husserl begins by pointing out that phenomenology is not "*a science of matters of fact, but . . . a science of essences* (. . . an "*eidetic*" science): . . . a science which exclusively seeks to ascertain 'cognitions of essences' and *no 'matters of fact' whatever*" (Ideas I, Introduction, xx). Accordingly, "pure phenomenology . . . is no more psychology than geometry is natural science" (Ideas I, Introduction, xix).

Recall that in the *Logical Investigations* Husserl makes the point that a direct awareness of essential principles, that is, "categorial intuition," is a ubiquitous feature of ordinary human experience. In *Ideas I* he stresses that a shift of focus away from the contingent particularity of matters of fact and toward essential principles, with their characteristic universality and necessity, can also be self-consciously adopted as a methodological tool of phenomenological practice. Husserl's name for this shift of focus is "the eidetic reduction": "The relevant reduction which leads over from the psychological phenomena to the pure "essence" or, in the case of judgmental thinking, from matter-of-fact ('empirical') universality to 'eidetic' universality, is the *eidetic reduction*" (Ideas I, Introduction, xx).

Husserl also reminds us that an essence disclosed by the eidetic reduction, when viewed in an unprejudiced way, based solely on what is given in experience, must be considered a genuine object. It is directly encountered in experience, and it reveals itself in such a way as to make some of the statements we might make about it true, and to rule out others as false. Moreover, it is "intuited" [recall that this has no mystical connotations, but refers simply to the everyday experience of seeing or grasping something by directly inspecting it], rather than posited, hypothesized, or arrived at inductively.

> *The essence is a new sort of object. Just as the datum of individual or experiencing intuition is an individual object, so the datum of eidetic intuition is a pure essence.* . . . *Seeing an essence is also precisely intuition,* just as an eidetic object is precisely an object. The universalization of the correlatively interrelated concepts "intuition" and "object" is not an arbitrary conceit but compellingly demanded by the nature of the matters in question." (Ideas I, §3, 9)

Ideal entities, such as mathematical or logical objects, are experienced in a different way, and are disclosed by different acts, than are perceptual objects. But it would be a metaphysical prejudice to assume that they are for that reason any less real. They are still governed by laws affecting objects in their region, and have discoverable properties about which we can be mistaken. They are thus fully objective, even if their existence, like that of all intentional objects, is strictly correlative to acts of consciousness. (This is not psychologism, since the laws governing ideal entities are not psychological [or, for that matter, empirical]; and it is not Platonism, because of the correlativity thesis.) Moreover, essences are not merely psychological facts. A particular instance of thinking of the number "9" is a psychological fact that occurs at a particular time, but it hardly follows that the same is true of the number "9" itself. Consciousness of an essence is not to be confused with the essence itself.

We can see anything that we encounter in our perceptual experience as an individual thing; but we also can see it as an instance of a type (or, more accurately, as an instance of any one of an indefinite number of types). We can see a particular car as a big thing, or a loud thing, or a black thing, or a Prius, or a humanly manufactured thing, or an expensive thing, or a vehicle of transportation, or a car, and so on. To see it as an instance of a type is to see it as meeting certain essential conditions. To do so is not to impose sophisticated, abstract philosophy on what would otherwise by ordinary experience devoid of an eidetic dimension. Rather, in all experience, including that of the most mundane, everyday kind, we recognize things, and make sense of them, by seeing them as instances of a kind, as exemplifying principles: "The truth is that everyone sees 'ideas,' 'essences' and sees them, so to speak, continuously; they operate with them in their thinking and they also make eidetic judgments. It is only that, from their theoretical 'standpoint' people interpret them away" (Ideas I, §22, 41, translation modified). We experience things, ordinarily, and not on the basis of any special philosophical training or insight, as exemplifying principles or structures that are much more generic than are the specific things in front of us, and as subject to laws governing those essential structures. Essences are intuited in empirical phenomena, but the latter are merely a condition for the appearance of the latter. Otherwise, the particulars of the empirical phenomena are contingent. The essence of movement can be discerned from any moving thing, so no particular moving thing is necessary.

Moreover, though it greatly offends common sense to say so, eidetic intuition is more fundamental than sense perception, since the latter would make no sense without the former. Without a grasp of principles in terms of which they can be understood, we would fail to perceive particulars as forming any kind of meaningful pattern or structure. Instead, we would be confronted with an incoherent, riotous cacophony of sense data, analogous to the experience of listening to a speech in a language that one cannot comprehend.

The fact that our ordinary experience is nothing like that indicates that no strange method is needed in order for people to see and to grasp essences. They do that all the time. One cannot do anything without dealing competently with essences. The eidetic reduction is simply a method by which one focuses on the essence itself, not as exemplified by whatever entity with which we are immediately concerned, but as it is in itself, independent of any actual or possible concrete and specific exemplification or instantiation. One performs the eidetic reduction when focusing on the color of an object (or on its shape, or size, and so on indefinitely). It is to see the object as an instance or instantiation of an essence shared by many other objects. Essence is the key to intelligibility.

So while individual objects, such as this tree or this chair, can be present to us, so can universal meanings, such as "large," "round," or the number "five." Each of these universal meanings is an *eidos*, that is, an idea. It is grasped intuitively, by means of the eidetic reduction.

To see things in terms of essential principles requires neither abstraction nor construction. If I see two shirts together, one of which is dark blue and the other light blue, what is directly given in my experience, typically, is not only the fact that they are shirts, that there are two of them, and that they are blue, but also their relations of "lighter than" and "darker than."

Similarly, though perhaps more controversially, suppose that I observe a person directing a hurtful remark toward another person. I can *see*, in addition to the contingent particular facts of this incident, the principle of cruelty. Though this perception of cruelty is fallible—perhaps the incident in question really exemplifies only insensitivity; or maybe I misunderstand the context: the two are actors, practicing their lines in a play—it is a genuine datum of experience. Moreover, in order to probe this incident, in order to determine whether or not my initial perception of cruelty is correct, I need to have some knowledge of what, in principle, cruelty is (and, for that matter, what insensitivity is, what acting is, and so forth). In other words, I need knowledge of eidetic principles.

Such eidetic knowledge is not inductive. To "see," to "grasp" an essential principle is not at all the same thing as drawing general conclusions on the basis of the expectation that future experiences will continue to exhibit the identical patterns that one has found to hold in past experiences. Whatever we know by induction could have been otherwise; we simply find, instead, that it is the way it is. Induction generates no insight, as is shown by the fact that the contrary of what we learn by induction is always perfectly thinkable. It is always perfectly conceivable, even if unlikely, that the inductive inference will break down in any given case. If the mail has arrived at precisely 3:00 PM on fifty consecutive mail delivery days, there is no absurdity, no conceptual or intellectual barrier of any kind, in contemplating the possibility that it might arrive at 2:00 or at 4:00 (or not at all) on the fifty-first day. But the case is quite different with the intuition of essences. We cannot conceive of a sound without timbre, loudness, and duration, or of color without spatial extension. Notice also that these essential truths are not formal, or logical, but rather material. (Some essences are formal, but others are material, as in the essence of memory, imagination, or perception, or of material values). It is in the *material* nature of sound to determine that it must have timbre, loudness, and duration. So the intuition of essences, unlike induction, can yield material knowledge that is universal and necessary. It can yield synthetic a priori truths.

While a person might need more than one experience of an eidetic truth in order to see and grasp it, it does not follow that such insight is arrived at inductively. The other possibility, affirmed by Husserl, is that insight is often an achievement, and one that typically requires time, and repeated experiential exposure to the relevant principle across a range of experiences. But in principle such insight is accessible from any single example, in radical contrast to conclusions that are arrived at inductively. A small child may have to join two rocks with two rocks to get four rocks, and then repeat the process with pencils, pieces of breakfast cereal, and the like, before he or she fully gets the point. But, once grasped, it is clear that 2 + 2 does not merely happen to equal 4, but rather must do so—an insight that is in principle available through the contemplation of any one of its concrete exemplifications, or, indeed, even without any such exemplification at all. The need for examples is psychological, not logical.

The fact that we directly perceive eidetic principles exposes as false the widespread view according to which objective reality consists solely of individual physical things and forces, on the one hand, and purely subjective responses, attitudes, and the like, on the other. For example, eidetic intuition includes the perception of synthetic relations among things. Are "taller than," "to the left of," "equal to," and other such relations among things themselves part of the furniture of the universe? Are they "merely subjective"?

Experience would be chaotic and meaningless without eidetic intuition. Everything seen would be particular; nothing would exemplify or embody a principle. In radical opposition to the prejudice of common sense, what we typically see in our ordinary experience is not simply physical objects in the world, but rather the principles, or essences, that those objects and the relations among them exemplify. It is only in the light of these principles that our experience is intelligible, rather than a riotous, cacophonous jumble of particular sense impressions.

Similarly, most works of art would be utterly inaccessible to us without eidetic intuition. For how can we understand, for example, a story about people we have never met, who live in a place we have never visited, who do things we have never done, and whose lives differ from ours in a thousand significant details? The answer is that, while the contingent particulars of their lives and ours may differ, those particulars embody many general principles that we share in common. To be sure, the differences are important, and one value of art is that it can educate us about them, thus expanding our horizons. But such a process of education cannot even begin without a point of access to, or ground of intelligibility for, this alien world. And this point or ground is provided by eidetic intuition—the ability to see in the details of the story the essential principles they exemplify, and thus, for example, to recognize as disappointment, and to grasp it as such, the feeling of a character who fails to receive something that he or she had desperately wanted, even though the thing wanted and not obtained might belong to a form of life that I have never experienced.[5]

The eidetic reduction also helps Husserl to explain how we can know the truth of a priori (that is, universal and necessary) statements. We can know such propositions when they concern essences, rather than facts. For whatever is true of an essence is always true of it, in all times and places, and with regard to every individual instantiation of the essence. (This is another of the ways in which statements about essences are radically different in principle from inductive generalizations, such as those found in the natural or social sciences.) Logic and mathematics are a priori disciplines, since they deal with relations among essences. Husserl suggests that a genuinely philosophical ethics will also be an a priori discipline of the same sort.

In that vein, it is worth pointing out that the eidetic aspect of phenomenology provides Husserl with another resource in the critique of relativism, including moral relativism. Differences between cultures often have to do only with contingent, accidental, inessential details, rather than with fundamental principles. It is wrong to drive on the left in the United States, and wrong to drive

---

[5] A leading contemporary French philosopher, Alain Badiou, offers a similar analysis, though he references Plato, rather than Husserl. At the conclusion of a discussion of four paintings of horses, two, painted almost 30,000 years ago, from the Chauvet cave in France, and two by Picasso from 1929 and 1939, Badiou makes the point that, despite the vast temporal and cultural differences separating Picasso from the Chauvet artist (or artists), and despite the fact that Picasso's paintings could not possibly have been influenced by the Chauvet paintings, since the cave paintings had not been discovered until after Picasso had executed his works, the four paintings nonetheless deal with "an invariant theme" and communicate the same "eternal truth" (*Logics of Worlds*, trans. Alberto Toscano [New York: Continuum, 2009 (originally published in 2006)], 18). In complete agreement with Husserl's position, and also with Plato's Theory of Forms (though not with Plato's theory of art, according to which drawings and paintings are regarded as mere copies of individual objects of sense experience, and thus twice removed from the ideal Forms, which are objects of thought), Badiou argues that these works of art point "towards the light of the Idea. . . . The image, here, is the opposite of the shadow. It attests the Idea in the varied invariance of its pictorial sign" (*Logics of Worlds*, 19). Thus, in response to "a famous cynic" who "thought he was laughing behind Plato's back by saying: 'I do see some horses, but I see no Horseness,'" Badiou responds as follows: "In the immense progression of pictorial creations, . . . it is indeed Horseness, and nothing else, which we see" (*Logics of Worlds*, 20).

on the right in England, but this does not show that morality is subjective, or conventional, or entirely cultural, or anything of that sort. If one performs the eidetic reduction, that is, if one looks past the surface particulars and focuses on the reasons underlying these moral judgments, one finds that in both cases the fundamental principle is the same. When driving, one must minimize the chance of causing injuries and/or deaths in a crash. To do so, it is necessary that drivers going in the same direction remain also on the same side of the road, with the opposite side of the road being reserved for drivers travelling in the opposite direction. But it makes no difference whether the rule is "everyone on the right" or "everyone on the left." So the difference between the British and American systems does not illustrate, or derive from, a fundamental moral disagreement. Rather, it represents only a difference in the choice between two arbitrary conventions, either one of which equally supports the same fundamental moral principle. (The case would be otherwise for a culture which adopted the rule, "drive on whichever side of the road you want," or, even more radically, "when driving, try to kill as many innocent people as possible.") Or again, to take a famous example from Herodotus, if one culture burns the dead, while another eats the dead, this need not (contrary to Herodotus) indicate a deep moral disagreement. The eidetic principle underlying both practices might be the same: that one needs to treat the bodies of the dead with respect, and not dispose of them in the same casual way with which we throw away garbage. Rather, there must be a special method of doing so (even if the identity of that special method is fixed merely by means of an arbitrary convention).

Somewhat surprisingly, it turns out that even purely empirical noneidetic generalizations or "laws" are also always shot through with eidetic principles. For example, Newton's gravitational theory asserts that material bodies in space are attracted to each other to a degree that is determined by their respective masses and by the amount of distance between them. Here such concepts as "body," "space," "attraction," "mass," and "distance," to say nothing of the relevant mathematical laws, are all to be understood as pure essences, applicable to any contingent particulars whatsoever. Indeed, even the mere act of using language requires the eidetic reduction. We refer to and explain particulars with reference to general, essential concepts, as when we say something like "This is a red ball."

Similarly, there is an eidetic dimension to all contingent facts. The reason is that in some cases eidetic insight reveals that two traits must either always be joined (e.g. all sounds have duration and loudness) or never be joined (e.g. no sounds can be seen or touched). The realm of contingent facts, then, is the realm of the joining of traits where the conjunction is eidetically neither required nor excluded, but rather revealed as possible, that is, as allowed by the eidetic nature of the traits in question.

Husserl's ideas about the eidetic reduction, essences, and meaning are relevant to his solution to a problem that has plagued philosophy since Kant: How do we account for the unity of experience? One never sees a physical object all at once, but rather always in profile. So why is it that we always see, right from the word "go," the objective content of these perceptual experiences (which, from a sense-datum standpoint, might differ from each other quite radically), as perceptions of one and the same object? Husserl's answer, in part, is that consciousness is always concerned with meaning, rather than with, say, raw sense data. When I look at the front of a house, what I typically see is a house from the front, and precisely not "the front of a house." I spontaneously engage myself with the essential meaning of what is perceptually present, and "house" is, in most contexts, meaningful in a way that "front" is not. One can not go inside of a "house-front" as one can a house. The house-front is meaningful only insofar as it refers to a house. So I see the house-front as a house with sides and a back, even though those are not presently accessible to me perceptually.

Husserl's enthusiasm for eidetic intuition is unsurprising, given his background in mathematics, that most eidetic of intellectual disciplines. Prominently displayed above the entrance to Plato's Academy were the words, "No one who does not love mathematics may enter this building." Philosophy, and thought in general, requires an ability to think about essences, that is, to think abstractly. One has to be able to neglect the contingent, superficial, irrelevant aspects of the case and to focus instead on its essential principles. The color of a triangle is irrelevant to geometry. Numbers are ideal, essential, permanent, imperishable. One must learn to be able to think effortlessly about, to swim comfortably in an environment of, essential principles in abstraction from sensory contingent particulars.

Throughout his life Husserl retained the admiration for the achievements of the sciences that began in his early years as a mathematician. At the same time, however, he found something lacking in the sciences in that they show no concern for their own foundations. They do not address questions about the nature of knowledge or truth or rationality or evidence or logic. Rather, they are content to adopt prevailing conceptions of knowledge uncritically, so as to get on with work in their specific domain. It is philosophy that historically has (and rightly so, on Husserl's view) taken up the task of clarifying the all-encompassing criteria and standards of rationally defensible knowledge. But on the other hand, philosophy, unlike science, has no well worked out method for achieving its goals. This is what Husserl attempts to provide with his phenomenology. As a first step, all scientific investigations must rely on conceptions of what are the essences of some of the things with which they deal—that is, what is the nature of the things—what qualities belong to them necessarily if they are to be the kinds of thing that they are, as opposed to those qualities that belong to them only accidentally and contingently. Knowledge of such matters cannot be arrived at through the methods of the sciences. For that, eidetic intuition is required.

And there is a technique for arriving at such intuition. When using an object as an example of an essence, we can employ "free variation" imaginatively to determine what sorts of variations a thing can undergo and still remain an example of that kind of thing. The intentional object can be examined from all angles, as an indefinite number of attributes can be imaginatively added to or subtracted from it. Thus, imagination is an aid to eidetic insight. It can help to determine the boundaries of a concept. Husserl's slogan is "ideation through variation."

Why is it necessary to use imagination, the free variation of examples, in order to arrive at the intuition of an essence? Why cannot our understanding of an essence be based simply on abstracting from a number of perceived objects? The reason is that if we took the latter course, our conclusion would be merely inductive. We would never reach universality or necessity. To reach these we must actually *grasp* the essence intuitively. An essence is not the same thing as a mere empirical generalization.

This point exposes a connection between the eidetic reduction and Husserl's ideal of presuppositionlessness. To grasp an essence we need not posit the existence of anything, nor do we need to establish (or assume) any facts. Eidetic discoveries are just as valid for possible, imagined entities as they are for actually existing ones: "*Positing of* and . . . intuitive seizing upon *essences implies not the slightest positing of any individual factual existence; pure eidetic truths contain not the slightest assertion about matters of fact*" (Ideas I, §4, 11). So eidetic inquiry need not presuppose the existence of anything or the truth of any factual matter. Moreover, because the objects of such inquiry are ideal principles, rather than real, existing things, "merely imaginative" intuitions can "seize upon an essence itself," and allow us to see it "originarily" and, sometimes, "adequately" (Ideas I, §4, 11). To grasp the eidetic structure "on top of," for example, one need not see a plate on top of a book, or a book on top of a table, or a table on top of a floor. Indeed, these are precisely the sorts of irrelevant contingent particulars that one would have to disregard, in the eidetic reduction, in order to focus on the relevant eidetic principle. To be sure, perceiving one of these embodiments of that principle might help one to grasp it, but any one of these perceptions would be as good as another for that purpose, and no one of them is necessary. Anything that presents the principle for one's inspection, that makes it available for intuitive, insightful grasping, will do, and it appears that imagination is frequently at least as well suited for this purpose as is sensory perception of something exemplifying the principle. And imagination is superior to perception in that it can be used freely to probe the boundaries of the principle by means of varied examples. Little wonder, then, that Husserl concludes, despite his recognition that this phrase will bring ridicule from adherents of philosophical naturalism, that "fiction constitutes the vital element of phenomenology as of all eidetic sciences" (Ideas I, §70, 160, translation modified).

Philosophy, as Husserl conceives it, is conceptual, rather than empirical, and it concentrates on a priori truths, rather than the contingent truths of the sciences. Philosophy, properly understood, is most of all concerned with the laws of logic and with the necessary conditions and essential structures of experience. Phenomenology, on this view, is as purely philosophical as any endeavor ever undertaken.

Critique of Empiricism

Husserl announces, seemingly with some reluctance, that "we must enter into a controversy with empiricism. . . . The situation forcing the controversy upon us is that 'ideas,' 'essences,' 'cognition of essence,' are denied by empiricism." Such denials cannot be ignored, since "the natural sciences . . . favor philosophical empiricism." Indeed, it is "the predominant conviction, . . . almost the solely dominant one among empirical investigators." Such "hostility to ideas" must eventually "endanger the progress of the experiential sciences themselves because, owing to this hostility, the still uncompleted eidetic foundations of these sciences and the perhaps necessary constituting of new eidetic sciences indispensible to their progress have become inhibited" (Ideas I, §18, 34).

Husserl's apparent reluctance probably stems from his admiration for the essential thrust of empiricism—the idea that all genuine knowledge must be grounded in experience. Indeed, he fully shares in common with classical empiricism the desire to get back to the things themselves, to set aside theories, speculations, authority, and prejudices, and return to a careful examination of what is given in experience. As a result, he even goes so far, in one memorable passage, as to call himself a "positivist":

> If "*positivism*" is tantamount to an absolutely unprejudiced grounding of all sciences on the "positive," that is to say, on what can be seized upon originaliter, then *we* are the genuine positivists. In fact, we allow *no* authority to curtail our right to accept all kinds of intuition as equally valuable legitimating sources of cognition—not even the authority of "modern natural science." When it is actually natural science that speaks, we listen gladly, and as disciples. But it is not always natural science that speaks when scientists are speaking; and it assuredly is *not* when they are talking about "philosophy of Nature" and "epistemology as a natural science." And, above all, it is not natural science that speaks when they try to make us believe that general truisms such as all axioms express (propositions such as "a + 1 = 1 + a," "a judgment cannot be colored," "of only two qualitatively different tones, one is lower and the other higher," "a perception is, *in itself*, a perception of something") are indeed expressions of experiential matters of fact; whereas we know with *full insight* that propositions such as those give explicative expression to data of eidetic intuition. (Ideas I, §20, 39)

As this passage suggests, what Husserl objects to in the otherwise admirable program of empiricism is its dogmatic assumption that all facts are facts of nature, that only sensory particulars are given in experience, and that we do not experience essences and general relations. Empiricism denies the palpable fact that we have insight into some universal and necessary truths. The falsity of empiricism's arbitrary assumption that all experience is sensory in nature, and that it discloses only particulars, and never universals, principles, qualities, structures, or patterns, is revealed by its implication that we can see lowered eyebrows but never a *frown* or *sadness*; bodily movements but never an *act*; two objects but not the numerous relations among them (to the left of, darker than, bigger than, etc.); the fact that this color is extended in space, and that this sound has pitch, duration, timbre, and a specific degree of loudness, but not the universal and necessary principle that *whatever* is colored must be extended in space, and that *any* sound must have these properties.

The exclusion of these clear givens of experience makes it inevitable that empiricism would result in skepticism, as, in the work of Hume, for example, it obviously does. For if we insist on counting as experience "not what we in fact live and are aware of living but only those disjointed fragments represented by discrete sense data, then any order we might impose upon them would be inevitably suspect, invented rather than given."[6]

Moreover, Husserl demonstrates that classical empiricism is self-undermining. The *thesis* that all knowledge, indeed, all valid thinking, is based upon sense perception, is not *itself* something that can be observed with the senses. After all, direct sensory experience "only presents particular singularities and no universalities," so it cannot inform us about *all* valid thinking (Ideas I, §20, 37). Were an empiricist to claim to have insight into the nature of knowledge—insight sufficient to determine that all knowledge must be based on sense perception—this, too, would be self-undermining, since such insight is not sensory; and it would fly in the face of the empiricist's explicit rejection of appeals to nonsensory intuition. The empiricist might then appeal to inductive reasoning, but this would only raise the question of the grounding of our knowledge of the validity of the principles of inductive (and, for that matter, deductive) inference. To claim that our knowledge of such principles is intuitive, or in some other way nonempirical

---

    6 Erazim Kohák, *Idea & Experience* (Chicago: University of Chicago Press, 1978), 160.

(that is, not based on sense perception), would contradict the empiricist's expressly stated general thesis. But to claim that our knowledge of the principles of logical inference is based on sense perception is to commit all of the fallacies that Husserl diagnoses in his critique of psychologism in the *Logical Investigations*.

The "Principle of All Principles"

Husserl's *"principle of all principles"* holds that *"every originary presentive intuition is a legitimizing source of cognition*, that *everything originarily* (so to speak, in its "personal" actuality) *offered* to us *in 'intuition' is to be accepted simply as what it is presented as being*, but also *only within the limits in which it is presented there"* (Ideas I, §24, 44).

To understand Husserl's meaning, it is important to underscore the point that "intuition," as the term is used here, means direct awareness, whether sensory or otherwise. To intuit, in this sense, is to "take in," to "see," to grasp. It does not refer to a mystical hunch, an inspired guess, an obscure feeling, or anything of that sort. Nor does it refer to complex, inferential reasoning, in which many different pieces and kinds of evidence must be sifted through and evaluated, as when one is attempting to solve a crime, or understand the causes of a many-sided historical event, or figure out which applicant for the job, each of whom has a unique and detailed set of qualifications, skills, and limitations, should be hired, or determine which position on some multifaceted moral issue, such as abortion, euthanasia, or capital punishment, should be adopted. Intuition, rather, is the source of our knowledge that there is a bird on the branch right in front of me, that an elephant will not fit in my pants pocket, that whatever is colored is extended in space, that things which are equal to the same thing are also equal to one another, and that happiness is intrinsically better than misery. Husserl's appeal to intuition, especially in the light of his critique of empiricism, amounts to a plea that we not reject what is directly, powerfully, noninferentially evident—and evident because it is accessible to our direct inspection—merely because neither the datum seen nor the seeing of it is sensory in nature. His point is that

> *Immediate "seeing,"* not merely experiential sense perception, but *seeing in the general sense as an originarily presentive consciousness of any*

kind whatever, is the ultimate source of the validity of all rational assertions. . . . If we see an object with full clarity, if we have effected an explication and a conceptual apprehension purely on the basis of the seeing and within the limits of what is actually seized upon in seeing, if we then see (this being a new mode of "seeing") how the object is, the faithful statement expressing this has, as a consequence, its legitimacy. Not to assign any value to "I see it" as an answer to the question, "Why?" would be a countersense. . . . (Ideas I, §19, 36–37, translation modified)

But why would it be a countersense? Part of the answer lies in recognizing that not all knowledge can be inferential. Chains of reasons must start somewhere. To demand an inferential basis for every knowledge claim is to demand an infinite regress. If knowledge claim A must be justified in terms of reason B, then we will have to justify B in terms of C, C in terms of D, and so on forever. So not everything can be justified in terms of something else. If knowledge is possible at all, then some things must be capable of being known on the basis of a direct inspection of them. Moreover, what is intuitively evident, that is, that which presents itself to us directly, and clearly indicates to us an obvious truth, cannot be subjected to further evidence or proof; but then, none is needed. We have already obtained the best and most evidence we can. To deny this is to fall into absurdity. Husserl intends phenomenology to be the descriptive science of these foundational, intuitively evident truths. This is part of his conception of philosophy as a "rigorous science," a foundational, "presuppositionless," science, one that begins at the very beginning. Phenomenology, which is concerned with essential principles, rather than with facts, is thus neither deductive nor inductive, but rather intuitive.

Many critics of intuition point out, however, and rightly so, that intuitions are far from infallible. We make mistakes sometimes when we claim that something is intuitively evident or obvious. But all bases for making knowledge claims are fallible. Sense perception, too, is imperfect, but its errors are correctible, and frequently on the basis simply of further sense experience. Husserl holds that the same is true for nonsensory intuition: the corrective of errors derived from experience is further experience. Errors of "seeing" of whatever kind (including insightful "grasping") are corrected by more, and closer, and clearer, and better, seeing. Husserl points to "the possibility that, under some circumstances, one seeing conflicts with another and likewise that one *legitimate* assertion conflicts with another," and comments that this

> no more implies that seeing is not a legitimizing basis than the out-weighing of one force by another signifies that the outweighed force is not a force. It does say, however, that perhaps in a certain category of intuitions (and that is the case precisely with sensuously experiencing intuitions) seeing is, according to its essence, "imperfect," that of essential necessity it can become strengthened or weakened, that consequently an assertion having an immediate, and therefore genuine, legitimizing ground in experience nevertheless may have to be abandoned in the further course of experience because of a counter legitimacy outweighing and annulling it. (Ideas I, §19, 37, translation modified)

The Natural Attitude

"The natural attitude" is Husserl's term for what might otherwise be called "common sense." It refers to the beliefs that we adopt habitually and uncritically, usually without ever making them the objects of our focused attention. Husserl's interest in the natural attitude has mainly to do with the ways in which he takes it to stand as an obstacle to the project of studying what is given in lived experience. He sees it as doing so in a variety of ways, but with two taking on special importance.

First, in the natural attitude we tend not to focus on experience at all, but rather look past it, so as to focus on what we take it to be telling us about the world. For example, if I have a headache, I do not typically direct my attention to what this experience discloses about the nature of pain, or about what it is like to "feel" in general, or anything of that sort. Rather, I am much more likely to think about what might be causing my headache, and what I might be able to do to alleviate it. In the natural attitude we take the independent existence of objects in the world for granted, and we assume that they cause us to have the experiences we have, so that those experiences can be read for clues as to what the independent objects in the world are like. And it is this information that chiefly concerns us.

The other major way that the natural attitude stands as a barrier to phenomenological investigation is that it imposes a meta-physical theory onto the data of lived experience, thus distorting our perception of those data. For example, the natural attitude assumes that individual physical objects are real, but that essences, principles, and values are merely subjective—things that we project onto a reality that does not in any sense contain, reveal, or present them. Husserl's primary objection to this metaphysical theory is not that it is false (though he does think that), but rather that it, in the natural attitude, it is given a status as prior to experience. So while it is not itself given in experience (and neither does it flow from it, or harmonize with it), we uncritically use it to interpret (or, more accurately, reinterpret, or explain away) what *is* given in experience. Thus, people who are overwhelmed by the beauty of a work of art, and who experience this beauty as flowing from properties and characteristics of the work itself, will nonetheless subsequently report that their experience flowed from something within themselves, since only this explanation fits their theory that "beauty is in the eye of the beholder."

The Phenomenological Reduction

In order to overcome these barriers to phenomenological inquiry, Husserl proposes a "phenomenological reduction," in which the theorizing and positing of the natural attitude are to be "bracketed," set aside, put in parentheses, so that all of our judgments about them are suspended.[7] The point of this reduction is not to

---

[7] Husserl makes use of a great number of synonyms for the phenomenological reduction, calling it, in various passages, the phenomenological "abstention," "suspension," "disconnection," or "*epoché*" (a Greek term, used by Sextus Empiricus and the Pyrrhonian skeptics to refer to a suspension of belief—a refusal to either affirm or deny something). He also refers to "bracketing" or "switching off" our commonsense assumptions, or to "putting them out of action" or "placing them in parentheses." Sometimes he uses the adjective "transcendental," rather than "phenomenological," when referring to the reduction/abstention/ suspension, etc. While it appears that, in context, there are sometimes slight differences in meaning or emphasis among these various locutions, the basic point of each of them is the same. However, none of them should be confused with the eidetic reduction (discussed above), by which we direct our focus to essential principles rather than to contingent particulars and matters of fact. As if this were not enough, it should be noted that Husserl also adopts a "philosophical *epoché*," which he says "consists of our *completely abstaining from any judgment regarding the doctrinal content of any previous philosophy and effecting all of our demonstrations within the limits set by this abstention*," adding that this is "not to be confused with" the "phenomenological reduction" (Ideas I, §18, 33–34).

deny or doubt any of the claims that comprise the natural attitude, but rather simply to turn our attention away from them so as to allow us to focus instead on what they tend to obscure, namely, the data, the contents, the "givens" of lived experience. Such focusing requires a methodological turning away from (again, not in the sense of denying, but rather only that of ignoring) our "natural," or "commonsense" tendency to impose on the givens of our experience some sort of theory about what causes or explains them. This reduction to phenomena is not a reduction to "mere appearances," but rather a reduction to experience—the domain of what is truly given.

One of the motivations for the phenomenological reduction is the realization that in the natural attitude we tend to operate with a crude objective/subjective dichotomy, which we from the outset impose on any analysis of, or reflection on, our experience. This theoretical screen obscures, and diverts attention away from, that experience itself. Common sense typically insists upon assigning a cause to whatever is experienced, and then to take much greater interest in that alleged cause than to the content or structure of the experience. Moreover, it usually bases its determination of cause on a general theory about what sorts of things are objective (in the sense of being caused by something external to and independent of us) and what sorts of things are subjective (in the sense of originating within us), as opposed to basing it on a careful consideration of evidence, including the evidence that is disclosed in the relevant experience itself. Thus, we assume that perception is caused by external objects, so we take little interest in the nature of perceptual experience, or in objects as perceived (as opposed to objects as we believe them really to be, apart from our experience); we assume that time and space are objective, so we pay little attention to the structures of temporal and spatial experience, or to time and space as they are experienced; we assume that ethical and aesthetic values are subjective, that is, projected by us onto a world that does not contain them, so we refrain from a careful study of experienced values or of the nature of value-experience.

This same pattern holds also for cases in which we do not have a general causal theory according to which the kind of experience in question has either an objective or subjective cause. For example, the natural attitude holds that fear sometimes has an objective cause (I am aware of a really existing external threat), and sometimes has a subjective cause (there is no threat; I am paranoid; I project a threat onto a world in which none is present). But in such cases the natural attitude's interest lies in determining whether the cause is objective or subjective, and then focusing on that cause (say, the snarling, unleashed pit bull, or, alternatively, my paranoia). It takes little interest in the experience of fear, or in the feared object as disclosed in experience, and within the limits of experience (that is, without reference to a theory about the status of that object outside of experience).

Another way to grasp the point of the phenomenological reduction is simply to recall that phenomenology is committed to relying exclusively on what is actually presented in experience. It follows directly from this that phenomenology can make no use of anything that we do not experience. Thus, if we habitually impose on our experience certain assumptions that are not themselves grounded in experience, or worse, ignore our experience entirely as a consequence of those assumptions, then we must take action so as to allow the givens of experience to emerge in clear focus.

The problem of nonexperientially grounded, experience-obscuring assumptions is exacerbated, moreover, by the fact that these assumptions are typically ones that we rarely (if ever) explicitly think about, focus on, or formulate to ourselves. The point of the reduction, then, is to bring these assumptions to our clear awareness, so that they can then be set aside, or put in brackets. The reduction allows us to thematize, to make explicit, to focus on, the natural attitude, which we ordinarily take for granted and fail to examine. This is another major theme of phenomenology—the attempt to make visible, and thus available for critical evaluation, what we ordinarily do not see because it is the taken-for-granted ubiquitous content of what is perpetually right before our eyes and right under our noses. The reduction does not deny our fundamental relation to the world. Rather, the point is that our engagement with the world is so basic, so intense, so thoroughgoing, that it is ordinarily invisible to us, like the air we breathe. The reduction is necessary as a methodological device to allow us to step back from our manifold connections to the world sufficiently as to allow us to see and describe them.

The phenomenological reduction can also be profitably understood as a response to the philosophies of Hume and Kant, both of whom had raised powerful criticisms of the idea that world is simply there, just as it appears to be, unaltered by our conscious engagement with it. Husserl sidesteps these criticisms with the reduction. The aim is to focus on the world as given in experience, and to describe it with unprecedented care, rigor, subtlety, and completeness, but without "the natural attitude"—the naïve assumption criticized by Hume and Kant. This applies not only to the objects of sense experience, but to all phenomena: moral, aesthetic, political, mathematical, and so forth. One can avoid the obscure problem of the true ontological status of the objects of experience in these domains by focusing on the objects, as experienced, themselves. These are to be described, together with their modes of givenness, and the acts of consciousness that disclose them. In this way, the reduction rules out a premature commitment to naïve realism or naturalism, or, for that matter, to psychologism, relativism, or subjectivism.

It is important to emphasize, however, that the point of the phenomenological reduction is not, as is sometimes thought, to shift our focus to "mere appearances" by ignoring the reality that allegedly stands behind or underlies those appearances. While it is true that the "phenomena" to which the reduction directs our attention are, in a sense, appearances, they are not, for Husserl (unlike Kant), to be contrasted with things as they are in themselves. Rather, phenomena are *manifestations* of things themselves, or ways in which things *show* themselves. To say that there exists, in addition to the world we experience, another one, hidden and inaccessible to us, which somehow causes us to experience what we (wrongly) take to be the real world, is to engage in pointless and warrantless speculation. No evidence supports such speculation, and it solves no problems, but rather generates new ones. On Husserl's view, appearances do not conceal the real thing, but rather reveal it, although any given appearance may reveal it only partially. The distinction between appearance and reality, then, is for Husserl not a distinction between two entirely different realms, but rather a distinction to be drawn entirely within the domain of phenomena. A "mere appearance" is a partial appearance, or an unclear or distorted appearance, and this can, indeed, be contrasted with "reality"—that is, with the object as fully and clearly given in experience.

According to Husserl, the reduction opens up a new region of being—that of intentional acts, intended objects, and the interrelations among them. This is new territory, never before explored. And this new region of being is not merely one among others. Rather, it is the primary one, the absolute with respect to which all other regions are relative. The other regions all essentially depend on it.

But the point of the reduction is not just to set aside the ontological commitments of the natural attitude, and thus to open up the region of the correlation of intentional acts and intentional objects; it also neutralizes any attempt to treat this correlation as one more natural fact, open to the same kinds of causal explanations as any other—perhaps psychologistic or anthropological/ sociological, and thus relativistic. Phenomenology under the reduction is not psychology, since psychology, while dealing with consciousness, does so from the standpoint of the natural world, wherein consciousnesses are seen as belonging to real persons in the real world, and as entering into causal relations with other things in the world. Psychology is empirical (in the classical, non-phenomenological, sense), and is concerned to provide explanations. It does not engage in the description of the essences of experiences and of the objects of experience.

Probably the most common criticism of the phenomenological reduction is that it allegedly amounts to a rejection of realism, and, indeed, an abandonment of any concern for the external world, or for questions about whether or not intentional objects actually exist. On this view, the point of the reduction is to bring about an exclusive focusing on the internal structures of experience, and on subjective representations of reality, to the exclusion of any kind of engagement with the world, or with reality, itself.

In response to this line of criticism, Dan Zahavi argues that it rests on a misunderstanding, that of succumbing "to what might be called a mentalistic misinterpretation of the phenomenological dimension. Rather than seeing the field of givenness, the phenomena, as something that questions the very subject/object split, as something that stresses the co-emergence of self and world, the phenomena are interpreted phenomenalistically, as part of the mental inventory." Zahavi adds that the objection slights

all the places where Husserl explicitly denies that the true purpose of the *epoché* and the reduction is to doubt, neglect, abandon, or exclude reality from our research, but rather emphasizes that their aim is to suspend or neutralize a certain dogmatic *attitude* towards reality, thereby allowing us to focus more narrowly and directly on reality just as it is given. In short, the *epoché* entails a change of attitude towards reality, and not an exclusion of reality. . . . The *epoché* and the reduction do not involve an exclusive turn towards inwardness. On the contrary, they permit us to investigate reality in a new way, namely in its significance and manifestation for consciousness.[8]

Indeed, Husserl never takes the position that intentional objects are contained within consciousness. Rather, he maintains that they are transcendent to consciousness, and are not reducible to it. Nor does he attempt to deduce or infer the world's existence from the structures of consciousness. Rather, his goal is descriptive—what is the meaning of the world's existence, as that is disclosed in experience?

The reduction is a return to experience. True, "reality," under the reduction, is methodologically defined as, or restricted to, the correlate of consciousness. If there are any unexperienceable or unthinkable realities, phenomenology, as a matter of method, gives them up. But it is unclear that this entails any real sacrifice—we are only "giving up" what we have never experienced or thought of in the first place. There is no difference in content between the world before the reduction and the world after the reduction. For example, there is nothing in the reduction that would prevent us from observing that things, that is, objects of experience, or intentional objects, typically present themselves as existing independently of us. The point of the reduction is simply to prevent us from going beyond what is given in our experience of that world.

A major obstacle to the understanding of the phenomenological reduction is the uncritical "commonsense" acceptance of the body/mind dualism that finds its most famous expression in the philosophy of Descartes. According to the popular understanding of this dualism, whatever does not exist as an independent physical thing (the realm of hard, objective, scientific facts) must, if it can be said to exist at all, exist as a "mere idea" in the mind. Thus, when Husserl proposes that we bracket the world as fact, he is often taken to be advocating that we focus instead on the world as

---

[8] "Phenomenology," in *The Routledge Companion to Twentieth Century Philosophy*, ed. Dermot Moran (New York: Routledge, 2008), 669–70.

something subjective, the world as mere idea. Instead, he is proposing that we focus on a third, previously unexplored, thing: the world as experienced, where experience is understood neither as objective nor as subjective, but rather in terms of the correlativity of conscious acts and the experienced objects and structures disclosed by them.

To make this point clear, recall what has been said above about intentionality, and about the eidetic dimension of experience. A particular rock exemplifies a limitless variety of eidetic principles. It is an example of a hard thing, a solid thing, a grey thing, a flat thing, a rock, a particular kind of rock, a natural object, an inanimate object, and so forth. Which of these principles emerge in my experience depends crucially on my focusing, which, in turn, usually depends on my projects and interests. If I am studying the rock in my capacity as a geologist I will probably experience it in a quite different way, and notice a quite different selection of the rock's qualities, than would be the case if I were an artist intent on including the rock as an element in a landscape painting. If I need to hammer in a tent stake, and find that I have forgotten to bring along a tool kit, it is the rock's hardness and flatness that are likely to attract my attention. So the rock-as-experienced differs substantially from the rock-as-it-is-in-itself (if one can even form a coherent idea of what that would mean). But none of this implies, even to the slightest degree, that the rock is not real, or that it does not exist independently, outside of my, or anyone's, conscious experience. To the contrary, if we are talking about a perceived rock, rather than an imagined one, then it gives itself in experience powerfully as having real, independent, physical existence.

Husserl's point, however, is not merely that the rock-as-experienced is an example of a neglected region of philosophical or scientific investigation. His claim is much more radical than that: It is not the case that the objective rock is primary, and that the rock-as-experienced is something derivative of that (such as the objective rock-as-colored-by-something-subjective-that-we-project-onto-it). Rather, our concept of the objective rock is an abstraction from our many encounters with the rock-as-experience. (We might arrive at this concept by synthesizing the information about the rock that we get from these various experiences; or, more likely, we might decide, based on some theory about what is real and what is not, that one of these perspectives, probably that of the geologist, rather than that of the artist, or of the camper putting up a tent, is the one that reveals the real, objective, rock.)

Another criticism of the phenomenological reduction is that it allegedly leads to a kind of relativistic subjectivism. If we are to ground our truth claims, not in objectively existing things, but rather in subjective experience, won't the result be a chaotic clash of "truths" flowing from the varied experiences of different individuals?

The problem with this objection is that it overlooks two important distinctions. From the standpoint of the subjective pole of experience, it overlooks the distinction between personal taste or preference, on the one hand, and the necessary structures of subjectivity, on the other. From the standpoint of the objective pole of experience, it ignores the distinction that the eidetic reduction addresses—that between the contingent particulars that pertain to things and the essential principles they exemplify. Though you and I may have led very different lives, we both have perceived, imagined, remembered, and doubted, and have experienced success and failure, joy and pain, friendship and enmity, kindness and cruelty. If you have the ability to see colors, then you and I have both seen red, green, blue, and yellow, even if we have never looked at any of the same objects. We both have the same access to "2 + 2 = 4," even if, when initially learning basic arithmetic, the objects we counted were entirely different. In short, our experience is not limited to particularities that are specific to our own unique stream of experience, but rather includes also a rich supply of structures, principles, essences that either are common to experience as such, or else are exemplified by a virtually limitless supply of objects of experience. So a turn to experience is not a turn to anything private or idiosyncratic. The data of experience always in principle, and usually in fact, are capable of adjudicating between competing truth claims. The radical experientialism of phenomenology is not a subjective relativism.

The Transcendental Ego

Not everything is excluded by the phenomenological reduction. What remain after the reduction are phenomena and "the transcendental ego," that is the subject of experience and cognition, the "haver" of the objects to which it is intentionally related. The empirical ego (that is, a natural subject—one that perceives, thinks, and wills from a particular perspective) is also placed in brackets, leaving only the transcendental ego (or the "pure ego," or consciousness as such) as something that cannot be bracketed. The subjectivity of the transcendental ego is not the idiosyncratic and peculiar subjectivity of particular individuals, but rather subjectivity in principle—the very condition of experience. The reason that the transcendental ego survives the phenomenological reduction is that the very activity of carrying out the reduction assumes it.

We do not notice the transcendental ego when we consider ourselves as physical beings in the physical world. Noticing it requires the phenomenological reduction, under which we discover the structuring activities of consciousness (that is, its intentionality, the "directedness" of all of its activities of perceiving, desiring, thinking, and willing).

Constitution

The experience of objects in a unified and coherent way requires considerable activity of consciousness. Different perceptual experiences must be synthesized and fused with memory and with imagination. (I have to be able to see that the house I am now seeing from the back is the same one that I just saw from the front, the same as the one I remember seeing yesterday, the same as the one I have imagined in the past, and the same as the one I anticipate seeing tomorrow). Moreover, I must be able to bring together many of the multileveled ways in which the object perceived relates to other objects if my world is to make any sense at all. "Transcendental consciousness" and "transcendental subjectivity" are terms that refer to the activity of consciousness and its role as a necessary condition for the unity of experience. Consciousness does not merely passively receive impressions, but rather actively shapes, unifies, and synthesizes information in such a way as to enable one to perceive unified objects and a coherent world. The experience of a physical object requires a synthesis of perception, expectation, memory, and imagination. This is one reason why Husserl describes the relationship between consciousness and the world in terms of "constitution," and argues that objects are constituted through acts of consciousness.

"Constitution" is a misleading term, however, since it suggests creation or fabrication, or perhaps the composition of a mental representation from sense data. But for Husserl it does not mean "create," "construct," or "invent," but rather, something closer to "disclose," "bring forth," "make available to experience," or "reveal."

The basic idea of constitution is that objects are disclosed, always, necessarily, and in principle, as meaningful only in the context of the intentionality of conscious, lived, experience. Moreover, they emerge within such experience as meaningful in only one or a few of the possible ways in which they might have been meaningfully encountered. Only some of their aspects will be revealed in any given experience, and which these will be depends crucially on the intention of the experiencer. Thus, to return to a previous example, depending on the specific focusing activities of the experiencer, a given rock might meaningfully appear, quite spontaneously in a particular experience, as a geological specimen, or as a hammer, or as an element to be included in a landscape painting. According to James M. Edie, "any phenomenology of human thought must" therefore

> recognize as its most essential characteristic the ability of consciousness to see and organize meanings (and relationships) in a field of ambiguity, to live in what does 'not yet have sense,' and to assist at the emergence of sense from non-sense, by 'zeroing in' . . . on those elements of a given and ambiguous field of awareness which, in terms of its present interest, enable consciousness to restructure that given field in a newly meaningful way.[9]

Part of what is involved in the constitution of objects as meaningful is the intentional "placing" of them within an ordered context. But this placing in context need not be, and typically is not, accomplished as part of some overtly conceptual or intellectual project. Rather, approaching the object while engaged in a practical project is generally sufficient to do the job. A paint brush is constituted as the kind of thing it is by virtue of the place it holds in relation to the paints and the canvas. If the same object were to be encountered in a different context it would be a different kind of object, and would take on a different mean-

---

[9] "Introduction" to *Phenomenology in America*, ed. James M. Edie (Chicago: Quadrangle Books, 1967), 12.

ing, even though it need not have undergone any significant physical change.

On the other hand, sometimes current engagement in a particular project is not necessary in order for the elements of one's perceptual experience to emerge as, and, indeed, to be constituted as, meaningful. The deep background of one's way of life, and corresponding interests and concerns, is often sufficient for this to happen. Erazim Kohák illustrates this point with the example of a Native American who witnesses hail beating down prairie grass. Kohák points out that, while a traveler who sees this by looking out of the dome of a railway car may appreciate it as sheer spectacle, and an "uncomprehending Martian" may merely record sense data, without being able to attach any significance to it at all, the case is quite different for the Native American

> who depends on the prairie grasses for his livelihood. The reality he sees is a meaningful whole, a destruction of food which spells a hungry winter. His perception is clearly intentional, partaking of an act-character: its hyletic contents [Husserl's term for sense data] are structured as coherent and meaningful. *The presence of the [Native American], not his preferences, not what he thinks or "feels," but his very presence, constitutes the experience as a meaningful whole.*[10]

Noēsis and *Noema*

Husserl distinguishes between sensual matter (*hylē*) and intended form (*morphē*), and between intentional acts of consciousness (*noēsis*), by and through which matter is disclosed and becomes an object of experience, and the object-as-experienced (*noema*). The noetic aspect has to do with the subjective side of the intentional act, that is, with the nature and quality of the conscious act of perceiving, remembering, imagining, doubting, and so forth. The noematic aspect relates to the objective side, that is, the meaningful intentional content (the intentionally constituted object perceived, remembered, imagined, etc.). The *noēsis* is the meaning-giving element in intentional acts, while the *noema* is the meaning given.

---

[10] *Idea & Experience* (Chicago: University of Chicago Press, 1978), 123, emphasis added.

Husserl uses the concept of *noema* to explain several phenomena that would otherwise be puzzling. For example, part of what it means to be conscious of an object is to be aware, right in one's present experience, that the object of which one is currently aware is the same one that one was aware of (or could have been aware of) previously, the same one that one could encounter in the future, and indeed, the same one that one could encounter in an indefinite number of acts. How is this to be explained? The conscious act which discloses an object is a fleeting event in time, and when it ends we no longer "have" the object. Moreover, when we once again encounter what we assume to be the same object, this will require a new conscious act, not identical with the earlier one; and what this act discloses may well on some level, for example, that of sense data, also be somewhat different from what was disclosed previously. So what can be the basis for our sense of the identity of the object? Husserl's answer is the *noema*, the intentionally constituted meaning, which must be distinguished from the object simpliciter. The *noema* is the object precisely as the perceiver is aware of it in the act of perceiving it. For the perceiver does not see the object in its entirety all at once. Rather, one sees it from a certain distance, from a certain angle, and in light of just one (or a finite number) of its aspects (for example, one may be noticing its size, but not its color, or the reverse, or thinking about it in terms of some practical use that could be made of it, or attending to the way in which it reminds one of a person or event from one's past, and so on indefinitely). Now notice that one can return again and again to this same *noema*. If, after having once perceived an object, I return to view it from the same distance and angle, consider it with respect to the same aspect, and so forth, as I did previously, I encounter the same *noema*. Husserl's explanation is that the *noema*, unlike the conscious act or the real object, is an ideal entity which, like other meanings or significations, is an atemporal entity. Thus, "the *tree simpliciter*, the physical thing belonging to Nature,...can burn up, be resolved into its chemical elements, etc. But the sense—the sense *of this* perception, something belonging necessarily to its essence—cannot burn up; it has no chemical elements, no forces, no real properties" (Ideas I, §89, 216). *Noemata* are independent of the concrete temporalized conscious acts that actualize and disclose them. Every intentional act is thus to be understood both in terms of a temporal aspect, since all conscious acts endure for a certain specific amount of time, and in terms of an aspect of permanence and identity, since such acts disclose meanings which do not come into or pass out of existence. The identity of objects is a fundamental, irreducible fact of consciousness, which any accurate description of what is given in experience will disclose. Consciousness is thus a correlation or a correspondence between acts (*noēses*) and meanings (*noemata*); but this is not a one-to-one correspondence, since one and the same *noema* can be disclosed by an indefinite number of acts. All intentional acts actualize a meaning or sense. This is part of the essence of consciousness.

And these meanings are not constructed out of sense data (*hylē*). Contrary to the picture painted by some classical empiricists, it is not the case that I first see splotchy shapes and colors, which I then interpret as "windows," "door," roof," "porch," etc., until I finally figure out that what I am seeing is a house. Rather (and consult your own experience to determine whether or not this description is more accurate—this is the phenomenological test), what happens is that I see all at once, in a flash, that this is a house. It is a gestalt. If I am then sufficiently interested in the house as to focus on its details, I am primed to interpret the *hylē* in terms of "house" categories. These categories (windows, door, roof, etc.) might at the outset of my scrutiny of the house be "empty," but as I scan the house they begin to be filled in. But some may be filled in only vaguely or indeterminately, as when the color of the house is somewhat obscured by dark or fog, and others may remain completely empty, in the sense that I have no sensuous presentation of them at all (for example, the back of the house if I never leave my vantage point in front of it).

While the *noema* is not constructed out of the *hylē* , the latter does constrain the former. While I can see the rock as a geological specimen, as a hammer, or as an element in a landscape painting (in other words, the *noema* is "underdetermined" by the *hylē*), I cannot see it as a giraffe, as an airplane, or as the *1812 Overture*.

Horizon

In addition to the object we are focusing on, and seeing one-sidedly in profile, we are also aware, but more dimly, less clearly, less attentively, of some of the background and surroundings of the object. Our experience of this background includes an important element of "anticipation" or "predelineation"—we have a sense of what these background and surrounding elements would look like if we were to focus on them attentively. This anticipation also holds for profiles of the thing that are currently entirely outside of our perceptual field. Intentionality always involves this aspect of "horizon."

Husserl distinguishes, further, between the internal horizon and the external horizon of every perceptual *noema*. Every such *noema* contains a part that is immediately given, but, as the object is given in profile, this given part also refers to not-immediately given aspects. The entirety of these not-immediately given aspects is the "internal horizon" of the perceptual *noema*. But every perceived *noema* also appears as a figure on a ground. This unfocused-on background is the "external horizon." Even though I do not focus on the external horizon, it is partially responsible for the constitution of what I perceive. I will not perceive an x as an x if I am in an environment in which the external horizon is incompatible with the presence of an x. (I won't see a big mass on top of a body of water as a car; a boat is a better candidate.)

A related distinction, that between "thema" and "thematic field" applies to other kinds of cognitive acts. In the act of thinking, for example, one focuses explicitly on some idea, concept, claim, problem, or argument. This is the thema. But it is surrounded by a thematic field consisting of related ideas, problems, etc.—ones the consideration of which may have led one to the present thema, or ones to which thinking about the present thema will lead. In short, thought takes place within a certain intellectual context, most of which is not explicitly focused on at any given time. This is the thematic field. Note that the thematic field is not completely analogous to the external horizon in perception, for the latter concept includes everything whatever that is present in the background, and thus it lacks the criterion of relevance of content that marks the thematic field.

This analysis of the concept of horizon carries with it the implication that "absolute" knowledge, absolute certainty, is impossible in connection with the deliverances of sensory experience, or with regard to any other kind of knowledge that is not absolute, complete unto itself, unvarying in different circumstances and contexts. Whenever a horizon belongs essentially to what is given, this fact alone entails that all knowledge pertaining to the thing in question is in principle presumptive, tentative, revisable, as is the generally accepted understanding with respect to knowledge obtained by scientific methods. In perception there is always a figure on a ground, and thus, it is always the case that there is more that is meaningfully present than is being focused on, and thus given, in any conscious act. There is always a "surplus of meaning," and this, always and in principle, would have to be investigated before adequate evidence could be attained.

Idealism

Because of the phenomenological reduction, and because of his emphasis on consciousness and the first-person perspective, many of Husserl's readers take him to be denying the importance of the world, or at least to be saying that all meaning and truth are "constructed" by a pure and worldless subject. Such an interpretation is lent further plausibility by Husserl's use of the term "transcendental idealism" to describe his position. But, as Dan Zahavi points out, "the subjectivity disclosed by . . . phenomenological reflection is not a concealed interiority, but an open world relation. . . . Had idealism been true, had the world been a mere product of our constitution and construction, the world would have appeared in full transparency. It would only possess the meaning that we ascribe to it, and it would consequently contain no hidden aspects, no sense of mystery. Idealism and constructionism deprive the world of its transcendence."[11]

Moreover, Husserl explicitly denies that his transcendental idealism is a metaphysical idealism or a subjective idealism (Ideas I, §55, 128–30). "Transcendental," in this context, means something like, "having to do with necessary conditions." Husserl's point is that all objects, all realities, as they are encountered experientially, are constituted meanings, which, in turn, require a sense-bestowing consciousness. A world without consciousnesses, without experiencing subjects, would be a world without meaning. But this is very different from holding that reality is mind-dependent, that all of existence is reducible to minds and ideas, or anything of that sort. Radical experientialism is not subjective idealism.

---

[11] "Phenomenology," in *The Routledge Companion to Twentieth Century Philosophy*, ed. Dermot Moran (New York: Routledge, 2008), 664–65.

3

Late Husserl

Without ever abandoning the "static phenomenology" of his earlier works, Husserl begins, toward the end of his career, to complement it with a "genetic phenomenology" that investigates the historical origins of meanings. This work is based, in part, on Husserl's increasing appreciation of the fact that the language, categories, and ways of seeing the world that we use when we focus on and constitute objects are not neutral, but rather are, at least in part, the accidental (it could have been otherwise, to some extent) result of history, culture, and tradition. We are historical beings, so, if we are to understand ourselves in the radical way that Husserl continues to favor, we will have to investigate our history. So history, in Husserl's later work, becomes part of philosophy, and phenomenology takes on a genetic component (that is, it becomes concerned with origins).

The establishment of meaning typically takes time. There is a social history behind the evolution of public meanings, but there is also a subjective, personal, evolution in the psychic life of an individual, so that, as the individual continually encounters certain phenomena throughout life, his or her understanding of the meaning of the phenomena deepens and becomes richer. Alternatively, a false, ungrounded, nonevident, unintuitive meaning might, because of social/historical forces, become "sedimented," so that it stands as an obstacle to the achievement of clear, evident, insight. This is one of the themes of Husserl's last great work.

The Crisis of the European Sciences and Transcendental Phenomenology

It is a poignant fact that Husserl wrote his diagnosis of the growing barbarism of European civilization between 1934 and 1938
(the book was only partially published before his death), when he
was experiencing it at first hand. As detailed in the "Introduction"
above, he suffered persecution because of his Jewishness, including, among many other indignities, the denial of a public platform
in Germany (the right to lecture, and to publish his ideas), despite
his age (he was in his seventies) and international eminence.

Husserl was struck by the observation that this astonishing barbarism was taking place against the background of an unbroken
succession of impressive achievements in the sciences and in technology. But how could this be? How could such remarkable progress
in science, a supremely rational human endeavor, go hand-in-hand
with an equally remarkable retrogression in politics? How could
one and the same culture simultaneously generate the finest
achievements of human rationality and the greatest imaginable
explosion of destructive irrationality?

In addressing these questions, one of Husserl's main points is
that a culture that produces great science is not necessarily a "scientific" culture, if that means a culture guided by norms of reason.
For science can become narrow and specialized, and lose its connection to human life. Critical thinking, the constant struggle to
test one's ideas, and to accept, provisionally, only those that are
well grounded in evidence, need not become a way of life and an
ethical standard for an entire culture. Rather, it can be relegated to
specialists (scientists), and then even in their case limited only to
their professional activities, as opposed to informing and guiding
their lives generally.

And indeed, this is precisely what Husserl claims has happened.
On his interpretation of history, the idea of a genuinely human
existence was first developed in the seventh and sixth centuries BC
in Greece. This would be a philosophical existence, based on the
autonomous use of reason, and on the ideals and norms generated
by such a use of reason. But Husserl complains that as science has
become more specialized, and more positivistic and technological
in its orientation, we have lost sight of the very idea of such a
human existence. All ethical questions, and questions of value

more broadly and generally, are eliminated from the sciences, if not dismissed as cognitively "meaningless." Scientists continue to advance human knowledge, but science has nothing to say about the meaning, or human significance, of these findings. Thus, science says nothing about the things that are most important for human existence. Since science is seen as exemplifying reason, this nihilism gives rise to skepticism about, and hostility towards, reason itself. The result is a proliferation of irrationalistic and anti-intellectual theories and world views. This leads to an estrangement from ourselves as rational creatures.

In response to this crisis, Husserl proposes a return to philosophy. To facilitate this return, he investigates the history of philosophy, attempting to find within the welter of competing theories an underlying coherence, a *telos* (goal), guiding the philosophical project. Not surprisingly, he ends up proposing phenomenology as a return to the idea of philosophy, and thus, to reason, and to a genuinely human existence, in which our self-estrangement will have been overcome.

Husserl's *Crisis* thus brings to the forefront and makes explicit the passionate ethical concern that underlies and pervades all his writing (though it is usually not directly stated). For in the *Crisis* Husserl is striving to help create a culture that would be based on rational insight into universally valid truths and values, rather than on traditions, prejudices, and unfounded opinions. He argues that "the universally, apodictically grounded and grounding science" is "the necessarily highest function of mankind," since it "makes possible mankind's development into a personal autonomy and into an all-encompassing autonomy for mankind—the idea which represents the driving force of life for the highest stage of mankind" (Crisis, Appendix IV: "Philosophy as Mankind's Self-Reflection; the Self-Realization of Reason," 338). "Reason is precisely that which man qua man, in his innermost being, is aiming for, that which alone can satisfy him" (Crisis, Appendix IV: "Philosophy as Mankind's Self-Reflection; the Self-Realization of Reason," 341).

Scientism

Though a great admirer of science, Husserl passionately criticizes "scientism"—the idea that the methods of the physical sciences are the only ones capable of producing knowledge, that "reality" refers only to the world as disclosed by such methods, and that whatever lies outside of their purview cannot be known. According to this view, philosophy is merely a historical forerunner to science, which is destined to die off once the culture becomes sufficiently scientific. Scientism alleges that science is comprehensive and much more rigorous than philosophy. Whatever cannot be addressed scientifically is cognitively meaningless. Consequently, defenders of scientism tend to claim that there is no such thing as ethical knowledge.

It must be emphasized that scientism is a philosophy, and is not to be confused with science itself. Husserl's critique of scientism is fully consistent with his great appreciation for the spectacular achievements of the sciences, and is in no way intended to reject, dismiss, or minimize them in any way. His objection is not to science, but rather to a bad interpretation of the nature, scope, and limits of science.

Science does not study questions of meaning, value, and purpose. These are taken to be subjective, immeasurable, and unquantifiable. If science is equated with reason, the despairing conclusion is that these questions cannot be dealt with rationally. The "crisis in the sciences," then, refers to a loss of meaning, especially with regard to a connection to human purpose. As Husserl puts it, scientism "excludes in principle precisely the questions which humanity, given over in our unhappy times to the most portentous upheavals, finds the most burning: questions of the meaning or meaninglessness of the whole of this human existence" (Crisis, §2, 6, translation modified).

Similarly, Husserl complains that

> the positivistic concept of science in our time [roughly, the thesis that experimentation and sense perception are the only legitimate sources of knowledge] . . . has dropped . . . all questions vaguely termed "ultimate and highest." Examined closely, these . . . excluded questions have their inseparable unity in the fact that they contain . . . the *problems of reason*—reason in all its particular forms. Reason is the explicit theme in the disciplines concerning knowledge (i.e., of true and genuine, rational knowledge), of true and genuine valuation (genuine values as values of reason), of ethical action (truly good acting, acting from practical reason). . . . All these "metaphysical" questions, taken broadly—commonly called specifically philosophical questions—surpass the world understood as the universe of mere facts. They surpass it precisely as being questions with the idea of reason in mind. And

they all claim a higher dignity than questions of fact, which are subordinated to them even in the order of inquiry. Positivism, in a manner of speaking, decapitates philosophy. (Crisis, §3, 9)

Little wonder, then, that we find ourselves living in an age of irrationality and barbarism. If we equate reason with science, and then find that science rejects questions of value and meaning, the result is hostility both to science and to reason itself. Moreover, insofar as human beings are themselves characterized by rationality, a further consequence is a kind of self-betrayal and self-alienation. These unhealthy developments, in turn, can easily metastasize into the irrationalism and anti-intellectualism that comprises such a large and influential portion of the cultural landscape, both in Husserl's time and our own.

Husserl blames the contemporary failure of rationalism on the widespread assumption that rationalism must be understood in terms of scientific naturalism, the idea that to understand something is to integrate it into the world as described by the natural sciences. On this view, anything that does not fit into this world is either to be rejected as unreal (or, at least, unknowable), or else reinterpreted (that is explained, or "explained away") in strictly objective, physical, scientific terms. The problem is that when people discover the limitations of scientific naturalism, in particular its inability to provide ultimate rational explanations, they abandon rationality entirely. It is against this background that Husserl champions his own project of defending rationalism phenomenologically, rather than on the basis of scientific naturalism.

One of the problems with naturalism is that the categories, concepts, and methods we use to make sense of natural events are often unsuitable for facilitating an understanding of conscious events. For example, while natural objects may indeed be governed by naturalistic causal laws, the phenomena of consciousness proceed in accordance with laws of intentionality (the relationship between consciousness and its objects).

Another problem is that naturalism regards only physical things as truly "real," and thus cannot make sense of ideal entities, such as numbers, logical principles, eidetic principles of all kinds, values, and the intentionally constituted meanings which, on Husserl's view, comprise the most fundamental reality with which we deal throughout our lives.

And a third problem with naturalism is that it sees itself as empirical, in the classical sense, and thus bound to the contingency of what we happen to find to be the case (which could, in principle, be otherwise). Thus, it cannot supply anything universal, necessary, absolute, or foundational.

The account of reality provided by natural science accords the highest grade of reality to properties things have "in themselves," quite apart from the qualities that we subjectively project onto them. So the reality of tools, for example, lies more in their chemical composition than in their uses. And how are we to make sense of money, nations, dance crazes, and wars—what is their status?

These difficulties are not confined to the natural sciences. As a result of the scientism of the social sciences, which tend to imitate the naturalistic and positivistic tendencies of the more successful natural sciences, there is no rigorous examination of the social world as it is experienced. Instead, this experience is reduced to what is empirically observable, measurable, and quantifiable.

Recall, in this context, Husserl's goal of returning to "the things themselves." This means returning to the most fundamental, basic, primitive, original, radical evidences to be encountered in conscious experience. It means setting aside all intellectual constructions, and returning instead to what underlies them. Empirical science, admirable as it certainly is, is a construction.

Life-world

What, then, is to be done? In answering this question, Husserl develops, in the *Crisis*, the idea of the "life-world," that is, the world of prescientific experience, the world of meanings that appear in life, prior to any philosophizing. He claims that this life-world is primary, and that technical worlds, like that of science, are derivative of it. But we have made the mistake, he thinks, of subordinating the life-world to the theoretical constructs of the sciences. We treat this artificial, abstract world—and it is *a* world, and a highly useful one—as if it were the ultimate reality ontologically. And we treat the life-world, which is in experience primary, as if it were a subjective projection or construct. This is disastrous because the life-world is a world richly laden with meaning and values. Husserl's thesis is that the life-world is the foundation of meaning in science, even though it (the life-world) has been forgotten by science. Previous philosophers and scientists had ignored the life-world because it was so familiar as to be invisible, like the air we breathe. But Husserl claims that the life-world is "the only real world, the one that is actually given through perception, that is ever experienced and experienceable" (Crisis, §9h, 48–49). So ignoring it leads to horrible distortions, since we end up rejecting what is most evident and obvious in experience whenever it does not line up with a particular interpretation (scientism) of one artificial, abstract world (science). This neglect of the life-world has led us to a crisis, requiring a rigorous return to first principles, basics, the obvious—and thus, to phenomenology.

The life-world is the world of our immediate lived experience. Gradually, since the time of Galileo, the idea that reality is the life-world has given way to the idea that reality is the world as it is presented by the sciences. The "objective" world of the sciences is seen as reality in a more basic and fundamental sense than is the life-world (to the extent that the life-world is conceptualized or thought about at all). In the words of Aldous Huxley, "the world of inferred fine structures" and of "quantified regularities" is taken to be more real than "the universe of given appearances," in which "human beings are born and live and finally die." This is "the world in which they love and hate, in which they experience triumph and humiliation, hope and despair." It is "the world of sufferings and enjoyments, of madness and common sense, of silliness, cunning and wisdom. . . ."[1] But this can't be right. For one thing, one cannot construct a scientific account of anything without drawing on our immediate experience of the life-world. The reverse, however, is not true. One can find the life-world meaningful without recourse to mathematical physics or its theories. Moreover, scientific theories, like mathematical and logical ones, depend heavily on idealization and abstraction, and the raw material for such idealization and abstraction is provided by the life-world, which serves as a kind of foundation for all of the sciences.

The problem, as Husserl formulates it, is that "we take for *true being* what is actually a *method*" (Crisis, §9h, 51). We come to think of the scientific method as something like a microscope, which is capable of directly revealing to us the world as it really is.

---

[1] *Literature and Science* (New York: Harper and Row, 1963), 8.

And what is not revealed by this instrument is assumed not to exist at all. But science, according to Husserl, is an instrument, not for improving our sight, but rather for interpreting and explaining what we see. Science is an abstraction from and interpretation of the life-world. Scientific theories are constructions made of materials from the life-world. Because of this constructed nature of scientific theories, the theories are typically not intuitively verifiable, and thus must be checked against the life-world, which is, according to Husserl, "the universe of what is intuitable in principle," and "the realm of original self-evidence" (Crisis, §34d, 127). Everything we think and do is rooted in the life-world, so a truly radical philosophy, one that gets to the roots of things, must deal with it. (So the life-world is important in its own right, and not merely in its capacity as serving as a foundation for science.)

Husserl contends, further, that the life-world, prior to our theorizing about it or even conceptualizing it, is ordered. For example, our conscious experience, as William James famously points out, is not a series of discrete events, but rather a stream, in which one event gives way to another, with the latter being experienced in part under the aspect of its having succeeded that which preceded it. This suggests that we are not trapped within language or texts. Not all order is created by language. There is a pre-linguistic order to which our language must be adequate.

Husserl argues that our failure to ground our thinking in experience, in the life world, leads to a crazy oscillation between scientism and relativism. This comes about, in part, because we tend, falsely, to assume that consciousness is reducible to its natural causes—it is merely a thing among other things. For notice that the relationship between consciousness and other things is nothing at all like the relations obtaining among nonconscious things. On this conception, the world has its meaning in itself, quite independent of any meaning-conferring activities of consciousness. Alternatively (and this goes to the relativism part of the equation), we see the world as created by consciousness, or else see the world as utterly closed off to it, so that we only have access to a subjective representation of it. For Husserl, by contrast, the meaning (as opposed to the existence) of the world is essentially disclosed by consciousness. It is a world for consciousness, just as consciousness is essentially a consciousness of something other than itself. Subjectivity and objectivity are inseparable, and essentially co-determining. Meaning resides neither in consciousness nor in the world, but rather in the intentional relationship between the two. Thus, Husserl rejects both realism and idealism. Because both of these, he maintains, reduce one side of the subject-object relation to the other, they fail to do justice to the experiential co-givenness of consciousness and world.

As the sciences and other intellectual disciplines advance, they increasingly tend to lose themselves in the world of their own abstract conceptual and theoretical constructions. The life-world, which grounds these constructions, and which the constructions are originally intended to illuminate, is increasingly forgotten, as the constructions take on a life of their own. After a while, we recognize only what is conformable to our concepts and theories, and are blind to any reality or any content of experience that does not fit our theoretical grid.

The modern way of practicing and understanding science allows us to improve progressively in our ability to understand nature and to manipulate and dominate it technologically. But it obscures for us our understanding of ourselves in our relation to the life-world, and stands as an obstacle to our thinking about all kinds of value questions. It does so, not only by declaring such questions to be, if not meaningless, then at least ones about which objective truth is unattainable and inquiry is fruitless, but also, and perhaps more importantly, by displacing our pretheoretical, prescientific understanding of such matters and then failing to replace it with anything else, let alone something more adequate. Husserl proposes phenomenology as the discipline needed to provide an analysis of the essence of the life-world, giving us rigorous understanding by means of clarifying descriptions, to supply the proper foundations of modern science, and to build a bridge between the two, showing that the sciences are grounded in the life-world.

Static, Genetic, and Generative Phenomenology

Static phenomenology investigates the formal structures of consciousness, and the correlation between conscious acts and intentional objects, taking both the structures and the objects as given. Genetic phenomenology, which Husserl explores in the *Crisis*, takes up the question of how these structures and objects have emerged and developed over time, and how some types of experience tend to enable and to motivate others. Husserl speaks of the "sedimented" structure of experience, as manifested, for example, in habits—they have a definite history. *What* we see depends in part on *how* we see, and this, in turn, depends, at least in part, on past experience. Finally, generative phenomenology expands its focus to include the intersubjective constitution of the world, as through history, culture, and tradition. The life-world is the central focus of generative phenomenology. For the Husserl of the *Crisis*, the one who experiences is not a mere formal experience principle, but rather a living body, an experiencing subject formed and influenced by its history of past experiences, who shares cultural meanings and an intersubjective life-world with others.

An important element of genetic phenomenology is what Husserl calls "passive synthesis." This refers to the part of intentional constitution that precedes the more explicit, schematized, active synthesis that occurs when one thinks about something and forms judgments about it. Husserl claims that "hyletic data" (roughly, raw data of sensation) appear to consciousness neither as a formless, meaningless series waiting to be organized by focusing activities of consciousness, nor as meaningful whole that have already been organized by such activities. Rather, prior to such focusing acts the elements in my perceptual field undergo some degree of organization "passively," in accordance with psychological "rules of association," such as prominence in the perceptual field, contrast, homogeneity, and heterogeneity.

Husserl thus comes to abandon the static analysis of the atemporal correlation of intentional act with intentional object in favor of a genetic phenomenology. An act of consciousness has a beginning, an origin, and Husserl wishes to take account of this. He claims that every intentional act carries within itself the residue of earlier acts. It is on the basis of this that conscious experience has the degree of coherence and dynamic unity that it has. Consciousness relates its current experience to previous ones through association and temporal contiguity.

4

Ethics

Husserl published little on ethics. However, since he frequently chose to lecture and to give seminars on this topic,[1] his decision not to publish probably indicates a dissatisfaction with his work in this area, rather than a lack of interest in ethics on his part. In any case, because Husserl's published works do not contain lengthy discussions of ethics, the resources that Husserlian phenomenology can provide for the study of ethics, and of value theory more generally, are rarely recognized. In this chapter I will attempt to show that those underutilized resources (I will mention nine of them) are quite substantial, and that they fill in some quite noticeable gaps in the contemporary understanding of the range of possibilities for ethical theory.

A Richer Conception of "Experience"

Husserl's phenomenology is, among other things, concerned to describe the objects of experience without accepting the classical empiricists' prejudice that all experience is sensory in nature. Thus, there is an experience of the hateful, the horrible, and the lovable, and of justice and fairness, and of the good and the right. These things are not physical objects, and they are not perceived through

---

[1] Unfortunately, Husserl's lectures on ethics are unavailable in English translation. They have been posthumously published in German, however, as *Vorlesungen über Ethik und Wertlehre. 1908–1914* (*Lectures on Ethics and Value Theory: 1908–1914*), ed. Ullrich Melle (The Hague: Kluwer, 1988).

167

the senses, but they are objects of our experience nonetheless, and we do not typically encounter them within our experience as having been created, invented, or arbitrarily chosen by us.

A Richer Conception of "Object"

In opposition to the widely-held view that only spatio-temporal entities, of the sort susceptible to measurement and quantification, can legitimately qualify as "objects," Husserl, as we have seen, leads the way in arguing that the realm of objects also includes such things as numbers, logical principles, meanings, and experiences—anything that can genuinely be encountered in experience, and which can present itself in such a way as to make some of our judgments about it true and others false. These arguments, if sound, pave the way for the inclusion of values within the category of objects.

Phenomenological Description Reveals the Ubiquity of Value Experience

Descriptive phenomenology reveals that we constantly and ceaselessly encounter values, throughout our experience, even at its most ordinary. To be conscious and engaged with the world at all is to be persistently and repeatedly struck by the value qualities of things, actions, and states of affairs, which we find to be, not only good or bad, but also, more specifically, wonderful, disgusting, outrageous, admirable, courageous, cowardly, just, unjust, and so on.

Both action and perception, perhaps the two most basic modes of human existence, are heavily value-laden. To act is to make a change, to attempt to bring about a new state of affairs and to negate the current one. I open a window to enable me to enjoy the feeling of cool air and to escape the oppressive heat; I study something interesting so as to gain knowledge and to overcome a particular area of appalling ignorance; I rest and take prescribed medicine in an effort to achieve renewed good health and to terminate an illness; and so on. Virtually everything we do is based on some sense, whether explicitly formulated as such or not, of what experiences or states of affairs are good, worthwhile, to be pursued, and which are bad, not worthwhile, to be avoided or overcome. This is a fundamental datum of everyday human experience.

With regard to perception, recall Husserl's point, developed in connection with his analyses of intentionality, eidetic intuition, and constitution, that what we see is a function, in part, of selective focusing. My perceptual environment generally includes a limitless number of items that could be seen, but these items do not organize themselves in such a way as to determine which we will elevate to the foreground and which we will relegate to the background. Nor do the objects on which we do focus dictate *how* we will focus on them. Will we pay special attention to color, or shape, or size, or chemical composition, or historical significance, or utility for some practice, or what? Our focusing, and thus our perception, is typically guide by values. We focus on what is interesting, or useful, or important, at the expense of what is boring, useless, or trivial.

Intersubjectivity

In maintaining that numbers, logical principles, and meanings are objective, one of Husserl's points is that they can be attended to, and seen or grasped, by anyone. When you and I think and understand that "2 + 2 = 4," we are thinking and understanding the same thing. Moreover, while we might think about this merely signitively, it is possible for us to bring this arithmetical truth to full intuitive givenness, in which case we both encounter experientially the same ideal object.

The same holds for sense perception of physical objects. To see a tree is to see it as "there for anyone." It is a datum of my perceptual experience (one about which I may be mistaken—there is no claim of infallibility here) that you can see the tree too, or, if you are not here, that you could see it if you were. The case is quite otherwise with the imagined tree—this is one of the phenomenological differences between the experiences of sense perception and of imagination.

Husserl points out that the same is true for value experience. Some, but by no means all, perceptions of, and judgments about, values are given in experience as "there for anyone." J. N. Findlay, the translator of Husserl's *Logical Investigations*, explains this clearly:

> 'Values' and 'valuations' must . . . , it is plain, permit of a distinction, not always wholly clear, but certainly always felt even by moderately

sophisticated persons, between such values and valuations as are freely
allowed to be 'personal', peculiar to the individual, and neither
expected nor required to hold for other persons, and other valuations
and values which are felt to impose themselves with a certain necessity or ineluctability, which it is felt must impress itself on *anyone*, or
at least on anyone who reflects at all carefully on the matter. Thus the
valuation of sitting on beaches or eating meals in the open or wearing
flowers in one's hair are obviously by their very nature and structure
matters on which no agreement can be expected or demanded,
whereas the valuation of being happy, of enjoying freedom and power,
. . . of being truly informed as to the state of things, etc., are obviously, in varying degrees, values disagreement with which tends to
seem absurd, unfeasible, perverse, mistaken, wrong. . . . Our impression may be mistaken, but the utterances 'I like bondage, I rejoice in
being discriminated against, I value a state of deep unhappiness' seem
to involve a certain deep absurdity, . . . a certain vein of deep nonsense
of which philosophy must take account. . . . [T]hese distinctions are
genuinely 'part of the phenomena', whether or not we decide that
they can ultimately be sustained.[2]

Findlay explains, further, that ethical disagreements rarely turn on
disagreements about fundamental values, or about the basic sorts
of considerations that show an action to be defensible, or mandatory, or unjustified:

While there may be vast disagreement on the relative choiceworthi-
ness of various characters of activity, experiences or states of affairs,
and extremely great disagreement as to what is to be sought, chosen
or preferred in the individual case, there is none the less a consensus...as to the *characters* of things that confer on them their desirability or worthwhileness, or the reverse. While the detailed content
of desirable living may be infinitely debatable, or open to personal
decision, its general direction (or range of directions) seems much
more uncontroversial. We seem always ready to justify our preference
of *A* to *B* by holding *A* to be more agreeable to someone, or to afford
greater insight and mastery in some field, or to involve less arbitrariness than its rival: we should not try to justify it by holding it to be
more nearly a square, or to require a greater amount of chewing than
B, or to be a considerably greater distance west of Greenwich. . . .
While our first reasons in justification of our preferences vary

---

[2] *Axiological Ethics* (New York: St Martin's Press, 1970), 8–9.

immensely, and are not necessarily acceptable or intelligible to others, they are for that reason also felt to be insufficient, and we are soon ready to justify them by falling back on one or other of a comparatively small range of reasons, which are in general acknowledged by others as well as ourselves. And this general acknowledgment has a queer air of the self-justifying and self-evident, just as its refusal would have a strange air of the absurd. While the last reasons cited are not mere synonyms of desirability, and while there is consequently no mere tautology in holding something to be desirable on their account, they seem none the less to have more than a merely factual or customary foundation. It is not, it would seem, merely because we belong to a certain species, or to a certain social group, that certain reasons strike us as compelling or at least relevant: they seem to have a not readily *avoidable* appeal. That things strike us in this manner is undeniable. . . . It is for philosophy to probe these beguiling appearances to the bottom, and to see what foundations (if any) they may have. This task remains obligatory even if contemporary philosophy largely evades it.[3]

On this issue of the intersubjectively valid and binding character of at least some value judgments, and the related question of how to integrate it with the more personal and subjective aspects of value experience and choice, Husserl offers some interesting suggestions. He notes that the classical ethical theories do a poor job of accommodating the differences among people. This is because of the universalizing aspect of these theories. They tend to claim that the right thing for me to do in any given situation is also what anyone in my situation should do. Universalizability is explicitly a major element in Kant's theory of the categorical imperative, but one finds it also in utilitarianism (everyone should act so as to maximize happiness and to minimize unhappiness, so that anyone in my situation should do the same thing—the one action that would be optimific), and in virtue theory (everyone should strive to be courageous, kind, patient, witty, generous, and so on for the entire list of traits that it is good for a person to have). This sets up something of a paradox. On the one hand, we want everyone to be moral. We want everyone to refrain from murdering or assaulting others, we want everyone to be kind, rather than cruel, and so forth, and yet we don't want everyone to be the same. We want to

---

[3] *Values and Intentions* (New York: Humanities Press, 1961), 19–20.

preserve something of the rich diversity of human types, a diversity that clearly makes life much more interesting than it would be if people were interchangeable with one another.

Husserl's remarks on ethics, though fragmentary, address this problem, and offer a solution to it. He says that my moral duty, though objective (in the sense that it is truly binding on me, such that if I neglect it I do wrong, and it is not established by taste, opinion, or convention, but rather by a rational will) is not universal (that is, my moral duty may not be the same as that of another person). Or, to be more precise, while my duty is the same as everyone else's formally, it differs from everyone else's materially. Formally, my obligation is to live the best life that I possibly can, just as yours is to live the best life that you possibly can. But because we are different people, this will amount to two quite different obligations materially—what is best for me is not what is best for you, and vice versa. There are at least two reasons for this. First (and this point becomes accessible to Husserl only subsequent to his development of genetic phenomenology), different people have undergone different experiences, have been influenced by different cultural and historical forces, have developed different habits, and so forth. In short, they are materially different in many ways that are relevant to the question of what is good for them, and to the question of what can reasonably be expected or demanded of them. Secondly, Husserl suggests that many of us are called to a vocation. We feel drawn toward a particular arena of value (he offers the examples of academic philosophy, economics, or child rearing). This gives our life a *telos*, an overarching goal, a sense of meaning. Moreover, the choice of living in accordance with this vocation entails a set of moral imperatives that are to some extent unique to the individual. There is a way that I must live if I am to live authentically as the unique individual that I am.[4] Moreover, while Husserl is no cultural relativist, he does acknowledge that part of what makes me me is my membership in a particular community and my participation in a particular culture. Thus, my obligations are not determined solely by my distinctive character and vocation, as my community and wider culture may also legitimately place certain ethical demands on me (and these

---

[4] See, for example, Husserl's *Aufsätze und Vorträge* (1922–1937), ed. T. Nenon and H.R. Sepp (Dordrecht: Kluwer, 1989), 118.

may differ somewhat from those emanating from a different cultural tradition.)

The Eidetic and Phenomenological Reductions

Husserl's discussion of the eidetic reduction clarifies the point that in our daily experience, even at its most mundane, what we primarily experience and deal with are abstract, general principles, rather than the concrete particulars of sense experience. This helps to overcome a resistance to value inquiry based on common erroneous beliefs, such as that values are unreal because unexperienced (but rather, as if by default, in spite of all descriptive phenomenological evidence to the contrary, subjectively projected onto experience) or nonsensory. Moreover, Husserl's elaboration of the technique of free imaginative variation offers something by way of method in connection with the investigation of values.

The phenomenological reduction, by bracketing a focus on the alleged causes of the data of experience, so as to allow a focus on those data themselves, aids value inquiry by removing one of its biggest obstacles, namely, the belief that since values (allegedly) do not exist, they cannot cause or in any way explain the contents of value experience. This belief typically leads to a distortion of what is given in value experience—the relevant data are explained away and interpreted as subjective projections, so that the results of the inquiry can be made to square with the inquirer's ontological commitments.

Intuition

Husserl's argument that intuition, the seeing or grasping of something by inspecting it directly, need not be sensory in character, undermines the commonsense position that ethical truths are unavailable to us, since there is no way to ground them in sense experience. He tells us that the arguments of the *Logical Investigations*, and in particular, the chapter on "Sensuous and Categorial Intuition" in Investigation Six, open the way for a clarification, not only of logical self-evidence, but also "its parallels in the axiological and practical sphere" (LI 2, volume II, part 2 of the Second German Edition, Foreword to the second edition, 178).

Moreover, his argument that the nonsensory grasping of eidetic principles is more fundamental than the sensory perception of physical things (both because it is only by seeing them as exemplifying ideal principles that we can see anything meaningful through sense perception, and because universality and necessity can be found through eidetic insight, but not through sense perception) restores value inquiry to a status, like that of mathematics and logic, that is out of reach of the (noneidetic) empirical sciences. That happiness is intrinsically better than misery, and that unprovoked injury must be rectified and compensated, hold universally and necessarily, and can be readily seen to do so, with genuine insight, in a way that it is not true of empirical truths, such as that water freezes at 32 degrees Fahrenheit.

The Material A Priori

Husserl's defense of the claim that there are material a priori truths, and that we have intuitive access to them, opens up the possibility of investigating a priori ethical truths based on the natures of specific values. Recall that a priori truths are those that hold universally and necessarily. Many of these are formal, meaning that their truth does not depend on the specific nature of the objects to which they are applied. "2 + 2 = 4" applies equally well to anything that can be enumerated. Similarly, the logical truth that "if either A or B is true, but B is not true; therefore A is true," holds good, no matter what material content is plugged into "A" or "B." But the a priori truths that anything blue must be extended in space, or that anything blue must not simultaneously be red, are based on the material essences of colors. This insight opens the door to the possibility that there might be a priori truths, accessible to eidetic intuition, concerning the values of happiness, health, intelligence, knowledge, friendship, courage, and so forth.

The Critique of Psychologism

All of the arguments Husserl presents in his critique of psychologism in connection with logic carry over to the attempt to reduce values to subjective states of liking or approving.[5] For example, to reduce a priori truths about values to the contingent empirical truths of human

---

[5]   I develop this argument at length in *Challenging Postmodernism: Philosophy and the Politics of Truth* (Amherst, NY: Humanity Books, 2003).

psychology or biology (a widespread contemporary tendency—perhaps it should be called "biologism") is to commit the evidentiary fallacy of subordinating the more evident to the less evident.

Axiological Ethics

Axiology is the study of values. It is noteworthy that, while an axiological approach to ethics would appear to be an obvious candidate for a serious and promising approach to ethics, it is rarely attempted. The field of ethical theory has for many decades been dominated by just three types of theories: utilitarianism (actions are right if they bring about the best possible consequences, usually defined either in terms of happiness and unhappiness, or else in terms of the subjective preferences of those affected by the action), deontology (roughly, actions are right are wrong because of the intrinsic nature of the acts, as opposed to their consequences [which might vary from case to case]; we have specific duties to fulfill, either to others in general, or to those with whom we stand in a particular relation [such as promisor to promisee, creditor to debtor, doctor to patient, employer to employee, and so forth), and virtue theory (the focus is not on the rightness or wrongness of actions, but rather a person's character—the important thing is to develop excellent character traits, such as honesty, courage, kindness, patience, and the like, and to act habitually on the basis of these traits).[6] While all of these approaches have their merits, there certainly would seem to be room for an ethical theory that would be based on our insight into the natures and merits of the entire rich range of values that we encounter in our daily experience. Husserl's phenomenological investigations lay the groundwork for such a theory.

---

[6] These are not the only ethical theories currently receiving significant attention. For example, I might also mention social contract theory, which sees ethics as arising from a kind of implied contract, in which, for example, the basis for the wrongness of assault and theft is the simple fact that it is rational for me to agree to refrain from assaulting or stealing from you in exchange for your agreeing to refrain from doing the same to me. But neither this, nor any other of the current leading "contenders" among ethical theories is even remotely axiological in its basic orientation.

5

Polemics

Husserl's work is certainly not without its faults, and many of the criticisms that have been leveled against him over the years are perfectly reasonable. However, in this book my major concern is to help the reader to achieve a solid introductory grasp of phenomenology. Toward that end, I think it is more important to attempt to refute criticisms that rest on misunderstandings, and that stand in the way of an accurate assessment of Husserl's ideas, than it is to pursue those truly penetrating objections that legitimately do call for revisions and modifications of some of his claims. The criticisms I will address are representative of what I take to be some of the most widespread and influential of current objections to Husserl's project.

I take the first set of objections that I will consider from an article by Gary B. Madison, who characterizes Husserl's work as "the culmination of a long tradition which is in fact the dominant, orthodox tradition in philosophy. . . . This is the tradition which has conceived of philosophy as the search for the Truth, for Knowledge, for, in a word, *Science*." Madison goes on to say that "the most fundamental of all the values of [this] tradition, the metaphysical value par excellence, [is] the intrinsic value of *Truth*" (PE, 249).

In response I would offer two brief comments: (1) The meaning of the capital letters is never explained. (2) What would it mean to question the value of truth?

Madison continues: "It is . . . a curious state of affairs that while Husserl possessed such an uncanny sensitivity for the spiritual history of Western consciousness, he yet failed so completely to see that if (precisely as he says) the notions of science and cosmos were conceptual innovations effected in the history of our culture [by the Greeks in the seventh and sixth centuries BC], they cannot, for that very reason, be accorded a transcultural or supratemporal . . . value and be accepted unquestioningly" (PE 250–51).

Comment: This criticism rests on a logical fallacy. From the fact that a given idea, or truth claim, or value judgment emerged at a particular time or place, it in no way follows that its validity is limited to that time or place, or even that it fails to achieve a validity that is universal and objective. To think otherwise is to think that, for example, the historical specifics (whatever they might be) of the realization that the world is round, rather than flat, would entail that the truth of the claim that the world is not flat must be relativized. This is a variant of the genetic fallacy. The origins of an idea are irrelevant to its truth (or scope or application). And as for the last part of Madison's comment, there are ample reasons to avoid accepting any idea "unquestioningly," but it is far from clear that the fact that the idea, like all others, was generated at some particular place and in some particular time is one of them.

Madison: "Science results in a . . . dogmatism, for science is possible only on the dogmatic (i.e., unquestioned) assumption that the truth is attainable, that man can, at least in principle, attain *certainty*, that reality is intelligible. Thus Husserl's philosophy is a form of (scientific) dogmatism" (PE 253).

Comments: (1) It is far from obvious that the very possibility of science requires it to assume dogmatically that truth is attainable. Must I assume, dogmatically, as a precondition for my undertaking the activity of taking a shot at a basket with a basketball, that I might make the shot? Might not the mere hope that I am capable of doing so be sufficient to justify my making this effort? Similarly, might not the hope (rather than the dogmatic, unquestioned assumption) that reality is intelligible and that truth about it is attainable, be sufficient to warrant a project of scientific investigation? (2) Just as the sight of the basketball going through the basket, together with the satisfying "swish" sound, after the ball leaves my hand, might well be taken as compelling evidence that I can indeed make a shot in basketball, are none of the results of scientific investigations to be understood as evidence that at least some aspects of reality are intelligible, and that some truths about them are attainable? (3) If reality is unintelligible, and truth is unattainable, then what would be the status of any claim that this is so? We couldn't after all, know it to be true. (4) While Husserl does sometimes aim for certainty, frequently he does not, as in his recognition that the evidence of the senses is never adequate for certainty, since physical objects are always given in profile. Moreover, science generally does not aim for certainty. Indeed, it is a hallmark of the empirical sciences that conclusions are always to be understood as tentative, provisional, subject to revision in the light of future evidence.

Madison: A "Greek," a "rationalist," an "idealist" (labels Madison applies to Husserl)

> is struck with awe when he contemplates the magnificent order of the world. This wonder is provoked by an experience of the world as *cosmos*, a marvelously ordered Totality. This type of wonder naturally culminates in *science*, for the question it evokes concerns the workings of nature. The idealist is provoked to ask: What is the secret of this wondrous order, what are the intelligible laws at work here? When, however, the "existentialist" asks, with Heidegger: "Why is there something rather than simply nothing at all?" he is experiencing the world in a radically different manner. For what awes him is not the *order* of the world but, more radically still, the fact that there *is* a world and not just *nothing*. This is an experience of the very real possibility of the *not-being* of the world, an experience not of its intrinsic rationality but of its utter contingency. It is an experience not of something but of nothing, not of hidden meaning but of fundamental, menacing absurdity. *It culminates not in science but in a heightened awareness of the final impossibility of all science.* What the "existentialist" experiences in wonder is the fact of the world's being, the world's *facticity*, and he experiences this fact as something fundamentally *opaque*. (PE 257)

Comments: (1) I agree that existence might, for all we know, be contingent, and that it is, in any case, unexplainable. The argument is simple. All explanation presupposes existence; therefore, existence itself is unexplainable. (This is the fatal flaw in the cosmological argument for the existence of God. If existence demands an explanation, so we posit God to explain the existence of the universe, then surely the existence of God also demands an explanation. To explain anything that exists, it would seem that one must always do so by citing an existing cause. Therefore, existence itself cannot be explained.) But it is unclear in what way or sense the recognition of this point, or, more to the point, the feeling of awe that might inspire the thought process leading up to it, is "an experience of nothing." The fallacy is the same as one finds in St. Augustine's argument against suicide, in which he claims that there is something logically absurd about the choice of nonexistence: "to choose nothing is not to choose." But if someone offers me a choice of coffee or tea, and I say, "no thanks, I'll have nothing," there is no logical absurdity in this, and I have made a choice—the choice of drinking nothing. To experience the contingency of the world is not to experience nothing, but rather something: the contingency of the world. (2) Why should any of this entail the impossibility of science? It is as if our failure to understand why, in some big metaphysical sense, there are dogs (or, better yet, our recognition of the contingency of the existence of dogs—the fact that the world might perfectly well have never contained any dogs) must for some reason preclude us from coming to understand anything about the "logic" of a dog's body—how the heart pumps blood through its veins, how the dog's brain and central nervous system allow it to feel pain, what is the function of its stomach, and so on. (3) The whole point of Husserl's phenomenological reduction was precisely to bracket huge metaphysical questions such as those concerning the origins and existence of the world, so as to enable us instead to focus on the logic and content of experience.

Madison:

> As a "philosopher of infinite tasks," Husserl concedes that a "total science" is a *de facto* impossibility, but he nonetheless would want to say that this does not invalidate the quest for such a science. What Husserl and the "sophisticated absolutist" do not see is that if the ideal of Science is not *actually* attainable, the search for it can only be, when all is said and done, a senseless pursuit after a meaningless will-o'-the-wisp. (PE 268, note 103)

Comment: So far as I can see, Madison gives no argument for this conclusion. Against it one can note that there are indefinitely many human activities that are worth doing—playing a sport, playing a musical instrument, studying a subject, pursuing a relationship, and so forth—about which it can truthfully said that perfection is utterly unattainable, but that pursuit of perfection can lead one to become progressively better at the activity, and that pursuing the activity endlessly, over the course of an entire life, is richly rewarding.

Madison approvingly quotes Hans-Georg Gadamer as saying, in opposition to Husserl's conception of philosophy, that "philosophical thinking is not science at all.... There is no claim of definitive knowledge with the exception of one: the acknowledgement of the finitude of human being in itself."[1]

Comments: (1) One can readily agree that human being is finite. But it is not clear that such finitude precludes the attainment of truth. Finite beings cannot do everything. It doesn't follow from this that they can't do anything, or that the establishment of some truths is one of the achievements beyond their reach. (2) Note the utter arbitrariness of Gadamer's exception. Why is this the *only* thing we can definitively know? Is it *more* evident than any other claim whatsoever? Is it more clear, evident, and obvious that human being is finite, and that, as a consequence, truth (with one exception) is unavailable to us, than it is that $2 + 2 = 4$, that elephants are heavier than beetles, that health is better than sickness, that LeBron James is a good basketball player, that colored things are extended in space, that sounds vary in their duration and loudness, that Australia is located in the southern hemisphere, that some interesting paintings do not feature bullfighters, that Descartes lived before Husserl did, and so on endlessly? It seems to me that Gadamer's exception is granted solely for the purpose of avoiding a contradiction. He wants to say that we know nothing, realizes that he cannot, without contradiction, claim to know *that*, and thus recognizes one exception to his general skeptical claim. But if human reason is capable of transcending its finitude sufficiently to recognize the truth that it (human reason) is finite, surely it is also capable of recognizing many other far more accessible truths as well.

Madison also speaks of Husserl's idea that philosophy, conceived, as he does, as a strict science, is an infinite task. Madison comments that "such a view can be very appealing for it offers people an assurance that Meaning, Truth, and Value do exist (as infinite Telos), and at the same time it also respects what they

---

[1] "The Science of the Life-World," in *Analecta Husserliana*, vol. 2, ed. Anna-Teresa Tymieniecka (Dordrecht: D. Reidel, 1972), 185.

nonetheless know to be a fact, namely, the *relativity* of all factual, finite knowledge" (PE 254).

Comments: (1) To what is our knowledge of the matters mentioned in the previous paragraph relative? Madison does not say. (2) What makes this a "fact," and what is the status of the claim that it *is* a fact? (3) How do we *know* this?

Despite Madison's rather harsh criticisms of Husserl, he suggests that his philosophy should be viewed as the culmination of the dominant tradition in the history of Western philosophy. This is the tradition, which Madison calls "rationalist" and "idealist," and which conceives of philosophy as, like science, engaged in the quest for truth. Its major figures include Plato, Descartes, the philosophers of the Enlightenment, and Hegel. With reference to this tradition, Madison remarks that his criticisms of Husserl should not "be interpreted as an attempt to disparage him or to deny his historical greatness. Husserl is without doubt one of the greatest philosophers of all time, philosophy being understood in the traditional sense . . ." (PE 262–63).

Comment: So if Madison's estimation of Husserl's place in the mainstream of Western philosophy is correct, but if his criticisms of Husserl and that philosophical tradition are, as I have argued, unsound, this leaves Husserl in a rather exalted position. (Note also that Husserl is "*without doubt*" one of the greatest philosophers of all time—even though the big problem with him is that he is naïve enough to think that some things can be known "without doubt!" Indeed, in this essay Madison peppers several of his hundreds of truth claims with such locutions as "of course" and "in fact.")

The other objection I wish to counter has been recently articulated by a former professor of mine, John McCumber, who, in spite of my disagreement with him on this issue, I greatly esteem. McCumber's objection is aimed at Husserl's theory of eidetic intuition. McCumber mentions the possibility that one might via eidetic variation "come up with *eidē* of things like tables, moral acts, and human beings." He then comments: "What controls will there be on this? The potential for abuse is enormous."[2]

McCumber does not say what kind of controls he would like to see placed on eidetic intuition (or who should be responsible for

---

[2] *Time and Philosophy* (Montreal: McGill-Queen's University Press, 2011).

implementing those controls, or why *that* wouldn't create a potential for abuse), or why the potential for abuse is enormous, or what the nature of that abuse would be. So some of my comments may not be responsive to his concerns. But here goes.

(1) *Anything* can be abused. Language can be abused (people tell lies). Friendship can be abused (as when one takes advantage of a friend's warm feelings for oneself). Feet can be abused (as one uses them to kick someone). But this does not mean that language, friendship, and feet are bad things, or that they are illegitimate in some way, or that we should abandon them, or that controls should be put on them, or anything of that sort. To be sure, some things should be banned or controlled or avoided because they pose enormous risks (nuclear weapons come readily to mind). But we need some sort of argument as to why a philosopher's claim that we are capable of achieving some insights into the essences of tables, moral acts, and human beings is dangerous. What specific threat does it pose?

(2) Note that there is nothing remotely authoritarian about Husserl's doctrine of eidetic intuition. He does not say that anyone should take on faith his, or anyone else's, testimony about the deliverances of eidetic insight. His position is that if you don't see what he sees in any given case, you would be well advised to reject his claims. (But that is very different from rejecting what he says on principle, even though you see it just as clearly as he does, on the grounds that the seeing that you and he share is inherently suspect, perhaps because there is always the possibility that appeals to such seeing might be abused.)

(3) On a related note, Husserl insists that the objects of eidetic insight are publicly available to everyone. They are not private. The ideal meaning content "whatever is colored is extended in space" is the same when you think and grasp it as it is when I do so. We do not have to trust anything that either one of us might assert on the basis of a claim of insight into something to which we allegedly have unique access.

(4) Husserl obviously does not propose that anyone who disagrees with him on some matter of alleged eidetic truth should be persecuted for his heresy. But in fairness, perhaps the worry is not that philosophers will directly hurt anyone as a result of having false beliefs about the essences of tables, moral acts, and human beings, but rather that people who actually wield political power

might do so if they are influenced by the philosophers. While there is no denying that power-wielding persons who have false beliefs about moral acts and human beings are capable of doing a great deal of damage, the only way to stop philosophers from inadvertently contributing to such harm is to demand that they stop philosophizing. Surely there is value in honest, informed, philosophical and ethical inquiry, even though there is always the possibility that such inquiry will result in the publication of wrong views, which then influence those in power, who then, as a result, cause harm.

(5) One worries that complaints like McCumber's might be based on a misconception as to what sorts of claims Husserl thinks can be justified on the basis of the evidence of eidetic intuition. Recall that such intuition cannot give us knowledge of anything factual. It cannot inform us about events in history, or about causes and effects in the realm of spatio-temporal objects. Nor can it tell us what conclusion to draw on any complex issue, where many different strands of evidence and argument must be assembled, sorted through, organized, and evaluated. Many-sided issues can't be intuitively "seen," for the same reason that physical objects cannot be seen in their entirety—they are given only in profile. Nor does eidetic intuition tell us anything vague and mystical, such as that "reality is one," or "the key is to drift downstream," or anything like that. The deliverances of eidetic intuition tend, on the contrary, to be simple and obvious: "$a + 1 = 1 + a$;" "if a is taller than b, and b is taller than c, then a is taller than c;" "health is better than sickness;" "any sound has a certain pitch, timbre, loudness, and duration;" "excellence in a work of art is compatible with its inclusion of a variety of different subject matters;" and so on. Does the claim to know such things through direct insight carry with it an enormous potential for abuse?

(6) Some people who issue criticisms of this sort do so from the mistaken belief that a defense of, and judicious reliance on, intuition is incompatible with the use of reason, argument, and evidence. But intuition does not preclude these valuable tools. To the contrary, logic, reasoning, arguments, evidence—all of these can be used to *facilitate* clear, intuitive, insight. To be sure, intuition, by definition, is direct. To know something intuitively is to know it on the basis of directly inspecting it. But direct inspection can be unfocused, unclear, obscured by some obstacle, attempted at too

great a distance, or defective in some other way. Rational arguments can be used so as to bring the object in question into clear focus, so that it can be seen intuitively. So the commonly-heard complaint about intuition, namely, that if two intuitionists disagree, all they can do is throw up their hands and call each other blind, is false. If you think my intuition is wrong, you can use arguments to show that there is an aspect of the thing that I am looking at that I have overlooked; or to show that I am confusing it with another thing that differs from it in some subtle, but crucial, way; or to show that I am confusing an aspect or an implication of the thing with the thing itself; and so forth. The situation is directly analogous to that of sense perception—the other, less controversial, kind of "intuition" that Husserl recognizes. If I believe that there is a cardinal on a branch of a tree in the backyard, I typically do so on the basis of intuition, that is direct inspection—I see, with my eyes, that the cardinal is there. My belief is not based on any kind of argument or indirect evidence. But if you do not see the cardinal, I do not give up the case as hopeless, since it involves intuition. Rather, I try to help you to see it: "It's on the third branch from the top, toward the end of the branch; no, not that tree, the one right by the fence," and so forth. That is what good arguments do—they enable you to focus on the right thing in the right way, so that you can see it, too.

(7) Finally, is there no concern about self-referential inconsistency here? Why is there a worry that claiming to know the essence of a table on the basis of eidetic intuition might be abused, so that it should be "controlled" in some way, but no apparent worry about claiming to *know* that such claims might be abused and should therefore be controlled? What is the basis and the warrant for *that* claim?[3]

---

[3] For Husserl's own response to a similar criticism, see Ideas I, §79, 188, author's footnote 18.

6

Successors

Husserl was spectacularly successful in attracting converts to phenomenology. However, very few of them worked as faithful disciples of his. Rather, they saw in his ideas, techniques, and basic approach, something that they could use in pursuing their own individual projects and visions. Indeed, it is hard to think of any philosopher who has inspired such a large and distinguished group of independent and original thinkers.

Since I have chosen to base this introduction to phenomenology primarily on its founder, Husserl, I have space only to offer a brief sketch or overview of four of the other important thinkers who have, to some degree, adopted the phenomenological approach in their work. It is my hope that these short introductory remarks, coupled with my suggestions for further reading (to follow) will inspire readers to pursue some of these thinkers in greater detail on their own.

Max Scheler (1874–1928)

Though Scheler was, during his lifetime, one of the most famous and widely read of contemporary European philosophers, he is considerably less well known today. The Nazi suppression of his work from 1933 to 1945 (he was Jewish, and an outspoken critic of Nazism and fascism) may have contributed to this neglect.

Scheler's *Formalism in Ethics and Non-Formal Ethics of Values* is perhaps the first major work of *applied* phenomenology, and remains the most important work on ethics ever written from a phenomenological perspective.

Scheler contends that the most basic acts of consciousness, which are foundational to all others, are emotional responses to values. Even to notice something is an evaluative act, that of taking an interest in the thing observed. The comprehension of values is, for Scheler, foundational to all existence. He claims that in every act there is either attraction or repulsion, a "draw" or a "push," that usually goes unnoticed. All thinking and all perceiving is preceded by this "value-ception."

Scheler's ethical theory is based on material a priori value judgments (an idea that is discussed in the chapter on ethics, above). Here are some examples of extremely basic conclusions about values. We know these to be true a priori, Scheler says, by means of intuition. They are not analytic truths, nor are they accessible to the senses, or arrived at inductively:

1. The existence of a positive value is itself a positive value.

2. The nonexistence of a positive value is itself a negative value.

3. The existence of a negative value is itself a negative value.

4. The nonexistence of a negative value is itself a positive value.

Scheler develops his own ethical theory by means of a detailed critique of Kant's theory. A well-known weakness of Kant's formalistic ethics is that it fails to address conflicting duties. Kant offers criteria by which we can determine that we have a duty to do A, and also that we have a duty to do B. But he does not tell us what to do if we find ourselves in a situation in which the only way to carry out our duty to do A is to violate our duty to do B (or vice versa). He tells us what our duties are, but offers little help as to how to rank them, so as to resolve conflicts between them. But a material value ethics that establishes an order of ranks among values could, in principle, solve this problem. Scheler attempts to provide this.

He offers five criteria for determining the order of ranks among competing values:

1. *Permanence.* The more enduring a value, the higher it stands in comparison to other values. Some values persist throughout history, withstanding all changes in fashion and taste. This is a mark of their higher status.

2. *Indivisibility.* The nutritive value of a loaf of bread is quite limited in that, if many people are to partake of this value, the loaf must be divided up. Those who do not receive a slice fail to receive any benefit at all; and the nutritive value of the loaf is very quickly exhausted entirely. In contrast, the aesthetic value of a publicly accessible great work of art does not need to be divided in this way. Moreover, it excludes no one, and is inexhaustible.

3. *Independence.* A value is higher the less it is dependent for its own worth on the existence of another value. The value of a tool, being dependent on an end, is less than the value of an intrinsic value (such as happiness or good health).

4. *Depth of satisfaction.* The realization of some values brings about a greater depth of satisfaction then does the realization of other values, indicating that the former have a higher status.

5. *Noncontingency.* A value is higher the less its value is contingent on the existence of beings of a certain sort. For example, the value of pleasure is contingent on the existence of sensitive, feeling beings.

Based on these criteria, Scheler offers the following hierarchy of values (from lowest to highest):

1. *Sensible values:* values of the agreeable and the disagreeable, of pleasure and pain, of enjoyment and suffering. Note that while people may differ in what (materially) they find agreeable or disagreeable, there is no relativism in the observation that the agreeable, as such, is better than the disagreeable.

2. *Values of life:* values of health and vigor (at one end) and values of disease and weakness (at the other).

3. *Spiritual values:* These include (a) the values of the beautiful and the ugly, and of aesthetic values in general; (b) the values of right and wrong, and of justice and injustice; and (c) the values of pure cognition of the truth. (These values have nothing to do with the body.)

4. *The values of the holy and the unholy:* values of the intuition of "absolute objects."

According to Scheler, good and evil are not material values. Rather, "good" has to do with the will to realize higher values, while "evil" consists in choosing the lower value over the highway. The moral values "good" and "evil" thus belong to a different logical order than do the material, nonmoral values described above.

Finally, "values" must be distinguished from "goods," that is, bearers or carriers of values. The latter are transient, variable, and relative in ways that the former are not. Friendship is a value, and its value does not change. But a bearer of this value, a particular friend, might die, or turn into an enemy.

Martin Heidegger (1889–1976)

Though Heidegger is an enormously controversial figure, he is without doubt currently the most influential, and the most widely read and studied, of all writers whose work might reasonably be characterized as phenomenological.

One of Heidegger's most basic criticisms of Husserl is that Husserl's project seems to assume (at least in his early and middle work, prior to the *Crisis*) that our primary or original attitude in our encounters with whatever is real is that of a scientist. But this assumption seems inaccurate. We do not initially confront things as contemplative theoreticians, or in any other primarily cognitive mode. Rather, we are always already doing things, in the midst of projects, with practical concerns. Science and philosophy are somewhat specialized projects, undertaken against a background of a more primitive, value-charged (though Heidegger would reject that language), practical engagement with the world.

Accordingly, Heidegger draws a distinction between entities that are "present-at-hand" and those that are "ready-to-hand." Present-at-hand items are "there," present to consciousness, in such a way as to be readily available for being thought about, scrutinized, theorized about, conceptualized. In short, they present themselves for intellectual inspection. Ready-to-hand items, on the other hand, are used unselfconsciously as tools or instruments. We typically drink, write, and go through doors without so much as noticing, let alone theorizing about, the cup, pen, and doorknob that we use in accomplishing these everyday tasks. Heidegger claims that readiness-to-hand is a more fundamental mode of experiencing objects than is theorizing about present-at-hand entities.

He criticizes Husserl for (allegedly) reversing this order, and treating presence at hand as the primary mode. This point is part of Heidegger's larger criticism that Husserl (allegedly) overrates thought and underrates practical, nontheoretical, activities when it comes to his account of our being-in-the-world.

Another innovation of Heidegger's is the turning of phenomenology in the direction of "hermeneutics," a term that refers to the principles of textual interpretation. One needs hermeneutics especially when dealing with an especially difficult text. Heidegger's hermeneutical turn, then, is motivated largely by his conviction that phenomena, like a recalcitrant text, are not typically simply there to be seen, fully accessible to a purely descriptive phenomenology. Rather, what is needed is a method for uncovering what had hitherto been covered up and hidden.

Here Heidegger builds on some of Husserl's findings, such as that physical objects can be seen only in profile (so that much of them remains hidden from view), and that events unfold over time (so that portions of them have already happened or have not happened yet, so that they are not available for direct inspection now). Heidegger emphasizes that this problem of the absence, the "hiddenness," of things is exacerbated by the fact that many things are covered up by our passive, uncritical acceptance of theories that render them invisible. Others are neglected because we have simply forgotten to ask about them or look for them. Many of these concealing forces are not natural, but rather are the products of history and culture. For example, the history of philosophy has developed in a certain way that could have been otherwise. Some questions have been asked, followed up, and continually investigated; others have been ignored. Some influential theories have been revelatory; others obfuscatory. What is called for, then, is excavation, and not mere looking and seeing. Partly for these reasons, Heidegger rejects Husserl's call for presuppositionlessness, and contends that we cannot help but begin where we are, as historically conditioned beings.

In his most important phenomenological work, *Being and Time*, Heidegger announces that he will investigate the question of the meaning of Being. While we seem to have some idea of what it means to say that a thing does or does not exist, we do not have a very clear idea of what Being itself—that in terms of which individual beings can meaningfully and truthfully be said to be—is.

The nature of the investigation of the meaning of Being is to be phenomenological, in that Being will be pursued through the manner in which it appears. But on the other hand, to the extent that it is hidden, the phenomenological investigation will also have to incorporate a hermeneutic dimension.

Heidegger's strategy is to approach the question of Being by interrogating the mode of being of Dasein (an ordinary German term, literally meaning "being-there," but which Heidegger uses to refer to human existence). For it is part of the being of Dasein, according to Heidegger, to question Being, to experience anxiety in the face of Being, to dwell in Being, to be open to it. We have a kind of inarticulate awareness of it that can be exploited, and sharpened by means of phenomenological investigation.

This strategy leads Heidegger to devote many pages to the description of human experience. Much to Heidegger's dismay, these passages have often been read as sociology, anthropology, or social commentary—as stinging indictments of the shallowness, pettiness, and mindless conformity that characterizes so much of modern life. They have also often been read as instances of existentialism (or existential philosophy), that is, philosophy that is concerned with the fundamental issues of human existence (for example, freedom, work, love, and death). Indeed, the term "existential phenomenology" has been widely adopted to refer to work, such as that of Heidegger, Sartre, and Merleau-Ponty, that combines the phenomenological method (careful description of the essential structures of lived experience) with the existential subject matter just mentioned. Heidegger has consistently rejected such interpretations, claiming instead that his discussions of the being of Dasein are strictly limited in their focus to the illumination of his ultimate ontological concern, that of uncovering the meaning of Being.

Thus, one of the difficulties in understanding Heidegger is that he insists that there is no ethical or evaluative aspect to his investigations in *Being and Time*, in spite of the fact that he chooses a value-charged vocabulary in explaining his findings.

For example, he distinguishes between authentic and inauthentic ways of being. If I lose myself in the crowd and passively go along with what others do and think, I live inauthentically, whereas if I think for myself, and act independently based on my own principles, which are in turn grounded in my full engagement with my own experience, then I live authentically.

He also suggests that inauthenticity, the flight from oneself, and the absorption of oneself into the anonymous crowd, can be an expression of one's refusal to face his or her own inevitable death—something that happens to each of us individually (in the sense that no one else can die my death for me, in contrast to doing my job for me, or cleaning my house for me, or raising my children for me). Recognition of one's own impending and inescapable death leads to anxiety, which one flees by melting into the undifferentiated mass of humanity. Death is something that awaits me as an individual, so I flee it by trying to evade my individuality. Authenticity, by contrast, goes hand-in-hand with resolutely facing one's own death.

Jean-Paul Sartre (1905–1980)

Sartre is the most versatile writer to have emerged from the phenomenological movement, as his enormous body of work includes novels, plays, short stories, biographies, essays on literary and art criticism (and scores of other topics), and journalism, in addition to his philosophical works. He was awarded the Nobel Prize for Literature in 1964. In a rather typical act of defiant independence, he declined the award.

The first several of Sartre's many philosophical writings are specimens of either theoretical or applied phenomenology. And in an interview conducted just five years before his death he reaffirms his phenomenological convictions, asserting that he had "never" left phenomenology, and that he "continues to think in those terms."[1] In response to the question, "was the real discovery, in terms of importance to you, Husserl?," he replied, "Yes...you're quite right, it was Husserl."[2]

Rejecting the prevalent criticism of Husserl's phenomenology as idealist in character, Sartre counters that "for centuries we have not felt in philosophy so realistic a current."[3] He explains that

---

[1] "An Interview with Jean-Paul Sartre," conducted and translated by Michel Rybalka et al., in *The Philosophy of Jean-Paul Sartre*, ed. Paul Arthur Schilpp (La Salle, IL: Open Court, 1981), 24.

[2] *Sartre by Himself*, trans. Richard Seaver (New York: Outback Press, 1978) [1976], 25–26.

[3] *The Transcendence of the Ego*, trans. Forrest Williams and Robert Kirkpatrick (New York: Noonday Press, 1957) [1937], 104.

Husserl's project of descriptive fidelity to what is given in experience utterly explodes the prevalent view that value-qualities do not really exist in things, but rather are projections based on our subjective reactions to them. To the contrary, Sartre maintains,

> it is things which abruptly unveil themselves to us as hateful, sympathetic, horrible, lovable. Being dreadful is a *property* of this Japanese mask, an inexhaustible and irreducible property which constitutes its very nature—and not the sum of our subjective reactions to a piece of sculptured wood.
>
> Husserl has restored to things their horror and their charm. He has restored to us the world of artists and prophets: frightening, hostile, dangerous, with its havens of mercy and love.[4]

If that description sounds a bit too dramatic to apply to the work of Husserl, it is perhaps better read as an account of what Sartre himself does on the basis of Husserl's inspiration. For Sartre's own richly detailed and innovative phenomenological analyses of imagination, embodiment, self-awareness, intersubjectivity, intentionality, and the emotions, among other topics, are not noted for their understatement. When Sartre errs, it is almost always on the side of provocative exaggeration.

As a philosopher, Sartre is probably best known for his phenomenology of freedom. He contends that it is in the experience of anguish that we are most directly conscious of our freedom. Sartre distinguishes between anguish and fear. I am fearful when I am conscious of an external threat. In one of his examples, I am walking in the mountains and suddenly find myself on the edge of an abyss without a guardrail. I experience fear when I recognize that an external force, such as a sudden gust of wind or a shifting of the dirt or rocks beneath my feet might cause me to plunge to my death. But in response, I might plan to proceed slowly and with maximum caution, paying careful attention to each step and noting at all times what is happening with the wind, the dirt and rocks, and any other potentially threatening elements of my environment. Knowing my own abilities, I might then conclude that there is no need for fear. So long as I am careful I will be fine.

---

[4] "Intentionality: A Fundamental Idea of Husserl's Phenomenology," trans. Joseph P. Fell, *Journal of the British Society for Phenomenology* 1, no. 2 (May 1970) [1939].

The problem, however, is that I cannot know now that I will be careful at the crucial moment. Perhaps, after having traveled a bit without incident, I will unwittingly begin to relax and to become overconfident, and thus cease to remain adequately vigilant. To be sure, I can promise myself now that I will not let my guard now. But how can I know now that my future self will keep this promise? My concern that I will fail to keep this promise is an example of anguish. It is not a worry about an external threat, but rather an awareness of, and apprehension about, my own freedom.

In part because we wish to escape our anguish, we frequently deceive ourselves about our freedom. This is "bad faith," a widespread phenomenon that Sartre describes and analyzes in detail, giving several examples. Bad faith is a paradoxical phenomenon, since it is hard to see how I could possibly succeed in deceiving myself. For bad faith is not simply a mistaken belief, but rather a (successful) attempt to persuade myself to believe something that in fact I don't believe. And yet, in spite of its apparent impossibility, it seems evident that bad faith occurs, and is even a widespread phenomenon. How can this be?

Sartre's answer to this enigma is based on his observation that we are always at a distance from ourselves. For example, I am temporally distant from my past and future. This is one source of my anguish. As in the case of the mountain climber example, I cannot now control or guarantee the actions of my future self. Or, to go at it from the other direction, I find that I am now free in the face of, and unbound by, past vows I may have undertaken, or promises I have made to myself. (Sartre illustrates this with a famous and dramatic example of a gambler who has taken a vow not to gamble anymore. When then confronted with the gaming table, he finds, in his anguish, that the vow has created no barrier at all, and that nothing prevents him from gambling again.)

We are also somewhat divided from ourselves in the sense that we are syntheses of facticity and transcendence (or freedom). "Facticity," roughly, refers to the factual givens of my situation— I am old or young, male or female, married or single, tall or short, healthy or sick, and so on. Sartre's point is that I am never simply identical with my facticity, since I am always hurtling past it as I act in the world. A table is simply a table, but a smoker, for example (as defined by facticity), might be in the midst of living intensely the project of not smoking. Unlike a rock or a table, I am conscious of some of my facticities, and can adopt attitudes toward them and undertake projects with respect to them.

The instability of my ambiguous existence as a synthesis of facticity and freedom facilitates bad faith because it allows me to deceive myself without having to lie to myself in such a bald fashion as to make my lie unbelievable. Bad faith is subtler than such outright lying, since it can be accomplished by a sliding between half-truths. If I wish not to confront the uglier aspects of my facticity, I can choose to look at myself in terms of my freedom: "I'm not a smoker; I'm the courageous guy who is quitting." And if I wish to evade the responsibilities that flow from my freedom, I can define myself in terms of my facticity: "You can't blame me. This is how I was raised. I don't know any better. I can't help it. It's not my fault."

Sartre argues, on the basis of a detailed phenomenological analysis, that freedom is inescapable. Every situation provides choices, and the choice not to choose is itself a choice. Responsibility cannot be evaded by passing it off onto others. If I defend my choices by pointing out that I am merely following the law, or the customs of my culture, or my boss's orders, or God's commands, then I am still responsible for choosing to do so. To take the last example, if I say that I am simply following God on some issue, I am still the one who is responsible for determining that there is a God, that I have correctly identified who is God, that God is indeed good, that I know what God's position on this issue is, and that the correct criterion for moral action is that the action follows God's position on the matter. So I'm up to my neck in inescapable responsibility.

Further, freedom is implicated in every perception, insofar as perception always involves a selective focusing not determined by the perceptual field itself. I have the freedom to focus on this or that, or even to move away from the mode of perception entirely, and instead imagine or remember something. Sartre argues, very much in a Husserlian vein, that when I am in the perceptual mode, what I see is largely determined by my projects and interests, as when, to return to an earlier example, the geologist, the landscape artist, and the camper in need of a hammer, each see quite different things when they look at the same rock. Sartre adds to this analysis that these projects and interests are often themselves to a large degree freely chosen.

Finally, in order to connect Sartre with earlier discussions of material value ethics in general, and Scheler's work in particular, I would point out that Sartre, in a posthumously published work, offers a sketch of an axiological ethical theory. He argues that "values reveal freedom," that freedom is the highest value, that the other highest values are those that are most closely connected to freedom, and that "any ordering of values has to lead to freedom." Accordingly, he calls for a classification of values in a hierarchy such that freedom increasingly appears in it" (NFE, 9). In Sartre's classification, the highest values, in ascending order, are passion, pleasure, criticism and the demand for evidence, responsibility, creation, and, at the very top, generosity (NFE, 470).

Maurice Merleau-Ponty (1908–1961)

Merleau-Ponty is perhaps the most scientifically oriented of all of the major phenomenologists. His work engages regularly with scientific findings in psychology and linguistics, among other disciplines. As a consequence, contemporary philosophers who are attempting to build a bridge between phenomenology and current scientific research (in neuroscience, for example), make extensive use of his work.

Merleau-Ponty argues that perception is primary, in that it is foundational to all knowledge, preceding both culture and science. As an excellent and pioneering student of the late (and often then unpublished) works of Husserl, he provides a clear explanation of one of his major sources of inspiration for this idea, namely, Husserl's concept of the life-world:

> The whole universe of science is built upon the world as directly experienced, and if we want to subject science itself to rigorous scrutiny and arrive at a precise assessment of its meaning and scope, we must begin by reawakening the basic experience of the world of which science is the second-order expression. . . . To return to things themselves is to return to that world . . . in relation to which every scientific schematization is an abstract and derivative sign-language, as is geography in relation to the country-side in which we have learnt beforehand what a forest, or a prairie or a river is. (PP, viii–ix)

But Merleau-Ponty rejects the claim, found in many of Husserl's works, that everything experienced can be analyzed either as an act of consciousness or as the object of a conscious act. For example, we seem to experience time, to be aware of it, without its being analyzable as either act or object.

Probably Merleau-Ponty's most important contribution, however, is his phenomenological account of embodiment. Drawing on previous work on this topic by both Husserl (in the second, then unpublished, volume of *Ideas*) and Sartre (in *Being and Nothingness*), but developing it in greater detail, Merleau-Ponty argues that the body is a locus of subjectivity. It is the site of our knowledge of the world. We do not experience our body as merely an object like other objects in space. Nor is it the case that the body is inhabited by a disembodied mind that directs it. Rather, the body itself is conscious, intelligent, and free. We do not so much take up space as inhabit it.

Because of his analysis of embodiment, Merleau-Ponty holds, in opposition to Sartre, that we are not perfectly free when it comes to the way in which we focus on, and thus structure, a perceptual field. In particular, such focusing is not solely determined by the particular project in which we are freely engaged. Merleau-Ponty gives the example of seeing mountains, and argues that, because of our bodily comportment in the world, we cannot help but see them as tall, irrespective of whether or not we are engaged in a project, such as climbing them, which would render their size relevant. "Insofar as I have hands, feet, a body," he remarks, "I sustain around me intentions which are not dependent upon my decisions and which affect my surroundings in a way which I do not choose (PP, 440).

Merleau-Ponty also goes beyond Husserl in his emphasis on intersubjectivity. For example, he maintains that eidetic variation should be conducted socially. I am not the only one who is intensely engaged practically with Being. Others are as well. We can compare notes. We can speak with others, and read their works. We can study past civilizations. This point also reveals the true value and importance of scientists, philosophers, and artists of all kinds.

Merleau-Ponty is a philosopher of "ambiguity." Our existence is, in several respects, characterized by a duality. For example, we are both freedom and contingency, and both incarnated and spiritual beings. Such ambiguities preclude the achievement of the sort of clarity that Husserl tirelessly sought.

Finally, Merleau-Ponty claims that what the phenomenological reduction reveals is the impossibility of a complete reduction. It shows that we are inextricably engaged with the world, and cannot tear ourselves apart from it. The world is inalienably present, given in perception, and manifested as neither meaningless nor clearly and precisely meaningful, but rather ambiguous.

Suggestions for Further Reading

Having read this book, I hope that you will have found the subject of phenomenology to be worth further exploration. If that is the case, rest assured that there is no shortage of material from which to choose. The available literature on this subject is so vast that no one could possibly hope ever to get through all of it. So, in an effort to provide some modest degree of help with this problem of selection, let me suggest a few works that I have found to be particularly interesting and helpful.

The three works on which I have concentrated in this book are: *Logical Investigations*, trans. J. N. Findlay, 2 volumes (New York: Routledge, 2001) [1900–1901]; *Ideas Pertaining to a Pure Phenomenology and to a Phenomenological Philosophy, First Book*, trans. F. Kersten (Boston: Martinus Nijhoff, 1982) [1913]; and *The Crisis of European Sciences and Transcendental Phenomenology*, trans. David Carr (Evanston: Northwestern University Press, 1970) [1954; portions published 1936].

The best commentary on *Ideas I* known to me is Erazim Kohák, *Idea & Experience* (Chicago: University of Chicago Press, 1978).

For a commentary on Husserl's *Crisis*, see Dermot Moran, *Husserl's Crisis of the European Sciences and Transcendental Phenomenology: An Introduction* (New York: Cambridge University Press, 2012). Essays on the *Crisis* can be found in *Science and the Life-World*, ed. David Hyder and Hans-Jörg Rheinberger (Stanford, CA: Stanford University Press, 2010).

Husserl's *Cartesian Meditations* provides an approach to Husserl's phenomenology by way of Descartes. It is available in a translation by Dorion Cairns (The Hague: Martinus Nijhoff, 1960) [1931]. For a commentary on this book, see A. D. Smith, *Husserl and the Cartesian Meditations* (New York: Routledge, 2003).

These two books show Husserl at his best at *doing* phenomenology, as opposed to introducing and describing it: *On the Phenomenology of the Consciousness of Internal Time (1893–1917)*, trans. John Barnett Brough (New York: Springer, 2008) [1893–1917]; and *Ideas Pertaining to a Pure Phenomenology and to a Phenomenological Philosophy, Second Book,* trans. Richard Rojcewicz and André Schuwer (New York: Springer, 1989) [1952; written 1912–1928].

"Philosophy as Rigorous Science," an interesting and important article published in 1911, captures Husserl's thought during the period of transition in his thinking from the philosophy of the *Logical Investigations* to that of *Ideas I*. It includes a detailed criticism of *Weltanschauung* philosophy (roughly, philosophy based on a subjective general worldview or ideology), and of the thought of Wilhelm Dilthey, in particular. It can be found, in a translation by Quentin Lauer, in *Phenomenology and the Crisis of Philosophy* (New York: Harper Torchbooks, 1965). The essay is also contained in *Husserl: Shorter Works,* edited by Peter McCormick and Frederick A. Elliston (Notre Dame: University of Notre Dame Press, 1981), a book which also contains Husserl's 1927 article on "Phenomenology" for the *Encyclopaedia Brittanica*, in a revised translation by Richard E. Palmer, his "Author's Preface" to the first English translation of *Ideas I*, that of W. R. Boyce Gibson, and several other short pieces.

For biographical information on Husserl's life, I recommend Ronald Bruzina, *Edmund Husserl & Eugen Fink* (New Haven, CT: Yale University Press, 2004), which covers his last decade (1928–1938).

Readers desiring further commentary on Husserl might want to try Dan Zahavi's *Husserl's Phenomenology* (Stanford, CA: Stanford University Press). It is brief and authoritative, as is Matheson Russell's *Husserl* (New York: Continuum, 2006); and James M. Edie's less systematic *Edmund Husserl's Phenomenology: A Critical Commentary* (Bloomington: Indiana University Press, 1987). David Woodruff Smith's *Husserl* (New York: Routledge, 2007) is longer and more comprehensive. Smith makes the case that

Husserl, along with Aristotle and Kant, is one of the three greatest systematic philosophers in the history of thought. But the single best scholarly discussion of Husserl's entire philosophical career, to my knowledge, is J. N. Mohanty's two-volume work, *The Philosophy of Edmund Husserl* (New Haven: Yale University Press, 2008), and *Edmund Husserl's Freiberg Years: 1916–1938* (New Haven: Yale University Press, 2011).

Leszek Kolakowski's *Husserl and the Search for Certitude* (Chicago: University of Chicago Press, 1987) is a clear and concise discussion and critique of Husserl's philosophical project. While Kolakowski rejects Husserl's conclusions, he argues that Husserl's attempt to find absolute foundations of knowledge is both admirable and culturally valuable.

A useful collection of essays is Barry Smith and David Woodruff Smith, eds., *The Cambridge Companion to Husserl* (New York: Cambridge University Press, 1995).

One of the few works on Husserl's ethics is Janet Donohoe's *Husserl on Ethics and Intersubjectivity: From Static to Genetic Phenomenology* (Amherst, NY: Humanity Books, 2004). Husserl's writings and lectures on ethics are not yet available in English translation. A collection of them, in the original German, can be found in *Vorlesungen über Ethik und Wertlehre. 1908–1914* (*Lectures on Ethics and Value Theory: 1908–1914*), ed. Ullrich Melle (The Hague: Kluwer, 1988).

Readers interested in a phenomenological approach to aesthetics should consult Mikel Dufrenne's *The Phenomenology of Aesthetic Experience*, trans. Edward S. Casey et al. (Evanston, IL: Northwestern University Press, 1973 [1953]); Roman Ingarden's *The Literary Work of Art*, trans. George G. Grabowicz (Evanston, IL: Northwestern University Press, 1973 [1965]); and Ingarden's *The Cognition of the Literary Work* of Art, trans. Ruth Ann Crowley and Kenneth R. Olson (Evanston, IL: Northwestern University Press, 1973 [1968]).

On the relevance of phenomenology to cognitive science and neuroscience, see Dan Zahavi, *Subjectivity and Selfhood* (Cambridge, MA: MIT Press, 2005); Evan Thompson, *Mind in Life* (Cambridge, MA: Harvard University Press, 2007); Matthew Ratcliffe, "Phenomenology, Neuroscience, and Intersubjectivity," in *A Companion to Phenomenology and Existentialism*, ed. Hubert L. Dreyfus and Mark A. Wrathall (Malden, MA: Blackwell, 2006),

329–45; Mark Rowlands, *The New Science of the Mind: From Extended Mind to Embodied Phenomenology* (Cambridge, MA: The MIT Press, 2010); and the journal *Phenomenology and the Cognitive Sciences* (which began publication in 2002).

While dated, Joseph J. Kockelmans, ed., *Phenomenology: The Philosophy of Edmund Husserl and Its Interpretation* (Garden City, NY: Anchor Books, 1967), is an excellent anthology, containing substantial selections from the writings of Husserl, Heidegger, Sartre, and Merleau-Ponty, as well as expository and critical articles on their phenomenological work.

Jan Patočka's *An Introduction to Husserl's Phenomenology*, trans. Erazim Kohák (Chicago: Open Court, 1996) is misleadingly titled. While it is probably too advanced and technical to serve as a first introduction to Husserl's work, it is an excellent resource for those who are no longer novices. Like most of the other major figures in the history of phenomenology, Patočka is a powerfully original thinker, and no mere disciple of Husserl. But whereas Heidegger, Sartre, Merleau-Ponty, and other post-Husserlian phenomenologists tend simply to take what they need from Husserl and then go off in their own direction, Patočka in this work develops his ideas in the context of a sustained engagement with Husserl's own problems and conclusions, on which he sheds considerable light.

An encyclopedic history of the entire phenomenological movement is Herbert Spiegelberg's *The Phenomenological Movement*, third edition (Boston: Martinus Nijhoff, 1982). More up to date and almost as comprehensive is Dermot Moran's *Introduction to Phenomenology* (New York: Routledge, 2000). See also Sebastian Luft and Søren Overgaard, eds., *The Routledge Companion to Phenomenology* (New York: Routledge, 2012).

Scheler's most important phenomenological work is *Formalism in Ethics and Non-Formal Ethics of Values*, trans. Manfred S. Frings and Roger L. Funk (Evanston, IL: Northwestern University Press, 1973) [1916].

Heidegger's *magnum opus* is *Being and Time,* originally published in 1927. It is available in two different translations: one by John Macquarrie and Edward Robinson (New York: Harper, 2008), and one by Joan Stambaugh, revised edition (Albany: State University of New York Press, 2010). A good commentary on this book is Hubert L. Dreyfus, *Being-in-the-World* (Cambridge, MA: MIT Press, 1990).

The clearest exposition of Heidegger known to me is Graham Harman's *Heidegger Explained* (Chicago: Open Court, 2007).

Sartre's early, phenomenological works include *The Transcendence of the Ego*, trans. Forrest Williams and Robert Kirkpatrick (New York: Noonday Press, 1957) [1937]; *Imagination*, trans. Forrest Williams (Ann Arbor: The University of Michigan Press, 1972) [1936]; *The Emotions: Outline of a Theory*, trans. Bernard Frechtman (New York: Wisdom Library, 1948) [1939]; and *The Imaginary*, trans. Jonathan Webber (New York: Routledge, 2004) [1940]. His *magnum opus* is *Being and Nothingness*, trans. Hazel E. Barnes (New York: Washington Square Press, 1992) [1943].

For commentary on *Being and Nothingness*, see Joseph S. Catalano's *A Commentary on Jean-Paul Sartre's "Being and Nothingness"* (Chicago: University of Chicago Press, 1980). My own book, *Sartre Explained* (Chicago: Open Court, 2008), emphasizes the role that phenomenology plays in all of Sartre's writing.

Merleau-Ponty's major phenomenological work is *Phenomenology of Perception*, trans. Colin Smith (London: Routledge & Kegan Paul, 1962) [1945]. For commentary, see Monika M. Langer's *Merleau-Ponty's Phenomenology of Perception: A Guide and Commentary* (Tallahassee: The Florida State University Press, 1989).

Index

Lightning Source UK Ltd.
Milton Keynes UK
UKHW011211210322
400383UK00001B/112